FRANCIS DE SALES

THE CROSSROAD SPIRITUAL LEGACY SERIES

Edited by John Farina

The Rule of Benedict: Insights for the Ages
   by Joan Chittister, O.S.B.

Ignatius Loyola: Spiritual Exercises
   by Joseph A. Tetlow, S.J.

St. Francis of Assisi
   by Regis J. Armstrong, O.F.M. Cap.

Francis de Sales: Introduction to the Devout Life *and*
Treatise on the Love of God
   by Wendy M. Wright

FRANCIS DE SALES

INTRODUCTION TO THE DEVOUT LIFE
AND
TREATISE ON THE LOVE OF GOD

Wendy M. Wright

CROSSROAD • NEW YORK

1997

The Crossroad Publishing Company
370 Lexington Avenue, New York, NY 10017

Copyright © 1993 by Wendy M. Wright

Printed in the United States of America

Library of Congress Cataloging-in-Publication Data
Wright, Wendy M.
   Francis de Sales : Introduction to the devout life and Treatise on
the love of God / Wendy M. Wright.
      p.   cm. — (The Crossroad spiritual legacy series)
   ISBN 0-8245-2508-6 (pbk.)
   1. Francis, de Sales, Saint, 1567–1622.   Introduction à la vie
dévote.   2. Francis, de Sales, Saint, 1567–1622.   Traité de l'amour
de Dieu.   3. Spirituality—Catholic Church—History—16th century.
4. Spirituality—Catholic Church—History—17th century.
5. Catholic Church—Doctrines—History—16th century.   6. Catholic
Church—Doctrines—History—17th century.   I. Title.   II. Series.
BX2179.F8175   1993
248.4'82–dc20
                                                              93-6022
                                                                 CIP

For Walter H. Capps

Contents

Foreword

Writing in the fourth century a North African Christian by the name of Lactantius offered the following definition of virtue. For him, virtue is nothing less than "enduring of evils and labors." How unlike contemporary notions this definition of virtue is and how odd it sounds for us to be told so plainly that the fullness of life can be had only through enduring evils and trials. Yet, despite our inclination to write off Lactantius as an overly pessimistic nay-sayer, we must admit that life does include a large dose of suffering. We can take it well or badly. We can flee it or embrace it, but it will come and find us wherever we hide, and then it will test our mettle. Virtue does involve suffering evils, not simply actualizing ourselves, or conquering our fears, or visualizing success, or learning techniques to cope with stress, or building better "relationships" with members of the opposite sex. There are things in life that simply cannot be so easily manipulated. Situations that don't get better. Unpleasant realities that won't go away. Where do we turn when confronted by them?

We can turn to the externals, to our comforts and our conveniences, to the superficialities of our lives, or we can turn to our depths. Many who have lived before us have learned the hard way that turning to the depths is the way to a fuller life. Their insights have been handed down, often in forms that are now hard to find and harder to read. Their language is archaic. Their morality out of sync with ours. Their clarity, offputting. Their humility, disconcerting. Yet they are there, waiting quietly to share with us their hard-won wisdom, waiting to dialog with us as we face situations that are different from those they encountered only in the particulars, not in the essences.

Simply put, that is the reason why Crossroad, myself, and a team of well-known scholars and spiritual leaders have joined together to undertake the Spiritual Legacy series. The need for spiritual wisdom is great. Our situation is critical. This then is more than an enterprise in scholarship, more than a literary exercise. It is an effort to convey life.

Certainly the idea of doing editions of the works of spiritual guides from the past is not new. There are a host of books available that do just that. How is the Spiritual Legacy series different?

The uniqueness of this series abides in its content and its style. In content it endeavors to present both texts from the spiritual guide and extensive commentary by a present-day disciple of the sage. It gives the reader the chance to encounter for herself the writings of a spiritual master. Nothing can take the place of that experience. However demanding it might be, whatever efforts it might require, there can be no substitute for it. One, for instance, cannot simply hear a description of the tenth chapter of Augustine's *Confessions.* No commentary, however skilled, can take the place of reading for oneself Augustine's words of unparalleled power: "Late have I loved Thee, O Beauty, so ancient, yet so new!"

While it is true that there is no substitute for encountering the text firsthand, it is also certain that for most people that encounter will be an excursion into a foreign land. Often many centuries and numerous barriers of language, customs, philosophy, and style separate us from the writings of bygone sages. To come to that point where we can understand the horizon of the author, we must be taught something about the historical context, the literary style, and the thought forms of the age, for instance. That is why we have included in this series extensive commentary on the text. That commentary is alternated with the text throughout the books, so that one can be taught, then experience the writings firsthand, over and over as one moves deeper into the text. At that point, the horizon of the reader meets that of the author, aided by the expert guidance of the editor of each book, who suggests not only what the text might mean, but how it might be made part of our lives.

The style of the Spiritual Legacy series is also unique in that it attempts to convey life with a certain degree of sophistication that befits an educated readership. Yet it does not assume that everyone will have a background in the material presented, nor does it purport to offer original or arcane scholarship. The editors' mastery of the texts is in each case complemented by their experience in putting the meaning of the texts into practice and helping others to do so as well. We are trying to present a series of books that will fit somewhere between the scholarly editions that pride themselves on their accuracy and originality and the popular pieces that offer too little substance for the healthy reader.

The series is designed to be used by a broad range of people. For those seekers who wish to journey toward spiritual wholeness as part of a group, the series is ideally suited. The texts presented can be easily divided into sections for discussion by a group meeting, say, on a weekly basis.

For those who are traveling alone, the series is a trustworthy and enjoyable tour book. The direct, simple language of the commentaries frames the memorable words of the classical texts and offers them in an attractive setting for meditation and practical application.

The publisher and editors of the Spiritual Legacy series join me in inviting you to undertake a journey that will take you back to an encounter with ancient wisdom and challenge you to an experience of self-understanding and, at its best, self-transcendence. It is our hope that that experience will help you to grow and to be a source of fresh life for all those around you.

John Farina

Acknowledgments

Thanks are due to a number of persons without whom this book could not have been written. First, thanks are due to Fr. Joseph Power, O.S.F.S., who is a constant source of bibliographic help, a wise counselor in the Salesian tradition, and a friend; next, to John Farina and the Crossroad Publishing Company for the inspiration and support to undertake this project; to John Crossin, O.S.F.S., of De Sales School of Theology and to the Georgetown Community of the Visitation for their respective reflections on what in Francis de Sales' writing is most revelatory for us today; to the numerous Visitandine communities who over the years have imaged Francis' dictum "Live Jesus!" to me, especially the communities in St. Paul, Minn.; Federal Way, Wash.; St. Louis; and Georgetown; to the De Sales Resource Center, Stella Niagara, N.Y.; and to Deans Michael Lawler and Michael Proterra of Creighton University, whose funding made the word processing possible; finally to Jackie Lynch, who did the word processing so competently, and to my husband, Roger Bergman, and to Grace McCormick, V.H.M., for their patient hours of thoughtful copy editing.

The first chapter, "Reading the Spiritual Classics," first appeared in slightly different form in the Spring 1992 issue of *The Way*. Permission to use the English translations of Francis de Sales' works was given by S.F.S. Publications and Paulist Press. The translations used (with minor modifications for inclusive language, clarity, and consistency) were *Introduction to the Devout Life*, translated by Fr. Armind Nazareth, M.S.F.S., Fr. Antony Mookenthottam, M.S.F.S., Fr. Antony Kolencherry, M.S.F.S.

(Malleswaram, Bangalore, India: S.F.S. Publications, 1990); *Treatise on the Love of God*, translated by Vincent Kerns, M.S.F.S. (Westminster, Md.: Newman Press, 1962); *Spiritual Conferences of St. Francis de Sales*, translated by Abbot Gasquet and the late Canon Mackey (Westminster, Md.: Newman Bookshop, 1943); *Francis de Sales and Jane de Chantal: Letters of Spiritual Direction*, translated by Peronne Marie Thibert, V.H.M. (Mahwah, N.J.: Paulist Press, 1988).

Although Francis de Sales himself did not cite chapter and verse when be quoted Scripture, it is usual to find such citations in later editions of his works. I have standardized this practice for the sake of consistency, adding citations in parentheses after his quotations. This gives the reader some sense of the pervasive influence of Scripture on Francis' thought.

To the Reader

This little volume has been written to introduce the modern reader to the person and thought of Francis de Sales, the seventeenth-century bishop and author who is considered one of the masters of the Christian spiritual tradition. My perspective in the writing of this volume has been focused by two considerations. First, I have wished to depict both accurately and attractively this man who has been pronounced a doctor of the church (which means that his teaching has been officially recognized for its wisdom and fullness). That is to say, I have hoped, as much as is possible across the centuries, to introduce you to a living person, someone who has struggled with the question of what it is to live the Christian life and to live it well. I hope that reading this book will be a little like going on retreat; that you take the opportunity to "sit with" and "pray with" Francis de Sales and to integrate some of his spirit and insight into your own struggle to live the Christian life.

Second, my perspective has been influenced by the belief that reading the spiritual classics of the past is not always a straightforward task. There is a certain sorting out and interpretation necessary to make the words of someone who lived four hundred years ago come alive and be meaningful for today. That has always been the challenge of appropriating Christian tradition — to remain faithful to the core insights of the past and yet to allow them to assume new forms appropriate to a changing historical reality.

So my tack will be to introduce you to Francis' own words, giving some sense of him and the moment in which he wrote them as well as the purposes and people for which and whom he wrote. Then I'll offer some reflections for your consideration, drawing out the heart of his spiritual message while at the same time pointing out some of the assumptions that he holds that seem applicable mainly to Christians of his own era and perhaps not useful or easily translated in today's world.

There will be, then, a frankly interpretive quality to the commentary that follows the selections of Francis' own writings. While historical accuracy will be respected, so you can rely upon the presentation of de Sales, you are free to agree or disagree with my interpretation of the usefulness of any of his teachings for today's Christians.

Indeed, the point of reading the words of someone who lived so long ago is not so that we can literally imitate or become that person and live in the era in which that person lived. The point of reading the spiritual masters is that we wrestle to know who we are and how we are called by God precisely through the interaction with others who have also wrestled in the uniqueness of their own lives. What connects us with them is the struggle, each in the immediacy of his or her own historical moment and personal story, to enflesh, to live out, the unfolding and everchanging mystery of God-with-us.

Francis de Sales was one of those remarkable individuals in our shared past who struggled with an unusual vitality and who was able to communicate the fruits of his struggle through his writings. The invitation in these pages is to come to know the truth of this man, which may ultimately aid us in knowing the truth about ourselves.

Reading
the Spiritual Classics

I will never forget when, as a very young college student in California, I was handed a copy of *The Cloud of Unknowing* by a medieval history professor who had intuited my budding interest in mysticism. Clutching the book tightly under my jacket to protect it from the rain, I scurried off to the library to find a secret place deep in the bowels of the musty stacks where I could be alone with my treasure. As I spread back the leaves of the first page, the words of the foreword fairly leapt off the paper.

> Whoever you are possessing this book, know that I charge you with a serious responsibility, to which I attach the sternest sanctions that the bonds of love can bear. It does not matter whether this book belongs to you, whether you are keeping it for someone else, whether you are taking it to someone or borrowing it; you are not to read it, write or speak of it; nor allow another to do so, unless you really believe that he is a person who, over and above the good works of the active life, has resolved to follow Christ perfectly.

I felt myself to be directly addressed by the author and trembled at the thought that I might not be a person truly resolved to follow Christ perfectly. But deep within I *knew* that this was *my* book. I was entrusted with a grave and holy responsibility. These were *my* words, meant for me at this very moment, uttered by some unknown person (I was totally unaware at what chrono-logical and spatial distance) with me clearly in mind. The book was a numinous and longed for companion teasing me deeper into some unfolding part of myself that I knew to be connected with God.

Several decades have passed since, in the innocence of my first naïveté, I encountered *The Cloud*. Along the way I have read many other spiritual classics, a few of them in the early years with that same sense that they fairly glowed on the page: Augus-tine's *Confessions* (about which I collapsed sobbing upon the desk of another history professor), fragments of St. Symeon the New Theologian, Br. Lawrence's *Practice of the Presence of God*, *The Inte-rior Castle* of St. Teresa of Avila. It was my feeling that these were timeless pieces of literature, gems of living wisdom undimmed by the passage of centuries. I suppose it was that feeling that caused me eventually to become a historian of Christian spiri-tuality. Over the years I have certainly learned to read the classic texts of our spiritual heritage differently, asking all the pertinent critical historiographical questions. Plus I no longer experience the life of prayer as some distant foreign landscape into which I am being invited. While the experience of prayer continues to unfold as mystery, I am no longer an outsider peering over the fence of an exotic garden but one gardener, among many, tend-ing the soil and delighting in the astonishing variety of fruits and blossoms that grow in the garden of the Christian spiritual tradition. So some of my earlier sense of these texts as missives breaking in from the spiritual realm is modified for me now.

First Naïveté

Many of my students, some of them of traditional college age, others of them older, come to the classic texts of spirituality with the same fresh wonder as I had done. They hear the advice of Jean-Pierre de Caussade's *Abandonment to Divine Providence* as constructed especially for them and calling them to a new level of trust in God's loving action working through the ordinary events of their lives. The text enjoins the reader to envision the present moment like a desert in which uncomplicated souls (those abandoned to providence) see and enjoy only God and attend to nothing but God's will, ignoring everything else. Or they read the dramatic *passio* of the martyrdom of Sts. Perpetua and Felicitas and find themselves overwhelmed by the heroic faith of these women and inspired to reexamine their own willingness to take their religious commitments seriously.

You need only go into a modern-day religious bookstore of any quality to find the shelves stacked with the classics of the Christian spiritual life. The readers of these volumes are not mainly scholars in the field (although in the last twenty years serious research, new translations, and groundbreaking interpretive work has been done in the area) but Christians from a variety of backgrounds and perspectives who are hungry for the living wisdom they uncover there. So you discover busy housewives and mothers receiving spiritual formation from the words of medieval women whose choice of lifestyle assumed that marriage and motherhood were antithetical to a life of true prayer. And you find (as in my own case with *The Cloud*) an active American university student imbibing the advice most likely intended for someone already well acquainted with communal monastic life and now being initiated into the contemplative life of a solitary. Or you discover a forty-five-year-old businessman making use of the writings of a sixteenth-century priest imprisoned for attempting daring reforms of his religious order to understand his twentieth-century midlife crisis.

Many of these readers come to the great texts of our heritage with what philosopher Paul Ricoeur termed "first naïveté." This does not mean simply that they read uncritically but that they also read with a freshness and openness that allows them to be eager recipients of what they read. They are like the "good soil" alluded to in the gospel that is fertile ground for genuinely hearing the Word (in this case the Word refracted through the lives and thoughts of the most faithful of the faithful).

For the most part, devotional readers of the classics like these hear well what I would call the heartbeat of the text's author.

When I collapsed in tears in my professor's office after read-ing *The Confessions*, it was not because St. Augustine's refutation of the Manichean philosophy of evil was so convincing or be-cause I too had come to understand my childhood as evidence of the tenacity of original sin. No, I sobbed my way through the text because I experienced the same overwhelming desire for the "something more" that the North African bishop did. I felt deeply the bishop's rhapsodic prayer, his passionate gratitude, his wonder at the marvelous discovery of the God-life within. Augustine mirrored for me my own ultimate vocation as lover of God. The hearts of the great writers of our contemplative tradi-tion are audible in the texts they have written. Readers hungry for God eagerly press their ears against those ancient beating hearts to detect the same God-ward movements beating in their own breasts.

The Chasm of the Centuries

But there are sometimes difficulties in reading from the vantage point of the first naïveté. Open ears take in everything uncrit-ically. So the words coming forth from one seeker of spiritual freedom may become words of spiritual bondage for another separated by time and place. I will never forget the anguish of a Lutheran pastor who attended a graduate seminar I offered on the history of spirituality. His seminary training, otherwise theologically sophisticated, had included no exposure to devo-tional classics. Later in life, longing for a deeper intimacy with God, he had begun delving into medieval literature on prayer. He heard there the most authentic beating of his own heart. But the books he was reading also told him that he had to flee the world to truly find God, that he must renounce all earthly ties to bind his life to the divine lover. Because of his wife's employ-ment in a nearby city, the pastor was not only immersed in a busy ministry but was primary caretaker of their two school-age chil-dren during after-school hours. Discouraged, sure that he would never achieve the deep spiritual intimacy he longed for, he began to experience his family as a hated and impassable obstacle in the path home to God.

Similarly, I remember the instance of a caring older woman who had made the letters of St. Margaret Mary Alacoque her spiritual nourishment for one Lenten season. Moved by the saint's profound intercessory prayer, she too began to imagine herself suffering for the souls in purgatory, desiring to take on herself their pains. She was a woman relatively new to prayer, of fragile ego boundaries and deeply concerned about the difficulties her own grown daughter was facing in an abusive marriage. At one point, during a group retreat at which participants were encouraged to engage in some exercises for depth spiritual healing, she decided she would "change places" with her daughter. When the exercises were concluded and retreat participants surfaced from their reveries to discuss what they had experienced, she remained deep in prayer. A neighbor finally noted her absorption when the group was dismissed for lunch. Gently, someone touched her shoulder. She did not respond. It took some vigorous intervention on the part of the other retreatants to bring her to. When she was able to speak, she recalled in terror "getting lost" and not being able to find her way back to ordinary consciousness. Her journey had not been one of intercession or of expansion of consciousness, but of psychic disintegration and possession by unbenign spirits.

In both these cases, writings intended to encourage spiritual freedom and maturity were encountered in a way that produced the opposite effect. In other cases, uncritical reading of words penned under circumstances very different from our own could lead to a kind of slavish literalism, intolerance, undue fearfulness (what used to be called scrupulosity), or narrow self-righteousness. Whatever the source, the wonderful sponge-like receptivity of the first naïveté can sometimes close in on itself. The heartbeat of God becomes obscured in the literal details of a text.

Most of our Christian spiritual classics were produced in eras separated from our own by the chasm of centuries. In our delight to find guides in the spiritual life we often forget that that life is not static. Rather, there is a history of holiness (as theologian Karl Rahner has pointed out) that has a unique and unrepeatable historicity in each generation. It is not the eternal return of the same; hence it must always be discovered anew. There is thus both a continuity to the Christian spiritual tradition and a distinctive unfolding quality. It does not stay the same. It is not static. The vast gulf of the centuries that separates us from Augustine and the author of *The Cloud of Unknowing* and Margaret Mary Alacoque is bridgeable in some ways — and not in others.

In reading the literature of our spiritual heritage it is best then to be aware that an author lived in an earlier century and wrote in a different language and thus comes to us as a historically bounded person rooted in a sociopolitical and ecclesial reality very different from our own. Human cultures change. Likewise the church has not from the beginning been the same polity. Its theological language has evolved. Its life vis-à-vis the surrounding culture has been ever changing. Its styles of praying and notions of the Christian life continue to grow. We may know this, but when we pick up the spiritual classics we tend to forget what we know. We tend to view spiritual advice as timeless, something that directly mirrors the eternal reality toward which it so ardently longs.

In part, this impression is reinforced by the literature itself. The witness of a life profoundly centered in God carries its own authenticity. This is the real thing, we intuitively sense. And, inevitably, spiritual wisdom is grounded in real experience so that the authors of our classics teach from the powerful vantage point of lived experience. They have done it, we say; let us do what they did. Further, our authors speak not merely out of the context of personal wisdom but out of the collective and cumulative wisdom of the entire Christian community. As such, they witness to religious values, practices, and lifestyles that have a validity well beyond their own experience. How many people have safely gone to God this or that way, we observe, and so believe it must be a way we might emulate.

Despite this, we would do well to try to analyze the values — both explicit and implicit — that inform a particular piece of spiritual literature. We can do this adequately only by knowing something of the history of the period, the author, and the audience to which he or she was writing. For example, the Lutheran pastor might have profited from knowing that the short anonymous text he was reading was a late fourteenth-century English treatise presumably written by a solitary for other solitaries at a time in Christendom when it was assumed that the life of withdrawal from the world was the most authentic response to the gospel. It was also a time when the writings of the Pseudo-Dionysius were being circulated and commented upon. This earlier contemplative author based his spiritual vision on Neo-Platonic precepts that posited that the surest way into intimacy with the divine was through the *via negativa*, the abandonment of all human capacities (the "knowing" discovered in verbal and visual imagery) and all ties. Had the Lutheran pastor known this, and also that our Christian spiritual heritage is a many-flowered garden that has continued to produce vigorous hybrid styles of spirituality from a common plant, he might have been better able to distill life-giving nectar from the particular plant he was enjoying.

Living with the Language

Developing a critical consciousness about these texts does not, for the Christian who is not a professional scholar, mean becoming an expert in the field. It simply means that we must become aware of the values that explicitly or implicitly inform the classic texts. It means being willing to accept an author as a person of his or her moment in history. It means being aware of ourselves as participants in an ongoing exploration of the Christian life. To participate in a tradition means that we must continually reappropriate it.

This is not something new. Sts. Augustine and Teresa or the author of *The Cloud* were similarly engaged in the task of making the holiness of Christ unfold in the uniqueness of their historical moment. Religious figures of the past always focused and emphasized the various aspects of Christian faith in response to the changing religious needs of their particular era.

I have found that for me, as a devotional reader, this means living with the language of the classic texts in two distinct ways. First, it means becoming aware of values, images, and assumptions that are so specific to the author's time that they do not translate. Sometimes an author's advice, for all her or his wisdom, may even be antithetical to a vital faith in our contemporary world. Let such language simply be sloughed off. Second, there may be concepts that appear foreign or distasteful but need to be lived with and lovingly contemplated, as it were, for the kernel of universal religious meaning to be hulled from the husk of its historical appearance. Let such language unfold.

Over the years I have spent a great deal of time with the writings of Sts. Francis de Sales and Jane Frances de Chantal, friends who sought to live vibrant lives of discipleship at the turn of the seventeenth century in France and Savoy. It is his works and life that form the subject of this volume. It is through wrestling with the witness of these two luminaries that I have learned to exercise these two critical options: letting some of their language simply be sloughed off and letting some of it unfold. Certainly when I am approaching their writings as a professional historian, I try as much as possible to recapture their vision in its specific integrity. But when I come to read them as devotional guides, I must meet them half way. Across the chasm of the centuries I must listen for words that give life in the twentieth century, an age of terrifying technological power and destructive capability, an age of ecumenism and interreligious dialogue, an age of ecological crisis, an intellectual age of postmodernism.

Language and ideas that might well be sloughed off are both explicit and implicit in a text. Sometimes the quaint antiquity of an idea makes this patently obvious. An example of this might be the advice given about "hearing Mass" in Francis de Sales' treatise *Introduction to the Devout Life*. St. Francis provides his readers with a list of meditations to undertake while attending Mass because at that time in the church's history the liturgy was said in Latin and people were usually not conversant with the ecclesiastical tongue. He also does not advise receiving communion daily, even if one attends Mass, a practice that has changed over the centuries. Such advice is obviously relevant primarily in his time and place.

Other assumptions of questionable contemporary value that inform texts such as *Introduction to the Devout Life* are less explicit; take, for instance, the Genevan bishop's perspective on "How to Practice Real Poverty While Remaining Rich." It is not his specific advice that might cause us to re-evaluate what he says: he counsels a holy indifference to wealth as well as responsible stewardship. The assumption that underlies his advice that might well be challenged is that wealth and position as well as material poverty and lack of viable participation in society are God-ordained. Francis de Sales lived at a time when the medieval notion of the divine right of kingship still hung in the air. Never having held the lens of the gospel up to the social and political institutions of his day, he did not see institutions as created primarily by human effort. He certainly is not to be blamed for this, for that insight was to come to Western European culture during the Enlightenment. For the bishop sin resided in personal response to a presumably God-given and fixed social situation. Certainly, it had always been seen as saintly to give everything away and become voluntarily poor for the sake of the kingdom. But the theological construct underlying such heroic gestures from our past was always cast in terms of personal salvation, as an individual desire to flee the world and be remade, through renunciation of all sorts, including renunciation of wealth, in the image of God in Christ.

Such assumptions might well be sloughed off.

On the other hand, we find in the pages of our classic texts some language which, at first glance, strikes us as antiquated or abstruse but to which we would be well advised to give more careful attention. Some language needs to unfold contemplatively in our prayer. We need the bite of an intellectual nutcracker to crack open the rich spiritual nourishment hidden in the inedible-looking husks.

For a number of years, as I was thick into my research for my dissertation on Francis de Sales and Jane de Chantal, I bridled at a phrase they would occasionally employ: "loving your abjections." Used in the context of the deepened virtue of humility, abjection in Jane and Francis' view refers to the "lowliness, meanness, and baseness that exist in us without our knowledge." As steady fare for spiritual reading I found this hard to take. It triggered for me a sense of unhealthy self-loathing that too often legitimates victimization. So I waited on the phrase. I left it alone as an area of study. I let it ripen in my prayer.

Gradually I began to find a referent, something that I knew to be deeply life-giving in my own spiritual journey, against which to evaluate the teaching on "love your abjections." I began to live into my own limitations, those pesky arenas of brokenness and blindness that seem always to be there whether we want them or not. Gradually I began (as midlife neared) to realize that my task was not so much to eliminate them, for this was in fact impossible, although I could certainly work on them. Rather my task was to recognize and accept them. My abjections were my unwanted limitations. It was then that the radical wisdom of the *Introduction* became clear to me. For its call was not simply to accept, but to *love*, my abjections. What could this mean? To embrace, to cherish those parts of the self that one would prefer not to claim, much less to make public. What an astonishing thought. But the more I lived with this and the more I let it unfold as an experience of self-revelation in prayer, the more I began to delight in it. To *love* our abjections is to love ourselves in our wholeness, *as we are loved* by God, and thus it is to enter into God's infinite compassion. To love our abjections is indeed a sublime spiritual teaching.

Yet it is a teaching I had to let unfold. It was one that caused me to work through false perceptions of the spiritual life and of self in order to come closer to God. The language of the spiritual classics is sometimes best sloughed off, but other times it is best waited upon to unfold in its own time in prayer.

With the Communion of Saints

On occasion I will find myself in the midst of a community of Christians who have departed so dramatically from the world of the first naïveté and entered with such vehemence upon the critical endeavor of seeing the religious classics across the chasm of the centuries that they no longer experience them as at all relevant to their lives.

One summer I taught a course in the history of Christian spirituality at a West Coast university where consciousness of contemporary ecclesial issues and debates was very high. Virtually every primary text from the tradition that I assigned was immediately dismissed with intense opposition. Augustine's *Confessions* were riddled with evidence of sexual dysfunction, the imagery of John Climacus' *Ladder of Divine Ascent* was too hierarchical, the desert fathers were mysogynist. The women's texts were greeted with somewhat less repugnance, but were generally chided for being too tainted with a body-denying ethos. In fact, I do not disagree with these evaluations. Awakening to the possibility of life-denying elements of a spiritual teaching is part of the process of coming into a mature relationship with a text. But one cannot stop there.

What happened to these students is that they had moved beyond the first naïveté but had not engaged with the texts on the level of second naïveté. They had learned to look hard, but in the process they had forgotten how to hear with their hearts. Perhaps, as in any vital and long-term relationship, we must fall in and out of love a number of times with the classics of our tradition. At each falling out we will have learned to see them a little more clearly, learned to know their faults and foibles more intimately. At each return we will learn to confront or refuse to embrace life-denying aspects of our relationship. Yet we will return. And our new falling in love will be richer, more mature, more grasped by the divine heartbeat that pulses through the hearts of our authors, less fixated on the particular manifestation of a divine/human love.

The dynamic goes both ways. It is not a bad idea to let an Augustine, a John Climacus, a Hildegard of Bingen, or a Francis de Sales, rooted as they are in their historical moment, become the catalyst for the discovery of our own limited frames of reference. If we can begin to read their words with both a sense of critical awareness *and* with a sense of our shared longings and our common life, I think we can become conscious of how we too are shaped by our moment, how we are given both the task of allowing new forms of holiness adapted to our times to emerge and the task of realizing ourselves as part of an ongoing tradition of searching for God.

Must *The Cloud of Unknowing* or the *Introduction to the Devout Life* be embraced as literal blueprints for all Christians searching for God? No. Must the *Introduction* be rejected because of the historical rootedness? Or, must *The Cloud* be utterly rejected because the Neo-Platonic philosophy forming it opposes our contemporary quest to live as reverent creatures on an endangered planet? No. But our task of reappropriation must be an active one. We must engage in it with as much energy as we would when cultivating an intimate relationship. We must be willing to be thoughtfully critical, sloughing off ideas and images that cannot sustain Christian life in the twentieth and twenty-first centuries and allowing those maddening and undecipherable gems of wisdom hidden in antique garb to gradually reveal themselves to us.

Most of all this active reappropriation of our tradition will be an experience of empowerment. We will discover that this is *our* tradition, one we are called to live creatively and with great risk. We are called to chart the vast and unexplored sea of holiness that floods forth from the inexhaustible source that is the holiness of Christ. But we will also have an experience of companionship, of being one with the women and men of our shared path who explored that same uncharted sea. We will discover ourselves in the communion of saints, straining to tack the fragile vessels of our lives in the direction of God as they did before us. We are certainly not alone. For the human heart, despite the centuries, has not changed; its fundamental rhythm is still the heartbeat of God.

Francis de Sales and the *Introduction to the Devout Life*

Annecy: 1610

In early 1610 the dynamic young bishop of Geneva, Francis de Sales, sat at his desk in the episcopal apartments located at the Maison Lambert in the village of Annecy, duchy of Savoy. The decor of his surroundings was remarkably simple and unadorned, especially considering that the era in which he lived, the Counter-Reformation, was one in which the office of bishop was greatly revered. Splendid religious ceremonies and beautiful vestments and all the accouterments of privilege were common to the Roman church hierarchy of his day. But the Genevan bishop preferred the simplicity of his modest dwellings. His apartments were located across the street from the Cathedral St. Pierre, where he exercised his episcopal ministry. In fact, the bishop's true cathedral church was in Geneva, fifty miles north of Annecy, but he could not preside there. This was the historical era of great conflict between the peoples of Christian Europe, who found themselves sharply divided in their religious loyalties. Barely a century before, Martin Luther had posted his famous ninety-five theses on the door of Wittenburg Cathedral, challenging, among other things, the sale of indulgences by the church. With the tap of his hammer Luther had unleashed the pent-up ecclesial, theological, and political tensions of Christendom, which exploded into what we have come to know as the Protestant Reformation. For the next hundred years all Europe was to reel from the bloody aftermath of the Reform. Most countries, provinces, or cities were either fiercely loyal to the church of Rome or tenacious adherents of the Reformed churches. In France, decades of battle between the two religious factions finally had produced an uneasy truce. Both Roman Catholics and the Reformed were legally allowed to practice their faith. But to the east in the city-state of Geneva, the Reform held sway. The Catholic bishop had been exiled from the city and all Catholic practice had been banned. The episcopal entourage had fled to the mountain hamlet of Annecy, just south of Geneva. By the time of de Sales' episcopal consecration in 1602, the bishop of Geneva had been in exile in the lakeside hamlet for nearly half a century.

Prelates accustomed to the elegance of church life in the great cities of Europe like Paris might have found Annecy something of a provincial backwater. But not Francis. He loved this quaint place, which he spoke of affectionately as "my dear Nessy." For him it was home. He had been born in 1567, just across Lake Annecy near the village of Thorens at the Château de Sales. His father was François de Boisy, a nobleman of some influence in local political affairs. Within the year before Francis' birth his mother, Françoise de Sionnaz, then a somewhat anxious young wife, had prayed fervently at the church of Notre Dame de Liesse in central Annecy, where the fabled Shroud of Turin was on display. She had prayed for a child. She promised that if her prayer was answered she would consecrate the child to God. It was and she did. These are some of Francis' deep roots in Annecy. He had frequented its narrow cobblestone streets as a boy, spending two years at the Collège Chappiusien and receiving his first communion and confirmation at the Church of St. Dominic. Later, after receiving an education in Paris and Padua, Francis had returned to Annecy to be made provost and then coadjutor of the bishopric of Geneva. When his predecessor, Bishop de Granier, died, he was made chief shepherd of the diocese from which he had come.

From the windows of his apartments, Francis could not see far beyond the cathedral edifice across from him except to peer down the tight winding streets that disappeared around the corner to his right and left. But he knew well where the curving avenues led. Annecy was not large and he generally moved through it on foot. A mountainside village, high in the Alpine regions, Annecy lay beneath the shadow of an ancient château perched on the side of the hills and above the shores of Lake Annecy. The town was crisscrossed by canals; lake water lapped gently at the feet of passersby and swirled under the town's many bridges. From his apartments it was not a long walk across the canals to the old prison, where he visited the imprisoned and condemned. Another short walk took him to the Saint Sepulcre quarter, one of the most destitute in the village, where he brought a message of consolation to the poor and those suffering from illness. The Street of St. Clare, just below the château, housed a convent of Poor Clare nuns where he often preached, as well as the Hôtel Favre, the dwelling place of his dear friend Antoine Favre, with whom he founded the Florimontane Academy, a center for intellectual and cultural exchange.

Francis frequently taught catechism to the children at the Dominican church down near the lakeside. From there he could easily round the edge of the lake to stop in at the Gallery House, where the widow Jane de Chantal and three other women were soon to begin an experimental community that they would call the Visitation of Holy Mary. Francis had dreamed for years of a community for such women: widows, the handicapped, and the frail, who felt a deep call to prayer and to give themselves to God and yet who could not find a welcome in any of the existing religious communities of the church. He had just the previous year made plans to establish the community with his friend Jane de Chantal, and the fledgling experiment was much on his mind.

In fact, there was hardly a corner of "dear Nessy" that had not felt its bishop's presence. Francis de Sales felt himself called to the formidable task of reforming his entire diocese according to the principles laid down by the recent Council of Trent. The church loyal to Rome was in the process of internal reform. Partly as a continuation of several centuries of foment within Christendom and partly as a response to the dramatic events of the Reform movement, church leaders had applied themselves to rethinking church policies, morals, doctrines, and institutions. At the core of Roman reform was the person of the bishop, the true shepherd of his flock, personally preaching the gospel, instructing the faithful, providing moral example, generously serving the poor, and encouraging dedication in religious life, zealousness in the priesthood, and piety among the laity. When he had been a law student at the University of Padua, Francis had been impressed by the spirit of the great Charles Borromeo, the bishop of Milan, which was so palpably present on the Italian peninsula. Like Bishop Charles, Bishop Francis gave himself unreservedly to the task of shepherding his people.

For Francis believed himself to be living in a unique period of the church's and Christendom's history. He saw the action of the Holy Spirit alive and working in the upheavals of his day. God seemed to be calling forth persons of generous, loving natures to respond to the divine initiative. From all walks of life and in all segments of society, God seemed to Francis to be raising up "devout souls" whose religious enthusiasm and desire to serve God would act as leaven in the loaf of society at all levels. The Genevan bishop envisioned little less than a renovation of Europe transformed by the standard of Christ. In this he believed himself to be a participant. This vision of Christian renewal that he identified with a revitalized Roman church motivated everything Francis de Sales did.

On top of Bishop de Sales' desk at the beginning of 1610 was the recently published book that bore the title *Introduction to the Devout Life*. It was the fruit of the bishop's pastoral experience serving as guide and spiritual director to a number of women, most particularly Louise du Chastel, Madame de Charmoisy, the young wife of an attendant at the French court who had confided to the bishop her desire to live a life of Christian principles and devotion even within the luxury and decadence of court life.

Francis had first pulled the book together rather quickly

between 1607 and 1608 in the midst of his busy schedule by reworking a series of memos he had written to Madame de Charmoisy and others like her. Because he often responded to people's requests for advice on the Christian life and because they often shared what he had to say with their friends, Francis had made it a habit to write, alongside his personal letters of spiritual guidance particularly tailored to respond to the needs of the addressee, more general memos of advice that could be circulated among a circle of acquaintances. He had reworked the memos sent to Louise de Charmoisy into chapter form and addressed them to an imaginary "Philothea," a feminine name that means simply "lover of God."

This little book, *Introduction to the Devout Life*, became an immediate success throughout the Europe of Francis' day. Both its popularity and the fact that after the first printing sold out, pirated and unauthorized editions were widely circulated, prompted the bishop to expand the work the next year. The version that lay on Francis' desk in 1610 was an enlarged five-part version of the original manuscript. In subsequent years he was to refine it even more, finally (in 1619) producing the work in the form familiar to readers well into the twentieth century. In the intervening three centuries the *Introduction* has gone through innumerable printings and been translated into dozens of languages, making it one of the most enduring of religious classics in the Christian tradition.

At the time of its first printing the book on the devout life filled a very real need in Catholic culture. Interest in the spiritual life was high among persons in all walks of life. Many of the classic works on prayer and spiritual practices were newly available in vernacular translations and people were hungry to read them. People were also seeking out guides to the spiritual life, and men like Francis, who had much to say on the topic, were in great demand. Yet because so many of the classic treatments on prayer were written for and by individuals in the monastic vocation and thus reflected a spirituality appropriate to a life of withdrawal, and because able spiritual directors were not easy to come by, there was a crying need for a book that could distill some of the collective wisdom of centuries of Christian experience and make it accessible to persons in various walks of life.

So Francis had responded to the need by gathering together his memos on diverse topics: thoughts on how to order one's day best to accommodate a life of devotion, perspectives on traditional Christian virtues like humility, ideas about what the life of "perfection" (usually, in those days, a life synonymous with vowed religious life) might mean "in the world," advice on widowhood, gentleness, and practices of meditation and prayer. These memos of advice became the backbone of the book.

The book began on a characteristically inviting note. Francis de Sales' writing, like his public speaking, affected people. And his writing reflected his personality, which was especially accessible. All sorts of persons — kings, courtiers, church officials, children, the poor, the handicapped, the simplest workers — flocked to see him, and each found an inviting presence and an empathetic ear awaiting him or her. Something about his message and the way he delivered it drew all these varied individuals. He had something to share that they were hungry to hear. He had assembled his memos into this little book that lay before him with the hope of reaching those he could not otherwise reach. His heart, moved by the love of God he experienced so deeply, was in those memos and in that book. He felt that if the desire he felt for God and the love of the kingdom of Christ he experienced could just be communicated, then others would be awakened to the deepest desires of their own hearts. The book began with a dedicatory prayer that came straight from Francis' own heart.

DEDICATORY PRAYER

Gentle Jesus, my Lord, my Savior, and my God. I prostrate before your divine majesty and dedicate and consecrate this writing to your glory. By your blessing give life to the words of this book so that those for whom I have written it may receive through it the holy inspirations that I desire for them. May they be especially inspired to pray earnestly that I may receive your infinite mercy, so that while showing the path of devotion to others in this world I may not be condemned eternally in the next. Rather, may I sing with them forever, as a song of triumph, the words I utter with all my heart as a sign of my faithfulness among the dangers of this earthly life:

LIVE JESUS
LIVE JESUS!

Yes, Lord Jesus, live and reign in our hearts forever and ever. Amen.

Right away in the opening prayer, one becomes aware of the young bishop's earnestness as well as his perspective on religious devotion, rooted as it is in the religious ethos of his age. There is an assumption, which is characteristic of Christian spirituality from its earliest postapostolic origins, that the Christian life is, to put it in contemporary terms, countercultural. "This earthly life," as Francis deems it, is an arena of choice. One may choose to serve Christ and espouse the values that Christ would (for Francis those values were upheld in the Roman church of his day). Or one may choose to serve another master, which means that one would live under the influence of "the world," where pride, greed, and the lust for power, self-aggrandizement and luxury held sway.

The notion that the life of Christ and the life of the world are antithetical goes back to the origins of the Christian spiritual tradition when fervent ascetics of the fourth and fifth centuries fled the cities of Christendom to seek the solitude of the Egyptian, Palestinian, and Syrian deserts. There, they believed, they could truly cultivate a life transformed in Christ, slough off the "old creation" in the fiery forge of silence and solitude, and be remade as a "new creation" in Christ. To do this they had to "die to self," to let go of the interior dispositions that tied them to worldly values and become gradually transformed through humility, charity, purity of heart, and continual prayer.

This countercultural thrust within the tradition was evidenced well into Francis' day, although by his time the cultural context had changed and the zealous didn't go to the desert. They went into religious life or — and this is where Francis' thought is original — they lived those countercultural values in a modest, interior, and hidden way in whatever situation they found themselves. Not that "true devotion," as Francis named it, didn't have exterior fruits. But the emphasis was on a radically countercultural change of heart that would gradually transform the person from within, rather than a change of lifestyle effected from without.

At the core of this interior change was the person of Jesus. Bishop de Sales ends his dedicatory prayer with a phrase very characteristic of him, Live Jesus! The phrase is the leitmotif of his entire life and it was to become the motto for the Visitation community he and his friend Jane de Chantal founded. In Francis de Sales' words, to live Jesus was to have the name of Jesus engraved on one's heart. It was to allow that name to become one's own true name, to allow one's entire self — body, thought, affections, actions, decisions, work, devotion — to be animated by the person known by that name. To allow Jesus to live, one did not simply learn about Jesus or pray to Jesus or even imitate Jesus. One surrendered the vital center of one's being, one's heart — understood as the core of a person's energy — to another. Authentic human living was for Francis the continual and ever-present bringing to life of the living Lord who bears the name Jesus.

This astonishing vision of life transformed by Jesus the Christ undergirded the entire *Introduction to the Devout Life*. For bishop de Sales, it was a countercultural reality available to all people in all walks of life.

MY DEAR READER, PLEASE READ THIS PREFACE FOR YOUR SATISFACTION AND FOR MINE

The flower-seller Glycera had such great skill in arranging flowers that with the same sort of flowers she would make a great variety of bouquets. In fact, the painter Pausias, wanting to make drawings of Glycera's different bouquets, was unable to do so, as he could not match his skill in painting to the profusion of bouquets she had prepared. In the same way, the Holy Spirit inspires and sets out the teaching on devotion in such a great variety, presenting it through the words and writings of his servants. While the doctrine is always one and the same, yet the compositions in which it is set out are very different according to the variety of ways used in putting them together....

My words are directed to "Philothea." In fact, I want to present for the general benefit of many persons what I had written in the first place for only one. So I use a name that can be given to anyone who wants to lead a devout life. "Philothea" means "one who loves God" or "one who is in love with God."

In all this my concern is for anyone who desires to be devout and so seeks to love God. Hence I have arranged this *Introduction* in five parts:

In the First Part, I make use of various counsels and exercises to change our simple desire for the devout life into a total commitment. We do this by concluding with a firm resolution after a general confession. Holy Communion follows when, entrusting ourselves to the Savior and welcoming him, we enter joyfully into his holy love.

After this, to help in advancing further, I give instruction about the two great means of uniting ourselves ever more closely to God: the sacraments, by which God comes to us, and prayer by which God draws us to himself. In this consists the Second Part.

In the Third Part, I explain the practice of various virtues that are specially suitable for our progress, giving more attention to some specific counsels that we would not get easily from elsewhere or discover by ourselves.

In the Fourth Part, I help to find out certain snares of the enemies and show how we can escape them and continue on our way.

Finally, in the Fifth Part, I teach how to withdraw for a while in order to refresh ourselves, recover breath, and renew our strength and so afterward be able to gain ground with greater joy and so make further progress in the devout life.

Certainly, I cannot write, nor do I want to write, nor should I write in this *Introduction* anything else than what has been published already on this subject by our predecessors. My dear reader, I offer you the same flowers, but the bouquet that I have made is different from theirs, because the arrangement is not the same.

Those who have written about devotion have nearly all had in mind the instruction of persons completely separated from life in the world. At least, they have taught a kind of devotion leading to such a complete separation. My purpose is to instruct people living in towns, in families, and those at princely courts. These are obliged by their state of life to lead an ordinary life to all outward appearances. Very often such persons do not want even to think of venturing into the devout life, finding an excuse in the false claim that it is impossible.

These people are of the opinion that just as no animal dares to taste of the seed of the plant called "palm of Christ" so no one caught up in the rush of living in the world should reach out for the palm of Christian devotion. But I want to make them understand that, just as the pearl oysters live in the sea without letting in a single drop of salt water, and just as there are springs of fresh water in the sea close to the Chelodonian islands, and just as a certain insect can fly about in the fire without burning its wings, so anyone with courage and determination can live in the world without being tainted by its spirit, finding springs of the fresh water of devotion in the world's salty waves and able to fly amid the flames of the temptations of the world without losing the wings of the holy desires of a devout life.

This task in difficult, it is true, and that is why I should like many to give it their attention with greater earnestness than has been shown until now. In spite of my great imperfection, I am trying to provide by means of this book some help to those who will take up this worthy task with a generous heart....

As this age is very peculiar, I expect that many will say that only members of religious orders and persons concerned with devotion should give such special guidance regarding the devout life; that this work requires more leisure than is at the disposal of a bishop who is entrusted with a diocese as burdensome as mine; that it is too great a distraction for the mind, which should be used for important matters. My dear reader, I tell you with St. Denis that guiding people to perfection is the task mainly of bishops, all the more so since their order is the highest among human beings as that of the seraphim is among the angels, and so their leisure cannot be put to better use than this.

The bishops of ancient times and the fathers of the church had at least as much concern for their responsibilities as we have. Even so, as can be gathered from their letters, they did not neglect taking care to give individual guidance to many persons who came to them for help. In this they imitated the apostles, who, while gathering the harvest in the whole world, picked up nevertheless with a special and particular affection certain outstanding ears of corn....

The guidance of persons individually is a difficult task, I admit, but one that brings comfort, as in the case of people gathering crops or picking grapes, who are happiest when they have plenty of work to do and heavy burdens to carry. It is a task that refreshes and enlivens the heart by the delight it brings to those who take it up, just as in Arabia those who carry cinnamon are refreshed.

A tigress, it is said, on finding one of her cubs, which the hunter has left behind to distract her attention while he carries away the others, places it on her back even if it is big. Rather than feeling its weight she finds it very light as she runs off to keep it safe in her den, because her natural love makes her burden less heavy. Much more gladly will someone with a fatherly heart take charge of a person whom he finds with a desire for holiness, showing tender love for such a one like a mother carrying her little child in her bosom without being weary of this burden that she loves so well. But definitely the fatherly heart has to be there. Hence, the apostles, and those like them, call their disciples not just "children" but even more lovingly "little children" (1 John 2:1).

My dear reader, in spite of all that I have said, it is true that

I am writing about the devout life without being devout myself. But I certainly want to be devout, and it is this very desire that encourages me to give you instruction. In fact, to quote a great and learned man, "A good way to learn is to study, a better way is to listen, and the best is to teach." ...

Now my dear reader, I am of the opinion that as bishop it is God's will that I should paint on the hearts of people not only the ordinary virtues but also God's most dear and greatly loved devotion. And I take up this work gladly, as much to obey and fulfill my duty as in the hope that while engraving the minds of others, my own would become filled with a holy love for it. And if God ever sees me enamored of devotion, God will give her to me in an everlasting marriage.

The beautiful and chaste Rebecca, watering Isaac's camels, was chosen to be his wife and received from him earrings and golden bracelets. In the same way, I hope from the infinite goodness of God that while I lead his sheep to the saving waters of devotion, God will make me wholly his own. He will put in my ears the golden words of his holy love and in my arms the strength to practice them well, for in this consists the essence of true devotion. I humbly ask God to grant this devotion to me and to all the children of his church. And to this church I want to submit always my writings, my actions, my words, my desires, and my thoughts.

+ FRANCIS DE SALES
Bishop of Geneva

In his preface, Bishop de Sales speaks "heart to heart" with his readers, extending an invitation to them to embrace the devout life. You will notice two things right away. First, he had a certain flare for employing metaphor and image in his writing. Some contemporary readers find his "flowery" language off-putting. It seems too mannered for those who want their spiritual lessons taken straight with a shot of asceticism. But it is important to be mindful of the historical moment in which Francis de Sales wrote as well as his intent in using such language. On the one hand, communication in seventeenth-century aris-

tocratic society was more formal, more self-conscious than that
to which most twentieth-century readers are accustomed. And
Francis wrote this piece mainly for women like Madame de Charmoisy, for whom genteel or colorful allusions, such as the story of
the flower-seller Glycera, would be appealing. (That story, as well
as the story of the tiger cubs and many other tales in the *Introduction*, comes from the Roman author and naturalist Pliny, whose
Natural History Francis enjoyed quoting.)

In his creative use of metaphor and simile, which can be seen
throughout his writing, Francis was not only appealing to the
polite sensibilities of his female readers; he was employing the
rhetorical skills he had learned as a student. The point of writing and of speaking in the classical rhetoric in which de Sales
was trained was to move the hearts and minds of the reader/
listener. His intent was to draw people's attention to their innate desire for God. So he used the language of desire to describe
the spiritual journey. His aim was to capture the human imagination and stir up aesthetic sensibility — in other words the
longing for beauty — by creating beauty. This was not mere device or artifice. Frances de Sales believed deeply that all human
capacities had been given in order that human beings might return home to God. The arts, literature, music, and architecture of
his day proclaimed this. Creativity of all kinds was employed to
bring people to God. Put another way, Francis and many of his
contemporaries in the Roman church believed that God created
human beings with the longing and the capacity to be united
with God. All life, especially human life, is infused with this divine restlessness, this ardent seeking. Human beings should call
upon all their innate potential to realize their longings. So beautiful words, colorful images, and carefully turned phrases are to
be employed to draw the imagination, the heart, and the mind
toward their source and final end: God.

Second, you will notice that Francis is rather self-effacing
about claiming he was not saying anything very original. By this
he meant that he was basing much of what he said upon his wide
reading of the spiritual classics. Versed in the Latin language,
he was familiar with the writings of the luminaries in the tradi-

tion of prayer. Deeply steeped in Ignatian spirituality through his Jesuit schooling and continued contact with Jesuit spiritual directors, Francis also absorbed all the spiritual influences of his day. He was well acquainted with current trends. He carried about with him a copy of the *Spiritual Combat*, a popular Italian guide to the spiritual life. And he was conversant with the writings of the Spaniards Louis of Granada and Teresa of Avila, whose influence was being newly felt in France. It was an era, not unlike our own, of peaked interest in spiritual practice and the rapid dissemination of spiritual literature. When in Paris de Sales was a familiar visitor at the salon of Madame Acarie. Here the individuals who were to become the beacons of the French mystical renaissance were to be found.

So de Sales knew his tradition, both past and present. He knew that the bias in the tradition was toward monastic life or the life of withdrawal and that most of the classic literature of prayer was articulated from that perspective. He also knew that devotion was in fact possible in all walks of life. Certainly he was not the first person to suggest such an idea. The history of Christian spirituality is crowded with people and movements that experimented with different lifestyles for individuals and communities to realize the ideal Christ life. In his own day Francis de Sales was not unique in believing that vitally lived Christian commitment was not the prerogative of monks, nuns, and priests only. (The Protestant Reform was suggesting the same idea in a very different way.) But Francis was the person who articulated this idea and gave practical form to it most persuasively in seventeenth-century Roman Catholic circles. He had a knack for being able to pull out from the monastically oriented classics the universal gems of wisdom that were hidden there and to integrate them into contemporary concerns and idiom.

At the forefront of this new mood in Christendom was the Society of Jesus — the Jesuits — founded by Ignatius of Loyola in 1540. The Jesuits were a group of men who took the traditional monastic vows of poverty, chastity, and obedience but were not subject to the enclosure central to the monastic life. They embraced an active life of apostolic service, committing themselves to furthering the kingdom of Christ. By the seventeenth century one of their chief works was the operation of schools all over Europe. The Jesuits were educating many of Europe's young men, shaping them for various careers but always instilling in them a sense of mission — to further the values of Christ through all of their actions. Francis had attended one such school early in his educational career, the Collège of Claremont in Paris, and it had stamped him indelibly with its spirit.

Perhaps what formed him most was his experience of the *Spiritual Exercises* devised by Ignatius. In many ways the *Introduction* might be seen as Francis de Sales' adaptation of this process of prayer and affective reflection to the lives of aristocratic women in France and Savoy. For the object of the *Exercises* was the ordering of life and affection in the service of the kingdom of Christ. The bishop's description of true devotion that prefaces his little book makes this clear.

A DESCRIPTION OF TRUE DEVOTION

You seek devotion, dearest Philothea, because as a Christian you know that it is a virtue very pleasing to God. Small mistakes made at the beginning of any project grow infinitely great as it progresses, and in the end are almost impossible to correct. Hence you should know, before everything else, what the virtue of devotion is.

There is only one true devotion while there is a very large number of false and meaningless ones. So if you cannot recognize true devotion, you could be deceived and waste time in following some devotion that is irrelevant and irrational.

Aurelius used to draw all the faces in the pictures he painted with the expressions and appearance of the women he loved. So each one represents devotion according to his liking and imagination. Those who are in the habit of fasting will think that because they fast they are very devout, even though their hearts are filled with hatred. They will not take a sip of wine, or even of water, anxious about sobriety, but they have no scruples to drink the blood of their neighbor by speaking ill or by false statements. Others consider themselves devout because of the very great number of prayers they recite every day, even though soon after this they speak words that are annoying, full of pride, and hurtful to those in their house and to their neighbors. Others very gladly open their purse to give alms to the poor but cannot take any gentleness from their hearts to forgive their enemies. Yet others will forgive their enemies but will not pay what they owe unless they are legally forced to do so. All such persons are generally looked upon as devout whereas in fact they are not.

When Saul's soldiers came looking for David in his house, Michal placed a statue on a bed and covered it with David's clothes and so made them believe that it was David himself asleep due to illness (1 Sam. 19:11–16). In the same way, many people cover themselves with various external actions related to holy devotion. The world takes them for people who are truly devout and spiritual whereas in reality they are nothing more than statues and illusions of devotion.

Dear Philothea, devotion that is true and living presupposes the love of God; rather it is nothing else than a true love of God. It is not, however, love as such. Insofar as divine love enriches us it is called grace, which makes us pleasing to God. In so far as it gives us the strength to do good, it is called charity. But when it grows to such a degree of perfection that it makes us not only to do good but rather moves us to do it carefully, frequently, and promptly, it is called devotion. Ostriches never fly, hens fly only awkwardly, quite low, and rarely; but eagles, doves, and swallows fly often, swiftly, and very high. In the same way, sinners do not fly toward God, but rather all their movements are on the earth and for the things of the earth. People who are good, but have not yet come to devotion, fly toward God by their good deeds, but rarely, slowly, and with difficulty. Persons who are devout fly to God frequently, promptly, and freely.

In short, devotion is nothing else than a spiritual agility and liveliness by means of which charity realizes its actions in us, or we do so by charity promptly and lovingly.

Just as it is the work of charity to make us keep all the commandments of God in general and without any exception so it is the work of devotion to make us do so promptly and earnestly. Therefore, whoever does not keep all of God's commandments cannot be considered either good or devout, because to be good one must have charity. To be devout one must not only have charity but a great liveliness and promptness in doing charitable actions....

In conclusion, charity and devotion are not more different from each other than the flame from the fire, all the more so because charity is a spiritual fire, which when it burns with intense flames is called devotion. In fact, devotion adds to the fire of charity only the flame that makes charity prompt, active, and diligent not only to keep God's commandments but also to put into practice God's counsels and inspirations.

DEVOTION IS SUITABLE TO EVERY KIND OF LIFE-SITUATION AND OCCUPATION

God commanded the plants, at the creation, to bear fruit "each according to its kind" (Gen. 1:11). Similarly, God commands Christians, the living plants of the church, to produce the fruits of devotion, according to each one's ability and occupation.

Devotion is to be practiced differently by the noble, the worker, the servant, the prince, the widow, the young girl, the wife. Even more than this, the practice of devotion has to be adapted to the strength, life-situation, and duties of each individual.

Do you think, dear Philothea, that it is suitable for a bishop to desire to live the life of a hermit like a Carthusian monk? If people with a family were to want to be like the Capuchins not acquiring any property, if a worker spent a great deal of time in church like the member of a religious order, and if a religious was always subject to being disturbed in all sorts of ways for the service of his neighbor like a bishop, would not such devotion be ridiculous, disorderly, and intolerable? However, this sort of fault is very common. The world, which does not distinguish or does not want to distinguish between devotion and the indiscretion of those who consider themselves devout, complains and finds fault with devotion that is in no way responsible for such disorders.

Indeed, Philothea, devotion in no way spoils anything if it be true; rather it makes everything perfect. When it conflicts with any person's legitimate occupation, it is without doubt false. "The bee," says Aristotle, "sucks honey from flowers without damaging them," leaving them as whole and fresh as it found them. But true devotion does even better. Not only does it not spoil any sort of life-situation or occupation, but on the contrary enriches it and makes it attractive. All sorts of precious stones when immersed in honey have a greater brilliance, each according to its color. Similarly, we all become more pleasant in our state of life by joining it with devotion. Devotion makes the care of the family peaceful, the love of husband and wife more sincere, the service of the ruler more loyal, and every sort of occupation more pleasant and more loveable.

It is an error, or rather a heresy, to try to exclude the devout life from the soldiers' regiment, the worker's shop, the court of rulers, or the home of the married. It is true, Philothea, that a devotion which is purely contemplative, monastic, and religious cannot be practiced in such occupations. However, besides these three sorts of devotion, there are many others suitable for leading to perfection those who live their lives in the world. This is attested in the Old Testament by Abraham, Isaac and Jacob, David, Job, Tobit, Sarah, Rebecca, and Judith....

THE NECESSITY OF A GUIDE TO BEGIN AND TO MAKE PROGRESS IN DEVOTION

When young Tobit was told to go to Rages, he said, "I do not know the way at all." The father replied, "Well, go and find someone to be your guide" (Tobit 5:2, 4). Similarly, I say to you, dear Philothea: If you want to set our earnestly on the path of devotion, find some good person to guide and direct you. This is the most important advice. The devout [John of] Avila writes that in whatever way you search, "You will never find the will of God with such certainty as by following the path of this humble obedience so much recommended and practiced by all the devout persons of the past."

Blessed Mother Teresa [of Avila], knowing that a certain lady, Catherine of Cardona, did severe acts of penance, was eager to imitate her in this against the advice of her confessor, who had forbidden her to do so. Because she was tempted to disobey him on this point, God said to her: "My daughter, you are in a way that is good and safe. Do you see the penance she is doing? But I value more your obedience." So she loved this virtue so much that, besides the obedience owed to her superiors, she vowed a special obedience to a very good man and bound herself to follow his direction and guidance, by which she was very greatly consoled.

Similarly, before her and after, many good people in order to better subject themselves to God have submitted their will to that of God's servants, and this is very greatly praised by St. Catherine of Siena in her *Dialogues.* The devout princess, St. Elizabeth, submitted herself in absolute obedience to the learned Master Conrad. The great St. Louis, before his death, gave his son this counsel: "Make your confession frequently; choose a confessor, a suitable one, who is a prudent man who can teach you with certainty to do the things you need to do."

"A faithful friend," says Holy Scripture, "is a strong defense: whoever has found one has found a treasure. A faithful friend is the medicine of life and of immortality: those who fear the Lord will find one" (Sir. 6:14, 16). These divine words, you will note, refer principally to *immortality,* for which it is necessary to have, more than any thing else, this faithful friend to guide our actions by advice and counsel and so keep us safe from the snares and deceits of the evil one. Our friend will be like a *treasure* of wisdom to us in our difficulties, sorrows, and failures. Our friend will serve as a *medicine* to soothe and comfort our hearts in our spiritual illnesses. Our friend will protect us from evil and help to improve our good. When we are spiritually ill, our friend will prevent our illness from leading to our death since he will help us to recover.

But who will find such a friend? The Wise Man answers: "those who fear the Lord" (Sir. 6:16), that is, the humble who earnestly desire their spiritual progress. Since it is so very important for you, Philothea, that on this holy journey of devotion you travel with a good guide, pray very earnestly to God to give you one after his own heart, and do not doubt. Even if it is necessary to send an angel from heaven, as he did for young Tobit, God will give you a guide who is good and faithful.

Always look upon this guide as an angel, that is, once you find him do not consider him as an ordinary man. And do not put your trust in him or in his human knowledge but in God. God will give you grace and speak to you through this man, putting in his heart and in his mouth whatever is needed for your happiness. You should listen to him as to an angel come down from heaven to take you there. In your dealings with him open your heart, with complete sincerity and fidelity, clearly disclosing to him the good and the bad in you without pretending or concealing. In this way, the good in you will be assessed and made more secure, and the bad will be set right and cured. So you will be given relief and strength in your troubles and moderation and control in your joys. Have very great confidence in him along with a holy reverence, in such a way that reverence may not lessen confidence nor confidence hinder reverence. Entrust yourself to him with the respect of a daughter for her father, and respect him with the confidence of a son in his mother. In short, this friendship should be strong and gentle, entirely holy, entirely sacred, entirely divine, and entirely spiritual.

And that it may be so, choose one from a thousand, writes John of Avila. And I insist choose one from ten thousand, for those who are fit for such a task are very few indeed. He must be full of charity, of knowledge, and of prudence. If he lacks any one of these three qualities, there is danger.

But I tell you once again, ask God to give you such a person, and when you find one give thanks to God. Be faithful and do not look for others. Rather, move on with simplicity, humility, and confidence, for your journey will be full of happiness.

As his preface makes clear, the project Francis de Sales had in mind was less an initiation into a practice or form of life than an immersion into an entire attitude of being. Devotion was not simply doing something (good works or pious practices) but rather an orientation of the heart that flows forth in action. For de Sales the religious or devout person was not one who fulfills specific obligations but one who responds willingly and sensitively to the breath of the spirit animating his or her life. Thus flexibility and freedom are crucial to undertaking the devout life. One cannot allow narrow attitudes, habits, or concerns to hinder responsiveness to the touch of God, which is always surprise, always new life. At the same time, de Sales assumed that the spirit, as lively and unpredictable as it might be, works within the structures and choices of human life. Thus, to follow the voice of God is not always to be called to abandon the persons and occupations that make up one's life. In this, he modified somewhat the Roman religious ethos of his age, which was reasserting the primacy of the monastic or vowed life over against the churches of the Reform, which deliberately abandoned those lives in favor of marriage and "secular" work as the normative way for all Christians.

In fact, de Sales wanted to have it both ways. On the one hand, he affirmed that people in all lifestyles cannot follow a purely monastic devotion. In this, of course, he is in one sense correct, for monasticism is an entire lifestyle that involves renouncing family relationships and living in an ordered intentional community under the specific guidelines of a rule. It purposely cultivates separation, silence, and solitude as the appropriate stances for religious transformation. Not all lifestyles can encourage this in the same total way. On the other hand, the Genevan bishop wants to say that devotion is possible for all, no matter where they find themselves. It can be lived in any circumstance because it is not essentially outward but inward.

In the earlier centuries of Christianity it was assumed that if one wanted to truly live the Christ life one should first *do* something different. If the countercultural reality that Jesus came to initiate was to be embraced, then one should follow a practice that would break down habituated ways of seeing or adopt a style of life that clearly broke with the established cultural norms or wear clothing or live in a fashion that set one apart from the ordinary un-Christlike world. It was assumed that doing something different gradually had the effect of changing the doer. Francis assumed (and in this he is modern) that to change outwardly you needed to change inwardly first. He didn't mean that living the Christ life was a very private affair. He meant that external change or actions come from a changed heart. While this may seem obvious to us, it was not always the way early and medieval Christians went about living the Christ life. For them, adopting a practice (fasting, bowing, renouncing wealth, etc.) should gradually change the heart. De Sales starts from the inside out. That's where "Live Jesus!" fits. By this exclamation he asserts that one must have the name of Jesus engraved on one's heart. The outward fruits will follow.

There is one point that Francis de Sales makes emphatically clear in his preface: one should have a spiritual director to practice effectively the devout life. A word needs to be said about this assertion. Spiritual direction as it was practiced in the seventeenth century was somewhat different from spiritual direction as it is generally practiced in the contemporary Christian context. Perhaps a short historical survey might make this clear.

Christians from earliest times have always felt the need to encourage and support one another in their faith. Community is essential to any fully lived religious experience. Precisely because we are interdependent beings we do not grow in knowledge or love of God apart from the interaction of others who are wise and loving and more experienced than we. Even in the solitude of the early fourth- and fifth-century desert hermitages this was true. In fact, the Christian tradition of spiritual guidance has its beginnings in those hermitages. Neophytes in the desert sought out the abba (father) or amma (mother) to pass on a word of life. While it was assumed that the real teacher of the novice hermit was God or the Holy Spirit operating in the silence of the hermit's cell, nonetheless the insight of a teacher was seen to be of importance. The elder amma or abba was a charismatic figure known to embody the simple, profound wisdom of desert prayer. She or he gave to the seeker a particular word that corresponded to the spiritual needs of that seeker. The word was not so much an instruction as something to be lived into, a wisdom that was uniquely suited to the spiritual condition of the disciple, which would unfold as the years went by.

As the hermit life of the desert gave way to the cenobitic or communal life of monasticism, the tradition of spiritual guidance continued, but in a new form. The rule of the monastery became the word by which the disciple lived. The rule was a formative medium through which transformation of the monk into the image and likeness of God in Christ (as it was understood in that period) was achieved. The superior of the monastery — the abbot or abbess — was a spiritual guide in the sense that he or she guided the community in the way of the rule. While the superior was in authority over everyone in the monastery and while obedience in all things to him or her was due, an individual might also have a spiritual guidance relationship with another in the community who had lived the life longer and who had a special gift for guiding others on the spiritual journey.

The art and practice of spiritual guidance spilled out beyond cloister walls in the medieval world with the innovation of new forms of Christian life. With the creation of the mendicant orders — the Franciscans and Dominicans, who lived a mixed life of contemplative withdrawal and active work, especially preaching — came the institution of "third order" communities. These informal lay groups operated under the inspiration of the mendicants. Living in their homes and pursuing ordinary occupations, third order members followed a modified rule of life. They also received support from one another and spiritual mentoring from the orders. During this same period, a number of outstanding holy women, some members of third orders, some others living as anchoresses (hermitesses attached to a monastery or church), and others acting independently, gained prominence as spiritual guides. In fact, persons with an outstanding reputation for holiness had always been sought out for advice by ardent Christians groping for a foothold on the sometimes slippery spiritual path.

But in the Middle Ages, manifest holiness was enough to establish one as a guide who was sought out by others. Thus guidance was noninstitutionalized and charismatic. It was determined by the gifts of the one who served as guide.

The techniques of prayer and discernment (evaluating interior movements) that were transmitted from guide to disciple varied from period to period and person to person, but they all drew on a common store of images and accumulated wisdom that had been unfolding from the era of the desert hermits. The medieval world had a special propensity for affective meditation, especially upon the life and passion of Christ. This trend came to fruition in the sixteenth century in the process of spiritual guidance developed by Ignatius of Loyola. The method is sometimes termed "interventionist" because the guide is one who, having experienced the interior process outlined in Ignatius' *Spiritual Exercises*, leads a retreatant through a series of meditations, examinations of conscience, and imaginative contemplations. The guide discerns the meaning, source, and directionality of the retreatant's affectivity, commonly referred to as "spirits." The guide actively confronts the person doing the Exercises with processes and subject matter that are designed to initiate a dynamic that allows him or her to encounter and respond directly to God's initiative.

Frances de Sales himself had experienced the dynamic process of Ignatius' Exercises; and his style of direction, especially as it is revealed in the *Introduction to the Devout Life*, owes much to the Ignatian influence. His use of directed meditations and his practice of gathering a "spiritual bouquet" at the end of the meditation day are variant forms of what one finds in the Exercises.

But a new model of spiritual guidance was developing at the same period in the Roman Catholic Church, and Francis was in some ways an early example of this "director of conscience" model of spiritual direction. For centuries the practice of sacramental confession had been gradually becoming closely tied to the practice of spiritual direction. For persons who were not in a monastic community or under the jurisdiction of a bishop, the confessor often became a spiritual director. In the centuries after the Reformation much emphasis was placed upon doctrinal orthodoxy among the faithful, and spiritual experiences were often evaluated for their adherence to normative church dogmatic teaching. Thus a person's spiritual life, his or her unique intimate relationship with God, became less the focus of spiritual direction than the cultivation of approved methods of prayer and avoidance of dubious forms of mysticism or heretical ideas. Clerics became the chief spiritual directors. No longer was spiritual guidance a charism. It was a function of the office of the cleric-confessor. The terms "spiritual direction," "director," and "directee" come from this model of guidance, which dominated Catholic practice for three hundred years.

Francis de Sales as a director was an example of the best of this "director of conscience" style of guidance, which reflects the strongly hierarchical model of church that prevailed from the seventeenth to mid-twentieth centuries. It could be poorly exercised by someone without a real charism in the discernment of interior movements. But Francis had this gift. For him spiritual direction was not simply the passing on of a system of ideas or methods of prayer, although it was that in part, as seen in the *Introduction.* It was first and foremost a process of intuitive response practiced between two persons. The directee came to the director seeking guidance in how best to respond to the Christian imperative and bringing the nascent yearning of his or her heart. The director helped that person to discern these promptings, to lean toward what we today would term the center of the self, to distinguish movements of the heart that seemed to be from God and those that seemed to be aligned to purposes alien to God, and to propose practices that might encourage the free expression of those God-born impulses as well as practices that might curb the impulses born of other sources.

The Genevan bishop saw himself less as a professional dispensing information to the uninformed than as a fellow Christian walking the same road as the directee. In such a context all director/directee relationships were in some sense friendships although their intensity and mutuality differed. Much of what

Francis did as a director is remarkably modern in its feel. It is also in continuity with the charism of spiritual guidance as exercised over the centuries preceding him. Yet he was also firmly rooted in the thought world of this time and could insist that a directee look upon his or her director as an "angel, not merely a man."

Spiritual direction as it is generally practiced in the twentieth century is not of the "director of conscience" type. Although some priests and ministers are formally engaged in spiritual direction, many are not. And many spiritual directors are not priests or ministers. The practice of spiritual direction is formally separate from sacramental confession. There has been a return, in recent years, to seeing spiritual guidance as a charism discovered among all Christians: ordained, lay, men, women, celibate, married, single. In addition, the developing fields of psychology, counseling, and psychiatry have profoundly colored the way in which spiritual direction tends to be undertaken now. There is an awareness of life cycle development, personality dysfunction, addiction, family systems theory, and the dynamics of pastoral interaction that shapes what happens in a spiritual direction session. Further, the religious pluralism and ecumenism of contemporary life have generally been embraced in modern spiritual direction. Emphasis tends to focus upon the unique relationship between the directee and his or her own God and not on the theological vision that lies behind it. Attentiveness to the diversity of ways in which prayer can occur, the religious propensities of differing personality types, and the diverse ways of naming the divine has likewise influenced spiritual direction.

When Francis de Sales speaks of the necessity of a spiritual guide in the life of devotion, he is anticipating what many people say in today's world, that people need accompaniment in the life of deepening faith. Worship communities, small faith-sharing groups, friendships, or shared spiritual commitments, as well as formal spiritual guidance are all ways such accompaniment may take shape. Francis de Sales also stresses the point that such accompaniment is especially vital for persons not in formal religious vows — in other words, lay persons. The point is still well taken today because the community of support and shared vision that, at least in theory, exists in a religious order or among those professed to ministry is often absent in the lives of lay persons.

Meditations on the Purpose of Life

After the opening discussion of the nature of devotion, the *Introduction* continues with a set of meditations designed to prepare the individual to consciously and freely embrace a devout life. De Sales' meditations clearly reflect the influence of the Ignatian *Exercises*. The purpose of the meditations is to implant firmly the awareness in both mind and heart of humankind's true identity as children of God created to know, remember, love, and praise the Creator. Thus we are encouraged to look carefully at our life and to evaluate the ways in which we have or have not made use of talents and capabilities. Then, as we reflect on the goodness of God, the possibilities for beauty and goodness inherent in human life, the shortness of life, the consequences of neglecting or misusing our gifts, we come to the point of choice. In the language of the tradition, we make an election. We make a firm resolution to start anew, to serve God with all our capacities, and to use all the means at our disposal to embrace a life of devotion, a life oriented toward the love and service of God.

At the end of each of the little meditations that conclude the first part of the *Introduction to the Devout Life*, the reader is invited to gather a little "spiritual nosegay." The phrase may strike twentieth-century readers as a bit sentimental, but the gentlewomen for whom de Sales penned this piece were accustomed to delighting in the polite and the gracious turn of phrase. As a spiritual teaching, gathering a little nosegay is profound. Good intentions and meaningful thoughts are useless unless they take form in action. They need to be impressed upon consciousness, burned into the flesh of our lives. So to distill from a longer, amorphous meditation a short, memorable phrase or image is to make the branding iron that can effect a lasting mark. In the spiritual journey, remembering is always an essential, formative act. We constantly need to be reminded of who we truly are and what is most essential in life. De Sales' spiritual bouquets allow us, using an olfactory metaphor, to breathe in memories of who we most essentially are and what we are called to become.

The process described in the meditations engages the memory, intellect, will, and affections. The meditator is invited to recall the depth of God's love and the fact that we are God's children, to exercise the intellect on the topic of the meditations, to make deliberate choices based on insight gained, and to integrate affectively those choices into the fabric of our lives through prayer. The meditations are, obviously, directed toward the whole person, so that the choice of the devout life will be deep, lasting, and transformative.

FIRST MEDITATION: OUR CREATION

Preparation

1. Place yourself in the presence of God.

2. Ask God earnestly to inspire you.

Reflections

1. Consider that a few years ago you were not in the world and that you were just nothing. Where was I then? The world was already existing a long time but there was no news of me.

2. God has given you existence from this nothingness. God has made you what you are, without having need of you and only because of his goodness.

3. Consider the kind of being God has made you: the first in the visible world, capable of everlasting life and of perfect union with himself.

Give Vent to Good Movements of the Will and Make Deliberate Decisions

1. *Humble yourself profoundly before God:* Say from your heart with the psalmist: O Lord, "I am truly nothing before you" (Ps. 39:5). How did "you have remembrance" of me to create me

(Ps. 8:4)? Alas I was plunged in that ageless nothingness and I would still be there now if you had not drawn me out. And what would I do in that nothingness?

2. *Give thanks to God:* O my Creator, powerful and good, how much do I owe you, since you have taken me in my nothingness to make me in your mercy what I am. What shall I do always worthily to praise your holy name and to give thanks for your immeasurable goodness?

3. *Be filled with confusion:* Alas, my Creator, instead of uniting myself to you by love and service, I have made myself a rebel by my disorderly attachments. I have separated myself from you and gone away in order to take hold of sin. I have not honored your goodness, as if you were not my Creator.

4. *Cast yourself down before God:* "Know that the Lord is your God. It is he who has made you, and you have not made yourself" (Ps. 100:3). O God I am "the work of your hands" (Ps. 138:8).

5. *From now on,* I will no more be pleased with myself, since of myself I am nothing. In what can I find glory, I who am "dust and ashes" (Sir. 10:9), or rather, true nothingness? What have I to be proud of?

In order to humble myself, *I resolve* to do _____ , bear _____ humiliations. I am determined to change my life and to follow my Creator from now on. I shall honor the kind of being he has given me, making use of it entirely in obedience to his will. For this I will take the means taught me, which I shall find out from my spiritual director.

Conclusion

1. *Thank God.* Bless your God, my soul, "and all my being praise his holy Name" (Ps. 103:1), for his goodness has drawn me from nothingness, and his mercy has created me.

2. *Offer.* My God, I offer you with all my heart the being you have given me. I dedicate and consecrate it to you.

3. *Pray.* My God, strengthen me in these loving desires and

resolutions. Holy Virgin Mary, recommend them to the mercy of your Son, along with all for whom I have to pray, and so on.

Our Father. Hail Mary.

At the end of your prayer, walk about for a while and gather a little bouquet of devotion from your considerations and inhale its fragrance all through the day.

THIRD MEDITATION: GOD'S BLESSINGS

Preparation

1. Place yourself in the presence of God.

2. Ask God to inspire you.

Reflections

1. Think of the *bodily gifts* that God has given you: your body, the many conveniences for its care, your health, all the lawful comforts, your friends, so much that is helpful. While considering all these, compare yourself to so many other persons who are more deserving than you but who have not been given these blessings: Some have defective bodies or lack health or limbs, others are subject to rebuke, disrespect, and dishonor, still others are weighed down with poverty. But God has not allowed that you should suffer such miseries.

2. Think of *your gifts of the mind.* Many people in this world are stupid, insane, or foolish. But you are not one of these. God has shown you favor. Many others have grown up without manners and in complete ignorance. By God's providence you have been given a good education.

3. Think of *your spiritual gifts.* Philothea, you are a child of the church. From the days of your youth God has taught you about himself. How often has he given you his sacraments? How many times inspirations, interior lights, and warnings to correct you? How often has God forgiven you your sins? How many times has he saved you when you were exposed to spiritual ruin? Have not these past years been time and opportunity for you

to grow in goodness? Consider for a short while in detail how gentle and loving God has been to you.

Give Vent to Good Movements of the Will and Make Deliberate Decisions

1. *Admire God's goodness:* How good is my God to me. He is good indeed. "Lord, your heart is rich in mercy and full of loving-kindness" (Ps. 86:5). I will proclaim forever his numerous graces to me.

2. *Wonder at your ingratitude:* What am I, Lord, that you are mindful of me (Ps. 8:4)? I am most unworthy indeed. Alas, I have trodden underfoot your blessings. I have dishonored your gifts, turning them into insult and contempt of your sovereign goodness. I have opposed the abyss of my ingratitude to the abyss of your grace and goodness.

3. *Stir yourself up to gratitude:* My heart be no more unfaithful, ungrateful, and disloyal to this great Benefactor. Henceforth, "shall not my soul be subject to God" (Ps. 62:1) who has worked so many wonders and graces in me and for me?

4. Philothea, hold back your body from sensual pleasures and make it subject to the service of God who has done so much for it. Make use of your spirit to know him and acknowledge him by exercises necessary for this purpose. Use carefully the means the church offers to save yourself and to love God.

Yes, I pray regularly and receive the sacraments frequently. I will listen to the word of God and put into practice his inspirations and counsels.

Conclusion

1. Thank God for the knowledge he has now given you of your duty, and for all the blessings till now.

2. Offer him your heart with all your resolutions.

3. Pray to him for strength to practice them faithfully

through the merits of his Son's death. Pray to our Lady and the saints to intercede for you.

Our Father, Hail Mary.

Make the little spiritual bouquet.

TENTH MEDITATION: DELIBERATE CHOICE OF THE DEVOUT LIFE

Preparation

1. Place yourself in the presence of God.

2. Humble yourself before his face. Ask for his help.

Reflections

1. Imagine that you are in the open country again, alone with your Guardian Angel. On your left you see the devil seated on a great raised throne, with many infernal spirits near him. All around him is a vast crowd of worldly people, who with uncovered heads acknowledge him as lord and pay him homage, some by one sin and some by another.

Look at the attitude of all the wretched courtiers of this abominable king: See some furious with hatred, envy, and anger; others killing one another; others worn out, preoccupied, and anxious in gathering wealth; others obsessed with worthless things, without any kind of pleasure but that which is useless and unsatisfying; others dishonest, depraved, corrupted by their brutish longings. See how they are without rest, without order, and without composure. See how they despise one another and how they pretend to love one another. In short, you will see a kingdom marked with disaster, ruled tyrannically by this cursed king. It will move you to compassion.

2. On your right, see Jesus Christ crucified. He prays with a heartfelt love for these miserable subjects of the devils that they may run away from this tyranny, and he calls them to himself. See a vast multitude of the devout all around him with their angels.

Contemplate the beauty of this kingdom of devotion. How beautiful the sight of this assembly of virgins, men and women, whiter than the lily; this gathering of widows, full of holy self-denial and humility. See the group of numerous married persons who live together with such gentleness and in mutual respect, which cannot exist without a great charity. See how these devout persons join the care of their exterior house with the care of the interior, and the love of their earthly spouse with that of the heavenly Spouse.

Look generally everywhere. You will see that their behavior is holy, gentle, and friendly. They listen to our Lord and all want to plant him in the center of their heart. They rejoice, but with a joy that is courteous, charitable, and well ordered. They love one another, but with a love that is holy and most pure. Those among these devout persons who suffer distress are not too upset and do not lose their composure. In a word, see the eyes of the Savior consoling them and see that all of them together long for him.

3. From now on you have turned your back on Satan, with his sad and pitiful company, by the good movements of the will formed in you. But you have not yet come to Christ the King. Nor have you joined his happy and holy assembly of the devout. Rather you have always been between Satan and Christ.

4. Our Lady with St. Joseph, St. Louis, St. Monica, and a hundred thousand others, in the group of those who have lived in the midst of the world, invites and encourages you.

5. The crucified King calls you by your own name: *Come my beloved one, come,* that I may crown you (Song of Songs 4:8).

Election

1. Worldlings, horrid assembly, no, never will you find me under your flag. I give up forever your follies and trivialities. King of pride, king of misery, infernal spirit, I reject you with your worthless show. I detest you with all your works.

2. To you I turn, my loving Jesus, King of happiness and eternal glory. I cling to you with all the powers of my spirit. I adore

you with all my heart. I choose you to be my King now and forever. I am determined to be always faithful to you and I surrender myself to you forever. I dedicate myself to obey your holy laws and commands.

3. Holy Mary, my dear Mother, I choose you for my guide. I place myself under your protection. I want to show you a particular respect and a special reverence. My Guardian Angel, present me to this sacred assembly. Do not ever forsake me so that I may reach this happy gathering. With them I say, and I will say forever, in confirmation of my choice:

Live Jesus, live Jesus.

The heightened affectivity of the election or choice of direction strikes the reader immediately. Francis had been well taught by his Jesuit mentors to pray imaginatively with Scripture or meditation material. The idea was to become immersed in the life and mission of Jesus to the extent that one would make the deliberate and life-altering choice to enlist under the standard of Christ. Ignatius' original metaphors were military. One chose to be a soldier in the forces of Christ, not the forces of Satan (which meant everything not oriented toward God as its end). Bishop de Sales chooses the image of two contrasting kings to make his point.

In recent years it has been popular to recast some of the language and imagery of the Ignatian *Exercises* in terms more congenial to contemporary tastes. Perhaps the same might be done for Francis' images and language here in the *Introduction to the Devout Life*. While attractive new translations have appeared in print, to my knowledge no reworking of the *Devout Life* analogous to the many reworkings of the *Exercises* has ever been attempted. While for some people the image of the kingdom of devotion with its assembly of virgins whiter than snow, self-denying widows, and gentle married couples may speak powerfully, for others it does not. Perhaps a community of persons concerned with the implementation of God's justice and mercy on behalf of the poor and oppressed might be an equally compelling picture. Or alternatively a vision of a creation-centered Christian community committed to the preservation of the planet and the cultivation of a vision of ecological interconnectedness might speak persuasively to others. In any case, the point we need to remember here is that the choice for the kingdom of Christ is at the heart of the *Introduction*. How Christians have envisioned that kingdom and its anticipation in our lives has differed from age to age.

Clearly, both for the contemporary world and for Francis de Sales, the kingdom of Christ is not simply an otherworldly "place" to be aspired to only after death. While the fullness of Christ's kingdom may not be identified with any particular political system, national group, or even church community, the kingdom is a reality into which people live through their choices and actions.

Nourishing the Devout Life

After making the radical choice for God, the task is to continue to live faithfully according to that choice. Thus the second part of the *Introduction* is concerned with "raising oneself to God by prayer and sacraments." Prayer and participation in the sacramental life of the church are considered by Francis to be the necessary means of nourishment in that continuing fidelity. The bishop especially recommends a kind of mental prayer focused on the figure of Jesus the Christ.

PRAYER IS NECESSARY

1. Prayer is opening our understanding of God's brightness and light and exposing our will to the warmth of God's love. Nothing else purifies so well our understanding of its ignorance and our will of its sinful attachments. It is a spring of blessings, and its waters quench the thirst of the passions of our heart, wash away our imperfections, and make the plants of our good desires grow green and bear flowers.

2. I strongly recommend to you prayer of the mind and of the heart, and especially that based on the life and passion of our Lord. By looking upon him often in meditation, your whole being will be filled with him. You will learn his attitudes and model your actions on his....

Let us stay close to him, Philothea. I assure you we can go to God the Father only through this door. The glass of a mirror would not catch our reflection if its back were not covered with tin or lead. Similarly, we could not easily contemplate God in this world if the Divinity were not united to the sacred humanity of the Savior. His life and death are the most suitable, appealing, delightful, and fruitful subjects that we can take for our ordinary meditation.

The Savior calls himself, not without reason, "The bread come down from heaven" (John 6:51). As bread should be eaten with all sorts of food, so also the Savior should be meditated on, considered, and searched for in all our prayers and actions.

The incidents of his life and death have been arranged and presented as points helpful for meditation by many writers.

3. Spend an hour in meditation every day, sometime before the midday meal. If possible do it in the earlier part of the morning, as your mind will be less distracted and more fresh from the night's rest. Do not spend more than an hour, unless your spiritual director expressly tells you to do so.

4. If you find sufficient quiet in church it will be easier and more convenient for you to make your meditation there. No one, neither father nor mother nor wife nor husband nor anyone else is likely to prevent your staying there for an hour. Being in some way dependent on others, you might not be able to make sure of an undisturbed hour while at home.

5. Begin any kind of prayer, whether mental or vocal, by recalling the presence of God. Keep to this rule without exception. You will soon realize how helpful it is for you.

6. I recommend that you say the Our Father, the Hail Mary, and the Apostles' Creed in Latin. But also learn to understand the words well in your own language. Thus, while using the

common language of the church, you will be able to relish the wonderful and delightful meaning of these holy prayers.

You should say them fixing your attention earnestly on the words and allowing their meaning to stir up good movements in your will. Do not hurry in order to say many prayers, but take care to say those that you do say from the heart. One Our Father said earnestly is of greater value than many recited quickly and in a hurry.

7. The rosary is a very helpful way of praying, provided you how know to say it properly. For this get hold of one of the booklets that explain how it should be recited. It is also good to say the litanies of our Lord, of our Lady, and of the saints, and all the other vocal prayers to be found in approved prayer books. However, if you have the gift of mental prayer, it is your responsibility to give it always the first place.

If it happens that after mental prayer you are not able to say any vocal prayers, either because of your many duties or for any other reason, do not be troubled about it. Be satisfied with saying simply the Lord's Prayer, the Hail Mary, and the Apostles' Creed either before or after your meditation.

8. While saying vocal prayers, if you feel your heart drawn and invited to interior or mental prayer, do not turn away, but let your mind go gently in that direction. Do not worry at all that you have not said all the vocal prayers that you had intended to say. In fact, the mental prayer you have made in their place is much more pleasing to God and of greater benefit to yourself. I make an exception with regard to the Divine Office. If you are bound to say it, you must fulfil your obligation.

9. If it happens that the whole morning passes without your having spent time in mental prayer, either because you have been busy or for any other reason (you should not allow this to happen, as far as you possibly can), try to make up for this omission after the midday meal. But find a time as long after the midday meal as possible. If you try to make your meditation soon after your meal, while you are still digesting your food, you will feel very drowsy and it will harm your health.

In case you have not been able to find time for mental prayer during the whole day, make good this loss by saying numerous ejaculatory prayers, reading some spiritual book, and doing some act of penance to prevent the repetition of this fault. With all this, make a firm resolution to take up the practice of daily mental prayer from the following day.

A SHORT METHOD FOR MENTAL PRAYER.
FIRST POINT OF THE PREPARATION:
RECALLING THE PRESENCE OF GOD

Perhaps, Philothea, you do not know how to do mental prayer. Unfortunately, it is something that few people know nowadays. So I teach you a short and simple method for it. It will be of help until you are more fully instructed by reading the numerous good books on this subject, and above all by practice.

I begin with the preparation that consists of two points: the first is to place oneself in the presence of God, and the second is to ask for God's help. I suggest four principal ways of placing yourself in the presence of God that you can use for this preparation.

The first consists in a lively and attentive awareness of the omnipresence of God: God is in everything and everywhere; there is no place or thing in this world where God is not really present. Just as the birds always find the air wherever they fly, so wherever we go or wherever we are, we find God present. This truth is known to everyone, but not everyone is attentive to it to be conscious of it.

Blind persons do not see a prince who is among them. If they are told of his presence, they behave with respect. But in fact, since they do not see him, they easily forget his presence. Having forgotten it, they more easily lose respect and reverence. Alas, Philothea, we do not see God who is present with us. Though faith reminds us of his presence, since we do not see him with our eyes, we very often forget and behave as though God was very far from us. In spite of knowing well that he is present everywhere, we are not attentive to it at all. Hence it is just as if we did not know it.

For this reason, before prayer we must always rouse ourselves to think and consider attentively this presence of God....

The second way of placing yourself in the presence of God is to reflect that God is present not only in the place where you are, but that he is very specially present in your heart and in the very center of your spirit. He enlivens and animates it by his divine presence, being there as the heart of your heart and the spirit of your spirit. The soul is spread throughout the entire body and is present in every part of it, yet resides in a particular manner in the heart. Similarly, God, who is indeed present everywhere, is present in a special way in our spirit. Hence David calls God "the God of his heart" (Ps. 73:26), and St. Paul says that "we live and move and are in God" (Acts 17:28). Considering this truth you will awaken in your heart a deep reverence for God, who is so intimately present there.

The third way is to think of our Savior, who in his humanity sees from heaven all the persons in the world, but particularly Christians who are his children and most especially those who are at prayer, whose actions and behavior he notices. This is not mere imagination but most certain truth. Though we do not see him, yet he looks at us from on high. St. Stephen, at the time of his martyrdom, saw him in this way. So we can truly say with the Spouse: "Look, there he is behind the wall, gazing in at the windows, looking through the lattice" (Song of Songs 2:9).

The fourth way consists in using simple imagination to represent our Savior in his sacred humanity, as if he were near us, just as we are used to imagining our friends and saying, "I imagine I can see a certain person doing this or that, it seems to me that I see him," or some such things. But if the Most Holy Sacrament of the altar is present, then this presence will be real and not merely imaginary. The species and appearance of bread is like a tapestry, from behind which our Lord really present sees and observes us, though we cannot see him as he is.

Make use of one of these four ways to place yourself in the presence of God before prayer. Do not try to use them all together. Use only one at a time and that briefly and simply.

SECOND POINT OF THE PREPARATION:
THE INVOCATION, OR ASKING GOD'S HELP

The invocation is made as follows: Having become aware that you are in the presence of God, cast yourself down with profound reverence. Acknowledge that you are most unworthy to remain before such a supreme Lord. Yet, knowing that his goodness desires it, ask him for the grace to serve and adore him well in this meditation.

You may use, if you wish, some short and fervent words, like these of David: "Do not cast me away, my God, from your face, and do not take from me the favor of your Holy Spirit" (Ps. 51:11). "Let your face shine on your servant" (Ps. 31:16), "and I will see your wonders" (Ps. 119:18). "Give me understanding and I will consider your law, and keep it with my whole heart" (Ps. 119:34). "I am your servant, give me understanding" (Ps. 119:125), and similar words.

It will be of help to pray to your Guardian Angel and the holy persons who are associated with the mystery on which you are meditating. For example, if it is the death of our Lord, you could pray to our Lady, St. John, St. Mary Magdalen, and the Good Thief to share with you the experiences of heart and mind that they had at that time. If the meditation is on your own death, you could pray to your Guardian Angel, who will be with you then to inspire you with suitable reflections, and so on for other mysteries.

THIRD POINT OF THE PREPARATION:
IMAGINING THE SCENE

Besides these two general points to prepare for meditation, there is a third that is not common to every sort of mediation. Some call it the composition of place, and others the interior presentation. This consists in presenting to one's imagination the scene of the mystery taken for meditation, as if it was really and truly taking place before us. For example, if you wish to meditate on our Lord on the cross, imagine that you are on Mount Calvary seeing and hearing all that was done and said on the day of the passion. Or, if you wish, for it is the same thing, imagine that in the very place where you are the crucifixion of our Lord is being carried out, in the way the Evangelists describe it. Follow the same method when you meditate on death. So also for the meditation on hell and on all similar mysteries concerned with things that can be seen or that are perceptible to the senses....

By means of the imaginary scene we fix our mind on the mystery on which we wish to meditate, so that it may not wander to and fro, just as we shut a bird in its cage or as we secure a hawk. Yet, some will tell you that to represent these mysteries it is better to use the simple thought of faith and a simple understanding entirely mental and spiritual, or to think that the events are taking place within your own spirit. But this is too abstract for beginners. So until God raises you higher, I advise you, Philothea, to remain in the low valley that I have shown you.

THE SECOND PART OF MEDITATION: REFLECTIONS LEADING TO GOD

Having made use of the imagination, next make use of the understanding. This is what we call meditation. It consists in making one or many reflections in order to arouse good movements of the will toward God and the things of God. In this, meditation differs from study or other thoughts and reflections that are made, not to acquire virtue or the love of God, but for some other purposes and intentions, such as to become learned, to write, or to take part in a discussion....

As long as you find sufficient attraction, light, and fruit in one of these reflections, stop there without moving on to another. Be like the bees who do not leave a flower as long as they find honey to gather there. But if a reflection is not to your liking, after attending to it and trying it for a while, pass on to another. But go on very gently and simply in this matter, without any hurry.

THE THIRD PART OF MEDITATION:
GOOD MOVEMENTS OF THE WILL
LEADING TO DELIBERATE DECISIONS

Meditation produces good movements in the will, such as the love of God and of our neighbor; the desire of heaven and eternal glory; zeal for the salvation of others; imitation of the life of our Lord; compassion, admiration, joy; fear of God's displeasure, of judgment, and of hell; hatred of sin; confidence in the goodness and mercy of God; shame for the sins of our past life. Our spirit should give vent wholeheartedly to these good movements of the will.

But, Philothea, do not linger too long with these general good movements of the will. You have to change them into deliberate decisions, precise and particular, for your correction and improvement.

For example, the first words spoken by our Lord on the cross will surely arouse in you a good movement of the will to imitate him. That is, you will desire to forgive your enemies and to love them. But I want to make it clear that this will be of little value unless you make a particular deliberate decision like the following: "I will not take offense anymore at such and such annoying words that such and such a person — my neighbor or my servant — may say about me"; or, "I will not be displeased any more by this or that insult from this or that person"; and, "On the contrary, I will say and do such and such a thing in order to win the person over and make him friendly"; and so on with regard to other matters.

CONCLUDING THE MEDITATION AND SPIRITUAL NOSEGAY

Bring the meditation to a close with three acts, which must be made with as much humility as possible:

1. The first is an act of *thanksgiving.* We thank God for the good movements of the will and the deliberate decisions he has given us and for his goodness and mercy that we have discovered in the mystery on which we have been meditating.

2. The second is an act of *oblation.* We offer to God his

goodness and mercy, and the death, the suffering, and the virtues of his Son, and along with these our own good movements of the will and our deliberate decisions.

3. The third is an act of *petition.* We ask God and implore him to give us the graces and virtues of his Son and to bless our good movements of the will and our deliberate decisions so that we can practice them faithfully. We pray also for the church, for our pastors, for our relatives and friends, and others. We ask our Lady, the angels, and the saints to intercede for us. Lastly, as I have already mentioned, we should pray the Our Father and the Hail Mary, the general and necessary prayers for all the faithful.

I have also suggested that, after all this, we should gather a little nosegay of devotion. I shall now explain what I mean. After taking a walk in a beautiful garden, people hesitate to leave without taking four or five flowers in order to enjoy their fragrance the rest of the day. Similarly, having considered some mystery in meditation, we should pick one or two or three ideas in which we took special delight and which are helpful to our improvement. We should remind ourselves of them during the day, breathing in their spiritual fragrance. This nosegay of spiritual thoughts is to be gathered while we are still in the place where we made our meditation, or as we walk about alone for some time soon after.

Readers who are actively engaged in the work force, who have the charge of young families, or who otherwise have limited freedom of time, will note right away that de Sales' advice on when and how long to pray (an hour preferably before the midday meal) was offered to women who had the leisure and household help to arrange their time as they wished. While he does make allowances for days in which fulfillment of this obligation is impossible, in general he assumes that such a prayer discipline is possible and essential to the devout life.

While I would concur that fidelity to prayer (defined quite broadly) is essential to a quickened spiritual life, there may be periods of one's life where very different forms and disciplines of prayer are called forth. For example, a young mother at home with three or four preschool children without outside help may find regular uninterrupted time impossible to arrange. When the toddlers finally go down for their naps, the baby may wake for a feeding. If she tries to get up an hour before her early-rising youngsters in order to pray, she may find herself so exhausted by mid-afternoon that she is unable to deal rationally with her boisterous four-year-old. If she waits to pray until her husband comes home from the late shift at work, she may find precious time for spousal communication eroded. Her prayer at this point in her life may arise less out of conscious focus on Scripture than on a contemplative awareness of the miracle discovered in the baby at her breast or the feverish child she comforts in the middle of the night.

Similarly, not all persons may be temperamentally drawn to mental prayer of the type Francis de Sales describes. It was assumed in his era that mental prayer was a safe, accessible form of prayer at which everyone could succeed. More formative and "deep" than vocal prayer (saying specific liturgical or formulated prayers aloud), mental prayer was distinguished from contemplative prayer, which was considered to be a more advanced form of discourse with God. There were "professional" prayers for this latter prayer, persons called specifically to the life of withdrawal whose sole occupation was to give themselves unreservedly to the cultivation of interior prayer. Generally, this contemplative type of prayer was considered to be mostly nondiscursive and imageless. It was a resting in loving union with God or Jesus as spouse. While this vastly oversimplifies the discussion (for the theological science of the contemplative life was skillfully articulated in this period), de Sales, like his contemporaries, assumed that most lay people would do best to practice the type of mental prayer he outlined here and leave contemplation to "advanced souls."

In the last third of the twentieth century, these traditional notions about contemplative prayer have been challenged. Contemplation is no longer described today as it was in the sixteenth through nineteenth centuries as an elite form of prayer that was a gift of God and generally reserved for those embarked on the life of "perfection." Instead, with a return to assessments of the contemplative life enunciated in the patristic and medieval church, contemplation has come to mean a simple, nondiscursive, wholistic prayer to which anyone may find himself or herself drawn. The contemporary centering prayer movement is an example of the popularization of the practice of contemplative prayer. On the other hand, recent awareness of the variety of ways in which people are drawn to pray (due to temperament, personality, cultural context, gender differences, training, and so forth) brings into question the universality of these prescriptions for mental prayer.

Nonetheless, the great benefit of this type of prayer activity that de Sales describes, whether it is a form to which one is naturally drawn or which is easily accommodated within the confines of one's daily life, is that it is clearly formative. By this I mean it gives one the opportunity to reflect in a focused, narrative way upon the central mystery of the Christian faith. Praying imaginatively and affectively with the story of Jesus creates the conditions by which one's personal life story becomes woven into the fabric of the greater Christian story of God's love and purposefulness. The great overarching story becomes the locus of meaning through which the seemingly random events of one's small story become significant. Mind, heart, imagination, and will are shaped by the narrative into which one ventures in this type of mental prayer. It is in fact an exercise designed so that one might come eventually to "Live Jesus."

The Virtues of the Devout Life

At the core of the *Introduction to the Devout Life* are the teachings on what de Sales calls "the virtues." Nearly all of the third part of the book is concerned with the cultivation of those distinctive attitudes or qualities of person that the Christian tradition has long designated as characteristic of a life conformed to Christ. The virtues enumerated by tradition are many, but chief among them are faith, hope, charity (the three "theological virtues"), and prudence, temperance, fortitude, and justice (the four "cardinal" virtues). Tradition assumed that a person under the influence of God's grace and with attentive effort would grow into the possession of faith, hope, love, prudence, temperance, fortitude, and justice.

But there were a host of other personal qualities that tradition held up as exemplary as well. Many of them come from the desert traditions of spirituality. Humility and simplicity, for instance, were qualities that the desert abbas and ammas constantly praised. And from the monastic tradition come what is known as the counsels of perfection or the evangelical counsels. They are poverty (renunciation of personal property), chastity (abstention from sexual relations), and obedience (submission of the will to a superior in all things). These counsels of perfection form the basis of the vowed religious life in nearly all its forms throughout the centuries. Not listed among the seven classic virtues, the counsels nonetheless inform discussions of virtue and the life modeled on Christ.

Beyond this there are numerous other laudable personal qualities or actions that tradition came to include among the virtues. Francis could mention courage, generosity, honesty, fasting, almsgiving, and such and be understood by his readers to be referring to the virtues. The bishop and his contemporaries felt every person could cultivate the virtuous life. In other words, allowing Jesus to live in you was something that required a certain amount of effort or cooperation on your part. It was a process in which you were actively involved. The virtues were numerous, and it was thought they would be realized in different degrees in different persons. Further, certain virtues would be made more manifest in certain circumstances. For instance, tragic events might call forth great courage in a person.

What is so interesting and distinctive about Francis de Sales' treatment of the virtues is his choice of those to be actively cultivated. Every Christian is called to virtue. But Francis highlighted what he called the "little virtues." These he contrasted to the great heroic virtues that are only rarely called forth. The little virtues are those qualities that become manifest in the common routine of everyday life. Much of what is distinctive about Salesian spirituality is found in this cultivation of the little virtues.

The third part of the *Devout Life* begins by introducing this idea:

WE MUST SELECT THE VIRTUES TO BE PRACTICED

The queen bee never goes to the fields without being accompanied by her little subjects. Similarly charity never enters a heart without finding a lodging there for itself as well as for a retinue of other virtues that it exercises and sets to work as a captain does his soldiers. However, it does not put them to work all at once, nor uniformly, nor at all times and in all places. The just man is "like a tree planted near running waters that bears its fruit in due season" (Ps. 1:3). For charity waters the soul and produces in it virtuous deeds, each in its proper season....

There are virtues that are almost always practiced. These must not only produce their own acts but must also communicate their quality to the acts of all other virtues. Occasions of practicing courage, magnanimity, and great generosity are rare. But gentleness, moderation, honesty, and humility are some of the virtues by which every action of our life should be colored. The practice of these are more necessary, though there are virtues that are more excellent. Sugar is more enjoyable than salt but salt has a more frequent and more general use. We must always have a good store of these general virtues at hand since we ought to make constant use of them.

In the practice of virtues, we must prefer that virtue which corresponds more with our duties than with our tastes.... Every life-situation requires the practice of some particular virtue. Different are the virtues to be practiced by a bishop, by a prince, by a soldier, by a married woman, by a widow. Although all should have all the virtues, nevertheless all are not bound to practice them equally. But we all must devote ourselves to those virtues most needed for the state of life to which we are called.

Among the virtues that do not concern our own duties, we

are to prefer the most excellent and not the most showy. Usually, the comets appear bigger than the stars and occupy more space as seen by us. All the same, they are not comparable to the stars either in their size or in their importance. They appear great because they are closer to us and are of a coarser substance than the stars. Similarly, there are some virtues that, since they are close to us, are more visible and in a way more physical. They are highly esteemed and always preferred by the common people. Thus they usually prefer temporal to spiritual almsgiving; a hair-shirt, fasting, going barefoot, discipline, and mortifications of the body to gentleness, good-naturedness, modesty, and other mortifications of the heart, which, however, are more excellent. Choose then, Philothea, the best virtues and not the most esteemed, the most sublime and not the most spectacular, the most excellent and not the most showy.

It is useful for each one to choose a special practice of some particular virtue. This is not to abandon the other virtues but to keep one's mind more precisely ordered and occupied....

St. Louis, king of France, used to visit the hospitals and serve the sick with his own hands as if he were being paid for it. St. Francis of Assisi loved poverty above everything else and called it his Lady. St. Dominic cherished preaching, from which his order took its name. St. Gregory the Great was happy to take special care of pilgrims, following the example of the great Abraham, and like him received the King of Glory in the form of a pilgrim. Tobit practiced charity by burying the dead. St. Elizabeth, though a great princess, loved humiliations above all else. St. Catherine of Genoa, when she became a widow, devoted herself to the service of a hospital. Cassian narrates that a devout young lady desirous of practicing patience had recourse to St. Athanasius. At her request, he put with her a poor, irritable, ill-tempered, troublesome widow. She constantly scolded the young lady and so gave her sufficient opportunities for worthily practicing gentleness and kindness.

Thus among the servants of God some dedicate themselves to serve the sick, some to help the poor, some to impart Christian doctrine to children, some to bring together lost and wandering persons, some to decorate the church and adorn the altars, and some others to bring about peace and harmony among people. In this they imitate the embroiderers who make all kinds of flowers by placing silk, gold, and silver on different backgrounds in such beautiful variety. Thus these devout persons who undertake some particular practice of devotion make use of it as a background for their spiritual embroidery. It forms the basis for the practice of a variety of other virtues, keeping their actions and affections so united and ordered in their relationship with the principal exercise that they thus reveal their spirit.

> In a robe of golden cloth so beautiful to see
> And adorned with figures fair in rich embroidery.
> (Ps. 45:13)

When we struggle against some vice, as far as possible we ought to embrace the practice of the contrary virtue, relating all the others to it. By this means, we shall overcome our enemy and we shall not cease to advance in all other virtues. If I am attacked by pride or anger, I should in all circumstances incline and direct myself to the practice of humility and gentleness, and make use of the practices such as prayer, the sacraments, prudence, constancy, and temperance to the end.

Wild boars sharpen their tusks by rubbing and polishing them with their other teeth, which thus become very pointed and sharp. Thus virtuous persons, undertaking to perfect themselves in that virtue of which they stand most in need for their protection, should strengthen and perfect it through the exercise of other virtues. By refining it, all other virtues become more excellent and quite complete.

Francis de Sales had, as you have just seen, a fondness for the little, common virtues. Throughout his writings he lists them. Which are they exactly? His lists vary. Usually included are humility, gentleness, simplicity, patience. I would single out especially gentleness as the most distinctive virtue of the spirituality that Francis exemplified. The French term that is usually translated as gentleness is *douceur.* Sometimes it is rendered in English as "sweetness," "meekness," or "suavity." But those translations do not convey the fullness of the virtue of *douceur.* I like to think of it as "gracefulness" and "graciousness" as well as "gentleness." Gracefulness extends from external demeanor to the internal ordering of a person's heart. One is both gracious in interactions with others and graciously ordered within. For the bishop being gentle or gracious had everything to do with living Jesus.

Most people hold a particular image of Jesus in mind and heart. There are many such images found in the gospels themselves. Perhaps one favorite might be the Jesus of the Last Judgment (Matt. 25:31–46) who warns that external punishment will come to those who neglected him when they refused to welcome him in the stranger, clothe him in the naked, visit him in the sick and imprisoned. Perhaps a favorite image is the Jesus of John 6:54, who promises that anyone who eats his flesh and drinks his blood will have eternal life. Perhaps it is Jesus hanging on the cross who, in Luke's Gospel (23:33–34), in the midst of his agony offers forgiveness to his enemies with the words, "Father forgive them; they do not know what they are doing." The images are manifold. Different spiritual traditions and different historical eras will tend to focus attention upon a specific image and thus cluster thought and action in conformity to that image.

Salesian spirituality looks especially to Jesus as depicted in Matthew 11:28–30: "Come to me, all you who labor and are overburdened and I will give you rest. Shoulder my yoke and learn from me for I am gentle and humble of heart and you will find rest for your souls. Yes, my yoke is easy and my burden light." It is the central phrase of the passage that is most important in Francis de Sales' understanding of Jesus: "Learn from me for I am gentle and humble of heart." The invitation to learn from, to imitate, to follow, to be as Jesus receives the stress. And what is Jesus like? He is gentle and humble of heart. That is, the core of his being, his most essential self, the point from which all actions and thoughts flow — the heart — has the qualities of gentleness and humility. For Francis this was a radically countercultural idea, for most hearts are not gentle and humble but proud, grasping, and envious. There is a kind of subversiveness to Francis' understanding of the Christ-life; in this he is tutored by St. Paul. While it may appear that strength, power, and capability should be desirable qualities, these are in fact somewhat dubious virtues. Francis was quoted as saying, "Nothing is so strong as gentleness, nothing so gentle as real strength." For him, this truth had eschatological significance, for Jesus the Christ came to overturn the standards of the world and enflesh a new standard of reality. Gentleness and humility were signs of the presence of the kingdom. To live these little virtues was to begin to realize God's intent for humankind.

All of the little virtues are primarily relational. They offer the possibility of realizing a community of mutual love and respect. This, I think, is one of the distinctive features of Francis' thought and one that translates most easily into another historical era. What he was about was a very biblical enterprise: the creation of a human community that genuinely loved as it had first been loved by God.

At the root of this loving community is the art of living the gentle, humble Jesus. Gentleness or graciousness is one of his qualities. Another is humility. Humility, unlike gentleness, is not a virtue uniquely developed in the Salesian spiritual tradition, but humility is one of the most consistently admired virtues in Christian spiritual literature. It was a favorite of the desert hermits and then became a prime virtue of monasticism.

Bishop de Sales' exploration of humility reflects aristocratic lay life in the seventeenth century, but he sees true humility as essential to the devout life. He makes a distinction between external and internal humility.

EXTERNAL HUMILITY

"Borrow empty vessels," said Elisha to a poor widow, "and pour oil into them" (2 Kings 4:3–4). To receive the grace of God into our hearts, we ought to empty them of our own glory. The kestrel crying out and looking at birds of prey frightens them away by its characteristic secret power. Because of it, the doves love it more than all other birds and live in security close to it. In the same way, humility drives away Satan and preserves in us the graces and gifts of the Holy Spirit. Therefore all the saints and especially the King of saints and his mother have always honored and cherished this precious virtue more than any other moral virtue.

Vainglory is the glory we give ourselves for what is not in us, or for what is in us but is not ours, or what is in us and is ours but for which we do not deserve any credit. Nobility of race, the favor of the great, and popularity are not in us but either in our predecessors or in the esteem of others. Some feel themselves proud and haughty because they ride on a good horse, have a feather in their cap, or are splendidly attired. But who does not see that all this is folly? If there is any glory in these things, it belongs to the horse, to the bird, and to the tailor. What meanness to borrow one's esteem from a horse, from a feather, or from a garment.

Some take pride in their curled moustaches, a well-trimmed beard, crimped hair, soft hands, in their ability to dance, play, or sing. Are they not showing lack of courage in seeking to enhance their value and increase their reputation through such trifling and silly things? Some wish to be honored and respected by people for a little learning as if everyone ought to become their pupils and hold them as masters; they are, therefore, called pedants. Some strut like peacocks thinking they are beautiful and believe everyone is courting them. All this is extremely vain, foolish, insolent, and the glory based on such silly things is called vain, foolish, frivolous.

We know genuine goodness as we know genuine balm. We test the balm by pouring it in water. If it goes to the bottom and takes the lowest place it is judged to be the finest and most precious. Similarly to know whether a person is truly wise, learned, generous, noble, we ought to see whether that person's good qualities tend to humility, modesty, and submission, for then they will be really good. If they float on the surface and wish to show themselves there, the more showy they are, the less genuine will they be. Pearls conceived and nourished in wind and the noise of thunder are only shells devoid of substance. In the same way, the virtues and the good qualities received and nourished in arrogance, boastfulness, and vanity have only the appearance of good without sap, without marrow, and without firmness....

The quest for virtue and the love of it begins to make us virtuous. But the pursuit and love of honors begins to make us contemptible and blameworthy. The well-born are not interested in this petty jumble of ranks, honors, and salutations as they have other things to do; such things belong to the idle.

Those who are able to procure pearls do not burden themselves with shells. Similarly, those who are intent on virtue are not eager for honors. Certainly everyone may take rank and keep it without harming humility, provided it is done without attachment and contention.

Those who come from Peru bring, besides gold and silver, monkeys and parrots because they cost them scarcely anything and do not burden their ships much. Thus those who aim at virtue do not cease to take their ranks and honors that are due to them, provided each time it does not cost them much care and attention and it is done without trouble, anxiety, disputes, and contentions. I am not speaking about those whose dignity concerns the public nor about particular occasions of great consequence. For in such cases, we all should preserve what belongs to us with prudence and discretion accompanied by charity and courtesy.

INTERIOR HUMILITY

You desire, Philothea, that I lead you further in humility. For to do as I have already proposed is wisdom rather than humility; now I pass on further. Many neither wish nor dare to think and reflect upon the graces God has given them personally, for fear of vainglory and self-complacency. In this, they certainly deceive themselves. As the great Angelic Doctor says, the true means of attaining to the love of God is the consideration of his blessings. The more we know them the more we shall love him. Since the gifts received personally move us more powerfully than those shared in common, they are also to be considered more attentively.

Nothing indeed can humble us so much before the mercy of God as the multitude of his benefits, and nothing can humble us so deeply before his justice as the multitude of our misdeeds. Let us consider what he has done for us and what we have done against him. As we consider in detail our sins so also let us reflect in detail on the graces he has given us. There is no need to fear that the knowledge of the gifts bestowed on us will make us proud provided we are attentive to the truth that the good that is in us is not from us. Alas! the mules do not cease to be clumsy and disgusting beasts even when laden with the precious and perfumed goods of the prince. What good do we have that we have not received? If we have received it, then why are we proud? On the contrary, a lively consideration of the graces received makes us humble, for recognition of them begets gratitude.

But if the knowledge of the graces God gave us arouses some kind of vanity in us, the sure remedy is to have recourse to the consideration of our ingratitude, our imperfections, and our miseries. If we reflect on what we have done when God was not with us then we shall realize well that what we do when he is with us is not our work or of our thinking. We shall be happy and we shall rejoice in our deeds because we have done them, but we shall glorify God alone because he is their author. Thus the Holy Virgin proclaims that God has done great things for her, but it is only to humble herself and glorify God: "My soul," she says, "exalts the Lord because he has done great things for me" (Luke 1:46, 49).

We often say that we are nothing, that we are misery itself and the refuse of the world. But we would be very sorry if anyone took us at our word and made public that we are such. On the contrary, we make a show of running away and hiding ourselves so that we are pursued and sought after. We pretend to wish to be the last and seated at the lower end of the table, but it is only to pass to the top with greater advantage. Genuine humility does not make a show of itself. It scarcely says words of humility because it does not only wish to hide the other virtues but also and especially seeks to hide itself. If it were lawful to lie, to pretend, or to scandalize one's neighbor, humility would produce arrogant and proud actions in order to hide itself under them and to live there altogether unknown and concealed.

Humility, as an interior attitude to be cultivated, has fallen out of fashion in our contemporary society. We tend to be concerned to eradicate low self-esteem, cure depression, and help people feel good about themselves. We commonly equate the term "humility" with psychologically detrimental attitudes. But true religious humility is something other than this, although I think it is a tricky virtue to define. Religious humility involves a dual perception: first, of the immense potential of the human person made in the image and likeness of God, and second, of the very real limitations that keep us from realizing that potential. Humility is actualized in an awestruck surrender to the God-story that is so intimately woven into our own stories. We are children of God, intimates to divine life. How generously we are gifted. Yet in our efforts to realize our deepest nature we constantly find ourselves thwarted. We continue to stumble over ourselves both as individuals and community. Humility thus involves the two-pronged recognition of the gratuitous gift of life itself and our own inability to receive it joyously and fully.

My impression is that Francis de Sales understands humility, both external and internal, in a somewhat similar manner. But his era was not a highly psychologized one like ours. His approach, which is in keeping with longstanding traditional Christian interpretations, emphasizes the downward thrust of the trajectory of humility without much concern that such a thrust might, at some psychological juncture, become counterproductive. Today we realize that it might, in fact, erode or inhibit the sense of being a recipient of the astonishing gift of life.

What de Sales and other commentators before him seemed to assume was that people were intrinsically self-interested and

self-willed, that their actions sprang from what we would perhaps term a solid ego base. Their "sin" then would be pride,
overemphasizing the egocentric focus so that they would lose
sight both of themselves as blessed recipients and as very fallible participants in a reality that is considerably larger than the
boundaries of ego-identity.

What the discussion of humility in the *Introduction* overlooks,
from a twentieth-century view, is the possibility that people do
not always begin with stable ego-identities. Through family up-
bringing or life's experiences or the accidents of biology, we may
find ourselves grasping and in need of a firm self-identity. To
preach humility or the loss of self to someone without a healthy
sense of self is not only futile; it is dangerous both to the individual and to his or her immediate companions. It may push her into
a spiral of self-loathing or he may violently project his sense of
worthlessness on his unfortunate family members or co-workers.

So what is important to remember about de Sales' treatment
of the virtue of humility is that it is not self-loathing. Rather, it
involves another realistic and sometimes painful recognition that
we are essentially interdependent creatures, needful of God and
the assistance of others. True humility takes a spacious bird's-eye
view of ourselves and refuses to place ourselves at the center of
creation. It also sees the self as one among many of God's children, both blessed and broken, nothing more or less than a small
part of the vast and mysterious drama of divine life.

But to soar into that bird's-eye view we often, paradoxically,
find ourselves forced to descend into a few valleys or at least
walk for a long while on the level stretches of the plains. Francis
uses the delightful metaphor of balm being poured into water.

For the Genevan bishop humility is closely linked to gratitude
and trust, both attitudes essential to a deeply lived spiritual life.
Both orient one away from undue self-concern and toward God,
who is the source of all blessing and the final reservoir of love
and strength when all else fails. To become both grateful and
trusting of all experience, no matter how troubling it may be, is
to root deep into the Christian God of love, who is revealed as
being with us in all things, even death.

Francis ends his discourse on humility with a short and characteristic teaching. He teaches us to love our abjections.

HUMILITY MAKES US LOVE OUR OWN ABJECTION

I proceed further, Philothea, and I advise you that in all circumstances and everywhere you must love your own abjection. But you say to me: What does it mean: love your own abjection? In Latin, "abjection" means "humility" and "humility" means "abjection," so that when our Lady says in her sacred canticle, "because he has regarded the humility of his servant, all generations shall call her blessed" (Luke 1:48), she means that our Lord has graciously looked upon her abjection, littleness, and lowliness to heap upon her graces and favors. All the same, there is a difference between the virtue of humility and abjection. For abjection is the littleness, lowliness, and meanness that is in us without our thinking of it. But the true virtue of humility is the real knowledge and voluntary recognition of our abjection.

The highest point of humility consists not only in the voluntary acknowledgment of our abjection but in loving it and taking pleasure in it. This is not due to any lack of courage and generosity. Rather, it is to exalt the divine Majesty and to esteem our neighbor all the more in comparison with ourselves. To this I exhort you and, for a better understanding, know that among the evils we suffer some are abject and others honorable. Many adapt themselves to the honorable but scarcely anyone to the abject. You see a devout hermit in rags and shivering from cold. Everyone honors his torn habit and has compassion for his suffering. But if a poor artisan, a poor nobleman, a poor young lady is in the same state, people despise and mock them and thus their poverty is abject. A religious receives a harsh rebuke from the superior or a child from its father. All call this mortification, obedience, wisdom. Let a gentleman or a lady suffer the same treatment from someone, and it will be termed cowardice and lack of spirit, although it is accepted for the love of God. This also is abject evil. One person has an ulcer on his arm; another has one on his face. The former has only the evil; the latter besides the evil has also contempt, disdain, and abjection. Now I say that we are not only to love the evil by the virtue of patience, but we are also to cherish the abjection by the virtue of humility.

Moreover, there are some virtues that are abject and some honorable: patience, gentleness, simplicity, and humility itself are virtues that worldly people hold as mean and abject while they appreciate very much prudence, courage, and generosity. Even among acts of one and the same virtue there are some that are held in contempt and others in honor. To give alms and to forgive insults are both acts of charity. The first is honored by everyone, but the second is despised by the world. A young man or a young lady who will not fall in with the disorders of a dissolute group and will not speak, play, dance, drink, and dress like the rest will be ridiculed and criticized by others. Their modesty will be called either fanaticism or pretense; to love this is to love abjection. There is another type of abjection. If, when going to visit the sick, I am sent to the most wretched, it will be an abjection for me in the eyes of the world; I will, therefore, love it. If I am sent to important persons, it is an abjection according to the spirit for there is not much merit or virtue in this. So I will love this abjection. By falling in the middle of the street, besides the hurt, we incur shame; we must love this abjection.

There are even faults in which there is no evil at all except the abjection. Humility does not require that we should commit them purposely, but it does require that we do not worry about them when we have committed them: Such are certain follies, incivilities, and lapses that we ought to avoid before they are committed in order to keep up civility and prudence. We must also accept cheerfully the abjection that comes to us from them when they have been committed, and so practice humility. I say further that if I am led by anger or dissipation to say indecent words by which God and neighbor are offended, I will repent sincerely and will be extremely sorry for the offense. I will try to make reparation for it in the best way possible. At the same time, I will not fail to love the abjection and contempt incurred by me. If one could be separated from the other, I would earnestly reject sin and would humbly keep the abjection.

Francis' advice about loving one's own abjections can, at first reading, be profoundly disturbing. But, as I suggested in my brief introduction on "Reading the Spiritual Classics," this characteristically Salesian teaching has gone from being one of the mysterious cyphers in the text to one of my favorite teachings from de Sales' pen.

At first the phrase seems to conjure up a world- and body-denying ethos that would have humankind groveling in its own deprivation. Yet this perspective is difficult to reconcile with Francis' Christian humanist optimism. Gradually it is possible to discern what Francis means. The call is not simply to accept but to *love* our abjections. To love our abjections is to love ourselves as we are loved, in our wholeness. It is also to have compassion for ourselves. It is to see that the true place of transformation is not in our gifts but in our weaknesses. It is to know ourselves as wounded yet beloved and thus to know each other most truly. It is not in our strengths that we find each other, but in our lack. For in our need we call each other forth. To love our abjections is to shatter the images of self-perfection we would like to project. It is thus to enter into the mystery of loving all that is human, and from there to begin to love all humans most truly.

Poverty

Francis' exploration of the virtues also includes the traditional virtue of poverty. As one of the three evangelical counsels of perfection with chastity and obedience, poverty had long been a primary value in Christian spirituality. For centuries those considering a serious life of devotion to God in a monastic setting knew they would be expected to give up all private property. The religious value of poverty was also seen to extend beyond monastery walls. Excessive accumulation of wealth was generally understood to be antithetical to a conscientiously lived Christian life. Christendom consistently held up persons like Francis of Assisi as models of holiness. The saint from Assisi (who was a favorite of his namesake from Annecy, Bishop de Sales) made poverty, both inner and outer, the central focus of his imitation of Christ. For him, to live in the spirit of Christ was to emulate the impoverished, crucified man who was stripped of all power, position, comfort, and support.

Four centuries later the Genevan bishop would still be turning the same virtue over and over, exploring its contours and making it come alive in the specific context of his readers' lives. His treatment of poverty has a unique cast to it, and although he does make the distinction between inner and outer poverty, for him the inner reality is primary.

THE POVERTY OF SPIRIT
TO BE PRACTICED AMID RICHES

Happy are the poor in spirit for theirs is the kingdom of God (Matt. 5:3). Accursed then are the rich in spirit for theirs is the misery of hell. Those are rich in spirit who have riches in their spirit or their spirit in riches; those are poor in spirit who have neither riches in their spirit nor their spirit in riches. The halcyons make their nest like the closed palm of the hand and leave only a small opening from the top. They put them on the seashore and yet they remain so strong and impenetrable that, even when washed by the waves, water never enters them. Thus always floating, they remain in the midst of the sea, on the sea, and masters of the sea. Your heart, Philothea, is to be like that, open only to heaven, impenetrable to riches and perishable things. If you have them, keep your heart free from attachment to them. Let it always remain above riches, and in the midst of riches let it be without riches and master of riches. No, do not put this heavenly spirit within earthly goods. Let it always be their master, above them and not in them.

There is always a difference between keeping poison and being poisoned. The pharmacists almost all keep poisons to make use of them in different circumstances. But they are not for that matter poisoned because they do not have poison in their bodies but only in their shops. So too you can own riches without being poisoned by them. Such will be the case if you have them in your house, or in your purse, and not in your heart. To be rich actually and poor in affection for riches is the great happiness of Christians. For they have by this means the benefits of the riches for this world and the merit of poverty for the next.

Alas, Philothea, no one will ever acknowledge being covetous. Everyone disowns this meanness and pettiness of heart. They excuse themselves under the pretext of the urgent care of children or the prudence that demands that they be well-established in resources. They never have too much. They always find the need to have more. Even the most avaricious not only do not admit that they are such in their conscience; it does not even occur to them that they might be such. . . .

If you are strongly attached to the goods that you do not have, it is useless to say that you do not wish them unjustly for even so you will not cease to be truly avaricious. Those who desire to drink ardently, even though they wish to drink only water, show signs of fever.

Dear Philothea, I do not know whether it is a just desire to wish to have justly what another possesses justly. For it seems that by this desire we wish to take advantage of the inconvenience of another. Has the one who possesses property justly more reason to keep it justly than for us to desire to possess it justly? Why then do we extend our desire over another's possession to deprive that person of it? Even if this desire is just, it is certainly not charitable. In fact, we would not like that anyone else to desire even justly what we wish to keep justly.

If you are too attached to the goods you possess, if you are too occupied with them, setting your heart on them, concentrating your thoughts on them, and fearing with a lively, anxious fear of losing them, believe me, you still have some kind of fever. Those who suffer from fever, drink the water given to them with a certain eagerness, as well as earnestness and satisfaction, that the healthy do not usually have. It is not possible to take great pleasure in something we do not love very much.

HOW TO PRACTICE REAL POVERTY
WHILE REMAINING RICH

The painter Parthasius painted the people of Athens in a very ingenious way, representing their different and changing moods: angry, unjust, fickle, courteous, mild, merciful, haughty, glorious, humble, audacious, and timid, all these in one. But, dear Philothea, I would like to put into your heart both riches and poverty together, a great care and a great indifference for temporal things.

Have much greater care than the worldly people to make your wealth useful and profitable. Tell me, are not the gardeners of the great princes more careful and diligent in cultivating and beautifying the gardens they have in their charge than if they were their own? But why is this so? Certainly it is because they think of these gardens as the gardens of princes and kings. They like to make themselves acceptable to them by these services. Dear Philothea, the possessions that we have are not our own. God has given them to us to develop and wants us to make them profitable and useful and thus render him loving service in taking care of them. This care, then, ought to be greater and more dedicated than the care that worldly people have for their possessions. For they are busy only for love of themselves, but we must work for the love of God. As self-love is a violent, agitated, eager love, so too the care taken for it is full of trouble, vexation, and anxiety. As the love of God is gentle, peaceful, and tranquil, the care that proceeds from it, though it is for the good of the world, is kind, gentle, and considerate.

Let us then have this considerate care for the preservation of our temporal goods, and even for their increase, when a just occasion presents itself and insofar as our situation demands it. For God wishes us to do so out of love for him. But take care that self-love does not deceive you, because sometimes it imitates the love of God so well that it would appear to be genuine. To prevent it from deceiving us, and the care of temporal goods from degenerating into avarice, besides what I have said in the preceding chapter, we should often practice real and effectual poverty in the midst of all the possessions and riches God has given us.

Give up always a part of your resources by giving them to the poor with a generous heart. To give away what you possess is to impoverish yourself by that much, and the more you give the more you grow poor. It is true that God will give it back to you, not only in the next world, but even in this. In fact, there is nothing that contributes more to temporal prosperity than almsgiving. But as you wait for God to restore it, you will be deprived of it. How holy and rich is the impoverishment brought about by almsgiving!

Love the poor and poverty because by this love you will become truly poor; as Scripture says we become like the things we love (Hos. 9:10). Love makes the lovers equal: "Who is weak with whom I am not weak?" says St. Paul (2 Cor. 11:29). He could say: Who is poor with whom I am not poor? Indeed, love made him to be like those whom he loved. If therefore you love the poor, you will certainly share their poverty and be poor like them. Now if you love the poor, be often among them. Be happy to see them at your home and visit them at their homes. Talk with them willingly. Be quite at ease when they come near you in the church, in the streets, and elsewhere. Be poor in the language you make use of. Speak to them like their companions but have generous hands, giving them your gifts in abundance.

Would you like to do still more, dear Philothea? Do not be satisfied with being poor like the poor, but be poorer than the poor. How is this possible? The servant is less than his master (John 13:16). Make yourself then the servant of the poor. Go to serve them in their beds when they are sick, and this with your own hands. Be their cook and at your own expense. Be their tailor and washerwoman. Dear Philothea, this service is more glorious than that of royalty. . . .

There is no one who has not experienced at times some want or lack of convenience. Sometimes it happens that a guest comes to our house whom we would like to and should treat well, but do not have the means at the moment. We have fine clothes in one place, but we may need them in another where we are bound to appear in public. It happens that all the good wines in our cellar ferment and turn sour, and there are left only wines that are of poor quality and immature. We find ourselves in the country in some hovel where everything is lacking; we have neither bed, nor room, nor table, nor service. In short, it is easy often to be in need of something, however rich we may be. This is being effectually poor with regard to what we lack. Philothea, be quite at ease on these occasions, accept them with a good heart, bear them cheerfully.

You experience some misfortunes that will impoverish you either very much or a little, such as tempests, fire, floods, droughts, thefts, lawsuits. That is the best time to practice poverty, accepting with gentleness this decrease of wealth and putting up gently and perseveringly with this impoverishment. Esau presented himself to his father, his hands all covered with hair, and Jacob did the same. Since the hair on the hands of Jacob did not stick to his skin but to his gloves, the hair could be removed without hurting him. On the contrary, the hair on the hands of Esau stuck to his skin, which was hairy by nature. If anyone had tried to pluck off his hair, it would have caused him great pain. He would have cried aloud and would have been provoked to defend himself. When our resources stick to our hearts, if a tempest or a thief or a cheat takes any part of our property, what complaints, what troubles, what impatience we have! If our goods are attached only to the care that God desires us to have for them and not to our hearts, when they are taken away we do not lose our reason or tranquillity. This is the difference between beasts and human beings as regards their garments. The garments of the beasts are stuck to their flesh, and those of human beings are simply placed on it so that they can put them on or remove them at will.

The specific audience to whom Francis de Sales was writing is no doubt obvious. He was writing for people who were materially advantaged, for women like Madame de Charmoisy, an individual of social standing, wife of the ambassador of the Duke of Savoy. Francis himself was a nobleman of the house of Sales, well-educated and propertied (until he deeded his inheritance to his brother when he became a priest). His advice is thus directed to those in the upper echelon of society whose wealth was for the most part inherited.

While material poverty was held in high esteem in the tradition as a religious goal and while Francis himself as well as those who embraced the "perfect life" did indeed renounce all claims of private ownership, it was assumed that those of Francis' social status who lived "in the world" would in fact own a great deal. That there were imbalances and injustices in the way in which wealth was distributed in the society of his day is no doubt obvious to the modern observer. But when Francis' contemporaries asked the question, "How is the Christian to understand poverty and wealth?" they did not consider whether the hereditary ownership of vast reserves of property by a few persons or families was a Christian ethical issue. Rather, the status quo was taken for granted. If one was born into wealth, God must intend one to steward it responsibly. If one was born poor, God must intend for one to bear it well. The same idea held about political institutions. The theory of the divine right of kingship still held sway in the European mind. The idea that political power should be shared by all citizens was not yet in the air. Francis was very much a citizen of his age in that he absorbed this perspective. Thus he could write about poverty of spirit in the midst of riches without raising the larger questions that have arisen in later centuries.

In our contemporary church context the scope of the questions about poverty and wealth has been radically enlarged. More than one hundred years have passed since the publication of the first papal encyclical on social justice. In the ensuing century the church has come to analyze in a new manner the question that the author of the *Introduction* addressed. What has emerged is the tradition of Catholic social teaching. In this tradition of social ethics sin is no longer perceived as only personal but structural as well. Persons, communities, and nations may construct and support social systems that promote the full dignity of every human person (the bottom line for the social teaching tradition) or they may not. It is fully within the purview of Christian morality to confront (through the use of nonviolent means) governments, policies, or practices that diminish the dignity of any person. Thus poverty, which effectively marginalizes an entire segment of the population from full participation in society, must be seen not as an inevitable state of affairs or as a given, but against the backdrop of the excessive and unbridled accumulation of wealth. Questions of distributive justice understood to emerge from the imperative of the gospel itself may be raised. The questions confronting the "very rich" today are wider in scope than in the seventeenth century. If one finds oneself with great wealth, in what does stewardship consist? Is dismantling economic structures that created such imbalanced distribution imperative? How do the need for personal security and the needs of the marginalized coincide? What does it mean to confront structural sin? Is poverty created, not by the choices of the poor, but by the economic system itself? The queries are endless, the responses varied and complex. The point is: the changes in both the sociocultural and theological climates have been so marked in the past four hundred years that the bishop's specific advice must be weighed against new standards.

Similarly, the teaching in the *Introduction* on how to practice richness of spirit in real poverty must be reevaluated in light of the newly emergent Catholic social teaching tradition. In fact, this tradition is not "new" in the sense of being an invention of the modern era. Instead, it is a reawakening of the biblical perspective of justice. Through the eyes of the God of the Hebrew prophets, who cried out to divine justice on behalf of the widow and orphan, poverty is not God's will. It is the result of many human choices. Human beings create institutions and systems that impoverish and exploit. God's will, from this perspective, could only be to liberate and free people from the conditions that impoverish them.

Much of mainstream contemporary Christian social thought has run along these lines. However one might choose to evaluate these modern points of view, the fact is that de Sales' unhesitating affirmation that the poor are poor because God wills it is not shared by many contemporary people of faith. Thus his teaching that it is laudable to acquiesce cheerfully to the will of God in one's destitution might rightly be questioned today. Alternative responses of the poor have emerged in the twentieth century. Most notably the voices of the poor given a hearing in Latin American liberation theology would articulate the vision of a God (the God of the Exodus) who seeks to free those who are economically and politically enslaved. As God works in the world to effect this liberation through the people, suffering occurs. This is God's suffering. It is the crucifixion taking place today in the bodies of God's *anawim*, the insignificant ones.

Such a vision would never have entered Francis de Sales' field of consciousness. Yet we might well modify his advice here with the insights of contemporary believers.

HOW TO PRACTICE RICHNESS OF SPIRIT IN REAL POVERTY

If you are really poor, dearest Philothea, be such also in spirit. Make a virtue of necessity and make use of this precious stone of poverty for what it is worth. Its brilliance is not discovered in this world; nevertheless it is exceedingly beautiful and rich. Have patience; you are in good company: Our Lord, our Lady, the apostles and so many men and women saints have been poor. Although capable of becoming rich, they despised being so. How many are the persons important in society who, in spite of much opposition, went with utmost diligence to seek holy poverty in cloisters and hospitals! Saints like St. Alexis, St. Paula, St. Paulinus, St. Angela, and so many others took much trouble to find it. Showing you special courtesy, Philothea, poverty comes to present itself to you. You have met it without searching for it and without pain. Embrace it then as the dear friend of Jesus Christ who was born, lived, and died in poverty, which was his nurse throughout his life.

Your poverty, Philothea, has two great privileges by means of which you are enabled to acquire great merit. The first is that poverty did not come to you by your choice but solely by the will of God, who made you poor without the consent of your own will. What we receive simply from the will of God is always very pleasing to him, provided we receive it with a cheerful heart and love of his holy will. Where there is less of our will, there is more of God's will. Simple and absolute acceptance of God's will renders the suffering extremely pure.

The second privilege of this poverty is that it is truly poor. A poverty that is praised, caressed, esteemed, helped, and assisted is allied to riches and it is not poor at all. But a poverty that is despised, rejected, blamed, and abandoned is truly poor. Such then is the poverty of the laity. Since they are not poor by their own choice but by necessity, it is not taken into much account. The poverty of the laity, which is not held in great esteem, is poorer than that of the religious. However, religious poverty has great excellence and is more praiseworthy because of the vow and the intention for which it has been chosen.

Do not complain then, my dear Philothea, of your poverty, because we complain only about what displeases us. If poverty displeases you, you are no longer poor in spirit but rather rich by attachment. Do not be grieved at not being helped as well as required, for the excellence of poverty consists in this. To be poor and not to be inconvenienced by it is asking too much. In fact, it is to desire the honor of poverty and the advantages of riches.

Friendship

In the third section of the *Introduction to the Devout Life* Francis de Sales placed an extended reflection on friendship. Alongside the virtues of humility, gentleness, and poverty he saw fit to include a discussion of the values and possible dangers of the love known as friendship. Francis distinguishes between types of friends. There are frivolous connections, based primarily on mutual flattery, and there are what Francis calls "evil" friendships, especially between men and women, which seem to be basically a prelude to seduction. But the bishop insists, and in this he goes against some tendencies in the tradition, that human relationships, when they are based on mutual love of God, are essential in the spiritual life. It is especially in the content of the communications between friends that the beauty and value of these "genuine friendships" are discerned.

For Francis friendship is a special type of love, and love, all love, comes from and returns to God. For him there is no intrinsic difference between the love of God and the love of neighbor. After all, he states, we do not have two hearts, one made for divine and one made for human love, but only one heart that is the seat of all our love. For the Genevan bishop as a Christian humanist, all human capacities are given for the express reason of praising and returning home to God. Love, with its intense dynamic of desire, is given to unite persons with the Creator from whom they come and to whom they return. Among the different types of love (a schema Francis derives from his reading of classical authors) the love of friendship is unique. It is the one type of love that must be mutual and equal. All love is not friendship for one can love without being loved in return (in the case of an unrequited love), and one can also love and be loved in quite different ways (as in the case of parent-child love). But a friendship implies a love that is both mutual (if the love is not present on both sides there is no friendship) and equal (there is comparable level of exchange and a sharing of perspectives). Friendship is also the most open-handed of the loves, a delicate dance that does not involve the conjoining of lives (as does marital love) but instead receives and gives love as gift.

Bishop de Sales particularly suggests the cultivation of spiritual friendships (i.e., relationships based on mutual love of God) to persons living outside of intentional religious communities. For all people need the support and encouragement of community to grow in love of God, and such support is often lacking in the lives of lay people (both in the seventeenth and twentieth centuries). Francis continued to develop his ideas on love and friendship beyond the *Introduction*. Indeed, love became the central theme of his next great book, the *Treatise on the Love of God*. Moreover, his own voluminous correspondence testifies to the fact that he sought out and cultivated a variety of spiritual friendships that were deeply influential in his own development as well as the religious development of many of his contemporaries. That he nurtured such relationships and wrote so probingly about their contours remains one of his greatest contributions to the literature of the Christian spiritual heritage.

GENUINE FRIENDSHIPS

Philothea, love everyone with a great love of charity, but have friendship with those capable of communicating virtuous things to you. The more exquisite the virtue you put in your exchanges, the more perfect will your friendship be. If you share knowledge, your friendship is indeed very praiseworthy; it is more so if you communicate virtues such as prudence, discretion, fortitude, and justice. If your mutual and reciprocal exchange is about charity, devotion, or Christian perfection, precious indeed will your friendship be. It will be excellent because it comes from God, excellent because it tends to God, excellent because its bond is God, excellent because it will last eternally in God. How good it is to love on earth as one will love in heaven, and to learn to cherish one another in this world as we shall do eternally in the next!

I do not speak here about the simple love of charity, for it ought to embrace all people. I speak of the spiritual friendship by which two or three or more persons communicate among themselves their devotion, their spiritual affection, and become one in spirit. With good reason such happy souls can sing: "How good and pleasant it is for brothers to dwell together" (Ps. 133:1). Yes, this delicious balm of devotion distills from one heart to another, by a continual sharing, so that we may say that "God has poured out his blessing and life" on this friendship "forever and ever" (Ps. 133:3).

In my opinion, all other friendships are only shadows compared to this. Their bonds are only chains of glass and jet in comparison with this great bond of holy devotion that is entirely of gold. Do not form friendships of any other kind — I mean the friendships that you make. However, you are not to abandon or despise the friendship that nature and earlier duties oblige you to cultivate toward relations, kindred, benefactors, neighbors, and others. I now speak of those friendships that you yourself choose.

Perhaps many people may tell you that you should not have any kind of special affection and friendship since it occupies the heart, distracts the mind, and creates jealousies. But they err in their advice. For they have found in the writings of many saints and devout authors that particular friendships and excessive affections do very great harm to the religious. They think that it is the same for all other persons. But there is much to be said about this.

It is understood that in a well-ordered monastery the common purpose of all tends to true devotion. So it is required not to make these particular communications there, due to the fear of seeking in particular what is common and of passing from particularities to partialities.

But it is necessary that those who live among worldly people and embrace true devotion join together in a holy and sacred friendship. By this means they encourage, assist, and support themselves well.

Just as those who walk on level ground do not need a helping hand, but those who are on a dangerous and slippery path support one another to walk more safely, so too those who are religious do not need particular friendships.

But those who are in the world do need them, to save themselves and help one another along so many difficult paths they have to travel. In the world, all do not strive for the same end; all do not have the same spirit. Hence, without doubt, it is necessary to draw oneself aside and form friendships according to our aim. This particularity is indeed a partiality, but a holy partiality that does not cause any division except between good and evil, between sheep and goats, and between bees and hornets — a necessary separation.

Renewing Devotion

The *Introduction* that Francis de Sales perused that day in Annecy in 1610 contained two more lengthy parts entitled respectively, "Counsels Required for Overcoming the More Common Temptations" and "Exercises and Counsels to Renew and Confirm Oneself in Devotion." Both were designed as useful reference points for the person seeking to live out the "election" or choice of the devout life. Advice on how to deal courageously with anxiety, sadness, spiritual boredom, and such was followed by a set of exercises designed to renew and deepen one's original intention to pursue the life of devotion. Among these exercises is the "Examination of Conscience," a practice that Francis himself learned from his Jesuit mentors and that is an integral part of the Ignatian Exercises. De Sales elaborated on the Ignatian model and divided the examination into several discrete and focused parts concerned with examining one's progress in the devout life, one's state with regard to God, self, and neighbor, and one's inclinations. Included here is merely the brief examination of one's state with regard to one's neighbor.

The habitual practice of such an examination, in all its facets, weathers the test of time. However, the recommended focus in such a reflection today (Francis recommends doing it at the end of the day, even while in bed, or while walking) is not upon one's sinfulness or failure to progress in devotion, love of God, self, and neighbor, but upon one's general consciousness. Thus to become aware of the presence of God by rummaging back through the contents of one's experiences and feelings during the previous day, week, month, or year is a fruitful exercise. Contemporary renderings of Ignatian spirituality emphasize gratitude for the gifts of life — encounters with friends, small insights into self and God, moments of grace. They tend to concentrate on meeting God where we are, as we are, rather than meeting God in the yawning gap between where we are and where we think God would like us to be. They also admit of an openness to a variety of feelings, both positive and negative, and seek to wholistically integrate these feelings into the spiritual life by making them part of prayer and thus available for healing. This contemporary approach highlights in newly meaningful ways the Ignatian and, by extension, the Salesian spiritual "style" — finding God in all things, in all ways.

What the examination of conscience, in either its modern or historical forms, seeks to do is to make devotion a living reality, to integrate a person's love of God with the whole of his or her life's experiences, in a word, to incarnate that love.

EXAMINATION OF ONE'S STATE WITH REGARD TO ONE'S NEIGHBOR

Love for one's husband or wife should be tender and peaceful, firm and continuous. It must hold the first place since this is God's plan and will. I say the same of the love of one's children, close relatives, and friends, each in its place.

Generally speaking, what is your attitude toward your neighbors? Do you love them from your heart and for love of God? In order to discern this well, call to mind certain persons whom you think are troublesome and unpleasant. It is specially in such cases that we practice the love of God toward our neighbor, and still more so in loving those who do us evil by their actions or their words. Examine carefully whether you are sincere at heart with regard to them. Or do you have great difficulty in loving them?

Do you readily speak ill of your neighbor, especially of those who dislike you? Do you do anything evil to your neighbor, directly or indirectly? Provided you are a little reasonable, you will easily notice it.

The exercise of the examination of conscience or the practice at looking at one's own experience to discern there the presence of God is complemented in the *Introduction*'s fifth part by another exercise entitled "Five Reflections for Renewal." This quintet of prayerful ruminations looks at devotion not from the human side "up" but from the divine side "down." Reflections on the excellence of the soul, the virtues, the examples of the saints, the love of Jesus and God for us take an alternate perspective on the enterprise of devotion. The reality of the overarching presence of divine love is affirmed by recalling the stories of faith and the people (the saints) who embraced that living reality so intently. Central to these reflections is the reflection on Jesus' love for humankind. Francis uses all his rhetorical skill in bringing that love to consciousness. His use of the image of the woman preparing the cradle as a metaphor for Jesus readying the spiritual cradle for each devout soul is delightfully typical.

FOURTH REFLECTION: JESUS' LOVE FOR US

Be conscious of the love with which Jesus Christ, our Lord, suffered so much in this world, especially in the Garden of Olives and on Mount Calvary. You were the object of this love. By means of all these sufferings, he obtained from God the Father good resolutions and decisions for your heart. By the same means he also obtained all that you need to observe, nurture, strengthen, and carry out these resolutions. Firm resolutions, how precious you are, being the child of such a mother as the passion of my Savior! How much should I cherish you, since you have been so dear to my Jesus. My Savior, you died to win for me the grace to make my deliberate decisions. Grant me the grace to die rather than forsake them.

Remember, Philothea, the heart of our Lord saw your heart, and loved you surely from the tree of the cross. By this love he obtained for you all the good things that you will ever have, including your resolutions. Yes, Philothea, we can say with Jeremiah: "Lord, before I existed you beheld me and called me by name" (Jer. 1:5). This is indeed so; his divine goodness has prepared in his love and mercy all the general and particular means for our salvation, including our resolutions. Yes, without doubt. A woman with child prepares the cradle, the linen, and swaddling clothes, and even arranges a nurse for the child whom she hopes to bring forth, though it be not yet in the world. So our Lord, his goodness as it were pregnant with you, wishing to bring you forth to salvation and make you his child, prepared upon the tree of the cross everything you would need. He got ready your spiritual cradle, linen, and swaddling clothes, your nurse and everything suitable for your happiness. These are all the means, all the attractions, and all the graces by which he guides you and wants to lead you to perfection.

My God, how deeply this truth should be fixed in our memory. Is it possible that I have been loved, and loved so tenderly, by my Savior? That he thought of me personally, in all these little events by which he has drawn me to himself? How much then should we love, cherish, and make good use of all this for our benefit! This is extremely kind; this loving heart of God thought of Philothea, loved her, and obtained for her a thousand means of salvation. This he did as though there was no other soul in the world he could think of. The sun shines on one part of the earth, shining on it no less than if it shone nowhere else, and as if it shone upon it alone. In the same way, our Lord thought of and cared for each of his loving children as though he had not thought of all the rest. "He loved me," says St. Paul, "and gave himself for me" (Gal. 2:20), as if he said: for myself alone, as though he had done nothing for the others. Imprint this in your spirit, Philothea, in order to cherish and nourish with care your firm resolution so precious to the heart of the Savior.

Correspondence and Conferences

Francis de Sales as Letter Writer

The desk at which Bishop Francis de Sales sat in 1610 served as a resting place not only for his recent edition of the *Introduction to the Devout Life*. It was also the surface upon which he penned much of his correspondence. Since in the seventeenth century there were no other means by which one communicated with business associates, relatives, and friends, letterwriting was a skill (and an art) in which most literate persons were well versed. The bishop often spent the early or late hours of each day conscientiously writing letters. Some of the time was spent taking care of official episcopal business, but much of it was given over to what can only be termed spiritual correspondence.

Often early in the morning even before his private prayer or the celebration of Eucharist, Francis could be found bent over his writing desk applying himself to his letterwriting task, for the couriers that carried the mail from Annecy left before the busyness of the work day took over. The young bishop always worked in this way: with a sense of focus and discipline in the midst of numerous fragmenting concerns. When he had first become a bishop he had drawn up a *regula episcopa* — a rule of daily life — which helped him to order constructively his many duties. It is one of the hallmarks of Salesian spirituality that the love of God can be cultivated in the midst of great busyness. While the heritage of prayer emphasized silence and solitude as the optimal conditions for a reflective Christian life, Francis de Sales stressed that an equally reflective if different life could be lived "in the midst of worldly concerns." To one of his correspondents, in fact his own sister, Madame de Cornillon (whom he addressed as daughter), he wrote:

> Let us all belong to God, my daughter, in the midst of so much busyness brought on by the diversity of worldly things. Where could we give better witness to our fidelity than in the midst of things going wrong? Ah, dearest daughter, my sister, solitude has its assaults, the world its busyness; in either place we must be courageous, since in either place divine help is available to those who trust in God and who humbly and gently beg for God's fatherly assistance.

Francis wrote what could be termed letters of spiritual guidance to scores of people who sought his advice. He saw them all as friends, lovers of God who like himself were struggling to realize that love in its fullness. As the *Introduction* suggests, friendships based on shared spiritual aspirations were prized and advocated by the bishop. One of his dearest friends was Madame de Chantal, the woman with whom he co-founded the Order of the Visitation. Jane Frances Fremyot, Baroness de Chantal, was a thirty-two-year-old widow with four children when Francis first met her at a series of Lenten sermons he was preaching in mercantile Dijon in 1604. She had come to the sermons with her father. Since the death of her husband three years earlier Jane had increasingly felt drawn to a deeper relationship with God. Convinced that she was being called to something new by divine initiative, yet feeling pressure from her extended family to remarry, she found herself looking for a spiritual director to help her make sense of the chaotic and intense interior movements she felt. During the 1604 Lenten season she sought out and confided in Francis. Thus began one of the most notable of spiritual friendships in the annals of Christian history.

A letter of guidance written to Jane seven months after their initial encounter gives insight into Francis as spiritual guide and correspondent. He penned it at his family home, Château de Sales, located in the mountainside beyond Annecy. The concreteness of his advice, based on traditional normative principles; the gentleness and flexibility of his spirit; the psychological soundness of his teachings (sometimes referred to as inspired common sense) — all are evident in the letter. After exploring in Dijon the possibilities of entering into a directorial relationship, the two friends had then subsequently met at the hillside pilgrimage site of St. Claude. Francis had escorted his mother, and Jane was accompanied by two girlhood friends who also sought out the bishop's counsel. Jane had some time earlier attached herself to a quasi-director who had burdened her with the recitation of innumerable formal prayers and the performance of elaborate religious rituals as well as bound her to a vow of secrecy. Her hesitation in confiding in someone besides this early unscrupulous priest-director is reflected in Francis' careful response. At St. Claude they formally bound themselves to one another as seeker and spiritual guide.

The incipient depth of their friendship is clearly articulated in the bishop's hand. Later in their lives it would mature beyond the director-directee relationship and become a bond of great mutuality. In the letter one can see the way in which general principles of the spiritual life as understood in that day were applied to concrete situations. Francis alludes to Jane's immediate family and to the specific circumstances in which she at that point found herself. Her visit to Dijon had been only a brief respite from a difficult and indefinite stay with her cantankerous father-in-law, the old Baron de Chantal. She was living with her four children — headstrong Celse-Bénigne, gentle Marie Aimée, vivacious Françoise, and the baby Charlotte — on her father-in-law's remote country estate under the dominance of a vindictive housekeeper who had borne the old man several illegitimate children.

References to others close to her are woven throughout the letter: Those include her brother, André, who was the archbishop of Bourges, and her childhood friend, Rose Bourgeois, the superior of the abbey of Puits d'Orbe, who under Francis' tutelage would undertake a reform of her religious community. Current ecclesial events and trends are also part of the communication. The upcoming canonizations of two great figures of the militant Catholic renewal — Charles Borromeo, reforming bishop of Milan, and Ignatius Loyola, founder of the Society of Jesus, are mentioned. And the new interest in spiritual reading in the vernacular that was sweeping through society is reflected in Francis' recommendations of three classic authors of spirituality — Bonaventure, Tauler, and Augustine — and a more contemporary author, Andrew Capiglia, a Spanish Carthusian, whose works had been translated into French in 1601. It is worth noting that Francis was unable to refer his correspondents to the gospel texts since no approved Catholic translation was available to them, hence the referral to meditation books as a means of praying with the life and death of Christ.

To his friend and directee Francis recommends that several traditional practices be integrated into her devotional life: fasting, visiting the poor and sick (part of what are traditionally known as the works of mercy), using the "discipline" (a mild form of bodily mortification), and emulating of saintly figures like John the Baptist and King Louis of France. But mostly he initiates her into the dynamics of the devout life by commenting directly on her particular concerns that she had outlined for him in a previous letter.

Sales, October 14, 1604

Madam,

I have a very great desire to make myself clearly understood in this letter; please God, I will find the means to match my desire! I am sure that you will be encouraged by my response to part of what you asked me about, especially the part about the two doubts that the enemy is suggesting to you concerning your choice of me as your spiritual director. So I am going to tell you what I can, in order to put into a few words what I think you need to consider in this matter.

First of all, the choice you have made gives every indication of being a good and legitimate one; so, please, have no further doubt about this. Indications such as these: the strong impulse of your heart that carried you to this decision almost by force, yet with joy and contentment; the time I took to deliberate before agreeing to your wish; the fact that neither you nor I relied on ourselves but sought the opinion of your confessor who is a good, learned, and prudent man; the fact that we allowed time for your first enthusiasm to subside in case it had been misplaced, and we prayed about this, not for one or two days only, but for several months; without a doubt, all these are infallible signs that we acted according to God's will.

Impulses that come from the evil spirit or from the human mind are very different: they are frightening, vehement, vacillating. The first thing they whisper to the agitated soul is not to listen to any advice, or if it does, to listen only to the advice of persons of little or no experience. These impulses urge us to hurry up and close a deal before having discussed the terms, and they are satisfied with a short prayer that serves as a pretext in deciding most important questions.

Our case was not at all like this. Neither you nor I made the final decision in this matter; it was made by a third person who had no reason to consider anything but God's will. The fact that I hesitated at first — and this was because of the deliberation I was bound to make — ought to put your mind completely at rest. You may be sure it was not from any disinclination to serve you spiritually (my inclination to do so is great beyond words), but in a decision of such moment I didn't want to follow either your desire or my inclination, but only God and God's providence. So please stop right there and don't go on arguing with the enemy about it; tell him boldly that it was God who wanted it and who has done it. It was God who placed you under that first direction, profitable for you at the time; it is God who has brought you under my direction and God will make it fruitful and useful to you, even though the instrument is unworthy.

As to your second point, my very dear sister, be assured that, as I was just saying from the very beginning when you consulted with me about your interior, God gave me a tremendous love for your soul. As you became more and more open with me, a marvelous obligation arose for my soul to love yours more and more; that's why I was prompted to write you that God had given me to you. I didn't believe that anything could be added to the affection I felt for you, especially when I was praying for you. But now, my dear daughter, a new quality has been added — I don't know what to call it. All I can say is that its effect is a great inner delight that I feel whenever I wish you perfect love of God and other spiritual blessings. I am adding nothing to the truth, and I speak in the presence of the "God of my heart" and yours. Every affection differs in some particular way from every other affection; that which I have for you has a certain something about it that brings me great consolation and, when all is said, is extremely good for me. Hold that for the truest truth and have no more doubt about it. I didn't intend to say so much, but one word leads to another, and I think you will know what I mean.

To me it's an amazing fact, my daughter, that holy church, in imitation of her Spouse, teaches us to pray, not for ourselves only, but always for ourselves and our fellow Christians. "Give us..." she says, "grant us..." and similar all-inclusive terms. It had never occurred to me when praying in this general way to think about any person in particular; but since leaving Dijon, whenever I say "we" I think of particular individuals who have recommended themselves to my prayers; ordinarily you are the one who comes to mind first, and when not first (which is rarely the case), then last, so that I have more time to think of you. What more can I say than that? But for the honor of God, do not speak about this to anyone, for I am saying a little too much, though I say it in total honesty and purity. This should be enough to help you answer all those temptations in the future, or at least to give you the courage to laugh at the enemy and spit in his face! I'll tell you the rest some day, either in this life or the next.

In your third point you ask me what remedies there are for the suffering caused you by the temptations the devil suggests to you against the faith and the church. At least, that's what I understand to be the difficulty. I shall tell you what God inspires me to say. In this kind of temptation we must take the same stance that we take against temptations of the flesh, not arguing at all, but doing as the Israelite children did with the bones of the Paschal Lamb, not trying to break them but simply throwing them into the fire. In no way must we answer or even pretend to hear what the enemy is saying, no matter how hard he pounds on the door. We mustn't even say "Who is it?" "That's true," you tell me, "but he is so annoying and is making such a loud racket that those inside can't even hear each other speak." It's all the same; be patient, speak by means of signs: we must prostrate ourselves before God and stay there at his feet; he will understand very well from this humble gesture that you are his and that you want his help even though you are unable to speak. But especially, stay inside; don't so much as open the door either to see who is there or to chase this pest away. Finally he will grow tired of shouting and will leave you in peace. "It's about time!" you will tell me....

So, courage then! Things will improve soon. So long as the enemy doesn't get in, the rest doesn't matter. Still, it's a very good sign that he is raging and beating at the door; it's a sign that he doesn't yet have what he's after. If he had it, he would no longer carry on this way. He would come in and stay. Remember this so as never to get caught up in scruples.

And here is another remedy for you. The temptations against faith go directly to the understanding to draw it to argue, and to get caught up in all these things. Do you know what you should do while the enemy wastes his time trying to scale the walls of your intellect? Slip out the gate of your will and take the offensive against him. That is, when a temptation against faith starts raising questions in your mind such as, "How can this be? But what if this? What if that...?," instead of debating the enemy with arguments, let your affective side attack him with full force, and even let your thoughts be reinforced by your voice, crying out "You traitor, you wretch! You left the church of the angels, and you are trying to get me to leave that of the saints! Disloyal, unfaithful, perfidious one! You gave the apple of perdition to the first woman and now you want me to bite it too! 'Get behind me,

Satan! It is written: you shall not tempt the Lord your God.' No, I will not argue with you. When Eve tried to dispute with you, she was lost; she argued and was seduced. Live Jesus in whom I believe, live the church to which I cling!" Say these and similar impassioned words. You must speak also to Jesus Christ and to the Holy Spirit in whatever way inspires you, and even pray as well to the church: "O Mother of the children of God, may I never be separated from you; I want to live and die in you."

I don't know if I'm making myself clear. What I'm trying to say is that we have to strike back with the heart and not with our reason, with intense feelings and not with arguments. It's true that at such times of temptation our poor will is without feeling. So much the better. Its blows will strike the enemy that much harder. And when he discovers that instead of delaying your progress, he is giving you the opportunity of expressing countless virtuous affections, particularly that of affirming your faith, he will finally leave you alone.

As a third remedy, it would be good once in a while to take fifty or sixty strokes of the discipline, or only thirty, depending on what you can take. It's surprising how effective this measure has been for someone I know. Undoubtedly that's because the physical sensation distracts from interior suffering and calls forth the mercy of God. Moreover, when the devil sees that his partner, the flesh, is being subdued, he gets afraid and runs away. But this third remedy must be taken in moderation, depending on the good it achieves, as you will know after trying it out for a few days.

When all is said and done, these temptations are simply trials like any other, and you must calm yourself, for as Scripture reminds us: "Blessed is he who undergoes temptation; for having been proved, he will receive the crown of glory" (James 1:12). I have seen few people make progress without experiencing trials, so you must be patient. After the squall, God will send the calm. But make use especially of the first two remedies I have suggested....

If you really like the prayers you are used to saying, please don't drop them; and if you happen to leave out some of what

I am telling you to do, have no scruples about it, for here is the general rule of our obedience written in capital letters:

DO ALL THROUGH LOVE, NOTHING THROUGH CONSTRAINT;
LOVE OBEDIENCE MORE THAN YOU FEAR DISOBEDIENCE.

I want you to have the spirit of liberty, not the kind that excludes obedience (this is freedom of the flesh), but the liberty that excludes constraint, scruples, and anxiety. If you really love obedience and docility, I'd like to think that when some legitimate or charitable cause takes you away from your religious exercises, this would be for you another form of obedience and that your love would make up for whatever you have to omit in your religious practice.

I want you to get a French translation of all the prayers you will be saying, not that I want you to say them in French, for they are more devotional for you in Latin, but I want you to understand them better. The same goes for the litanies of the Name of Jesus, of our Lady, and the other prayers. But do all this without anxiety and in a spirit of gentleness and love.

Your meditations will focus on the life and death of our Lord. I approve of your using the *Exercises* of Tauler, the *Meditations* of St. Bonaventure, and those of Capiglia, for in the end, it is always the life of our Lord presented there, as it is in his gospels. But you must simplify all this in the manner I have written out for you. Meditations on the four Last Ends will be good for you, on condition that you always close your meditation with an act of confidence in God, never thinking about death and hell on the one hand, without picturing the cross on the other, so that after having been moved to fear by the first consideration, you will have recourse to the other through confidence. Your period of meditation should not exceed three-quarters of an hour. I like spiritual canticles, but sung with feeling.

As for brother ass, I approve of a Friday fast and a frugal supper on Saturdays. It's a good idea to hold him down during the week, not so much by cutting down on the quantity of food he is given (moderation must be observed), but by cutting back on the variety of foods you put before him. Nevertheless, I recommend that you treat him once in a while by giving him oats, as St. Francis did, to make him go faster. That's where taking the discipline comes in, for it has a marvelous power of quickening the spirit by stinging the flesh; but use it only twice a week.

Do not go to communion less frequently than you've been doing, unless your confessor tells you to. It is a special comfort for me on feast days to know that we go to communion together.

Now for your fifth point. True, I have a particular affection for Celse-Bénigne and your other children. Since God has put into your heart a desire to see them totally devoted to his service, you must bring them up with this in mind, gently encouraging them to think along these lines. Find the *Confessions* of St. Augustine and read carefully Book VIII and what follows. There you will see St. Monica, a widow like yourself, and her care for her son Augustine; you will find other things too that will encourage you.

As for Celse-Bénigne, you will have to inspire him with generous motives and plant in his little soul a noble and courageous ambition to serve God; and you will have to minimize the idea of purely human glory, but do this very gradually; as he grows up, with God's help, we shall think of specific ways of doing this. Meanwhile take care that he and his sisters sleep alone, as far as possible, or with persons whom you can trust as completely as you would yourself. I can't tell you how important this is. Experience teaches me this every day.

If Françoise wants to be a nun of her own accord, fine; otherwise, I do not approve of her being influenced by any recommendations, but only, as in the case of other young girls, by gentle inspirations. As much as possible, we must touch the hearts of others as do the angels, delicately and without coercion. Still, I think it's a good idea that you send her to be educated at the monastery of Puits d'Orbe, where I hope true devotion will flourish again very soon. I would like you to cooperate toward this end. Try to remove traces of vanity from the hearts of your daughters; vanity seems almost innate to their sex. I know you have the *Letters* of St. Jerome in French; read the one he wrote about Pacatula and the others about the education of girls. You will find them refreshing. But do all this in moderation. "Gentle inspirations" sums up all I have to say on the subject.

I see that you owe someone two thousand crowns. As soon as you can, get this paid, and be very careful not to withhold from others anything you owe them. Give alms in little ways, but very humbly. I like the practice of visiting the sick, the elderly — women especially — and very young children. I like the practice of visiting the poor, especially poor women — humbly and with kindness.

As to your sixth point, I agree that you should divide your time between your father and your father-in-law and that you try to obtain the good of their souls (the way the angels do, as I said above). It doesn't matter if you spend more time in Dijon; after all, that is where your first duty lies. Try to be more humbly attentive to both fathers, and work gently toward their salvation. I think it would probably be better for you to spend the winter in Dijon.

I am writing to your father. Since he asked me to write him something that would benefit his soul, I have done so in all simplicity, maybe too much so. My advice to him is twofold: first, he should review his life as a whole in order to make a general confession — this is something that any man of honor should do before he dies; second, he should try, little by little, to detach himself from worldly ties. Then I suggest to him ways of going about this. I present all this as my opinion, quite clearly and gently, giving him to understand that he must not suddenly break off all his worldly connections, but that he should loosen and untie them. He will show you the letter, I'm sure; help him to understand it and to put my suggestions into practice.

You owe him the great charity of accompanying him as he journeys toward a happy end of life. No human respect should stand in the way of your doing this with humble affection, for he is the first "neighbor" the Lord obliges you to love; and the first thing you should love in him is his soul; and in his soul, his conscience; in his conscience, his honesty; and in his honesty, his concern for his eternal salvation. The same goes for your father-in-law.

Perhaps your father, who doesn't really know me yet, will misinterpret the liberty I have taken; so help him get to know me for when he does, I'm sure that more than anything else about me, it's that very liberty that he will love. I have written a five-page letter to the archbishop of Bourges [Madame de Chantal's brother] in which I describe for him a method of preaching, and along with that, I tell him quite freely what I think about certain responsibilities in an archbishop's life. In his case, I have no fear of being misunderstood. So what more could you want? Your father, brother, uncle, children—all are infinitely dear to me.

In answer to your seventh point, about the spirit of liberty, I shall tell you what I think it is. Every good person is free of committing mortal sins and has no willing attachment to them. Such freedom is necessary for salvation, but that's not what I'm talking about here. The freedom I'm referring to is the "freedom of the children of God" (Rom. 8:21) who know they are loved. And what is that? It's the detachment of a Christian heart from all things so that it is free to follow the known will of God. You will readily understand what I'm trying to say if God gives me the grace to explain to you the characteristics and effects of this freedom, and the occasions when it is practiced.

We pray to God above all that his name may be hallowed, that his kingdom come, that his will be done on earth as it is in heaven. All this is nothing other than the spirit of freedom; for, provided that the name of God is hallowed, that his kingdom is coming in us, that his will is being done, a free spirit has no other concern.

First characteristic: The heart that enjoys this freedom is not attached to consolations, but accepts affliction with as much docility as nature can manage. I'm not saying that the person doesn't like or long for these consolations, but just that her heart isn't bound to them. Second characteristic: A person who has this spirit is not emotionally bound to her spiritual exercises; so, if she can't do them because of illness or some emergency, she doesn't get upset. Again I'm not saying that she doesn't like them, but that she is not attached to them. Third, she hardly ever loses her joy, for no deprivation can sadden a person whose heart is attached to nothing. This isn't to say that she can't lose her joy, but if she does, it's never for very long.

The effects of this freedom are a great inner serenity, a great gentleness and willingness to yield in everything that isn't sin or an occasion of sin; it's a flexible disposition, able gracefully to do the virtuous or charitable thing. For example: Try interrupting the meditations of someone who is very attached to her spiritual exercises and you will see her upset, flustered, taken aback. A person who has this true freedom will leave her prayer, unruffled, gracious toward the person who has unexpectedly disturbed her, for to her it's all the same — serving God by meditating or serving him by responding to her neighbor. Both are the will of God, but helping the neighbor is necessary at that particular moment. We have occasion to practice this freedom whenever things don't go the way we'd like them to; for anyone who is not attached to her own ways will not get impatient when things go otherwise.

This freedom has two opposite vices: instability and constraint or, in the extreme, dissoluteness and slavishness. Instability is a kind of excessive freedom that makes us want to change our practices or our state in life for no good reason or without knowing if to do so is God's will. The least pretext is enough to make us change a practice, a plan, a rule; for the flimsiest excuse we give up a rule or a good custom. Before we know it, our heart is scattered and loses its way; it becomes like an orchard open on all sides, where the fruit is not for the owner but for all who pass by (cf. Ps. 80:13).

Constraint or slavishness is a certain lack of freedom that causes the soul to be unduly anxious or angry when it cannot carry out what it had intended to do, even though it could now do something better. For example: Suppose I have decided to make my daily meditation in the morning. If I am unstable, then for the slightest excuse I will put it off until evening, e.g., a dog kept me awake, or I have a letter to write (though there is no urgency about it). On the other hand, if I have a spirit of constraint or slavishness I wouldn't give up my meditation even if a sick person had great need of my help at that very moment or if I had some pressing obligation that should not be postponed; and so on.

I still want to give you two or three examples of this freedom to help you understand what I'm not explaining very well. But first of all, I must point out two rules that must be observed if we are not to fail in this matter. First, we should never neglect our exercises and the common norms of virtue unless to do so appears to be God's will. Now the will of God is indicated in two ways: through necessity or charity. Example: I would like to preach the Lenten sermons in a small town in my diocese. But if I get sick or break a leg, there's no point in feeling sorry or worried about not preaching, for I can be sure that God wants me to serve him by suffering and not by preaching. However, if I'm not sick and an occasion comes along to go preach in another place where people might become Huguenots if I didn't go, this would be the will of God, signifying clearly enough that I should very simply change my plans.

The second rule is that when we use our freedom for charity's sake it must be without scandal or injustice. Example: I am certain I could be more useful somewhere far from my diocese. I must not use my freedom to follow through with this, for I would give scandal and act unjustly since my obligation is here. Therefore, it's a false use of freedom for married women to absent themselves from their husbands without a legitimate reason, under pretext of devotion or charity. Our freedom must never take us away from our vocation. On the contrary, it should make us content each with our own calling, knowing that it is God's will that we remain in it (cf. 1 Cor. 7:20, 24).

Now let's look at Cardinal Borromeo, who will be canonized in a few days. He was one of the most precise, rigid, austere men you could imagine; he lived on bread and water; he was so austere that after he became archbishop, in twenty-four years he went to his brothers' homes only twice when they were ill, and only twice did he go in his own garden. And yet, this strict man, who often dined with his Swiss neighbors (he did this in the hope of having a good influence on them), had no problem drinking a couple of toasts with them at every meal, over and above what he drank to quench his thirst. Here you have an example of holy freedom in the most austere man of our times. An undisciplined person would have drunk too much; one who is very constrained would have been afraid of committing a mortal sin; a person with a true spirit of freedom does it out of love.

Bishop Spiridion, a bishop of long ago, took in a pilgrim almost dead from hunger. It was during Lent and there was nothing to eat in his place but salt meat. He had some of it cooked and offered it to the pilgrim, who refused to take it, hungry though he was. Spiridion, who wasn't at all hungry, out of charity ate some first in order to remove, by his example, any scruples the pilgrim might have. That's the loving freedom of a holy man.

Father Ignatius of Loyola, who will also soon be canonized, ate meat on Wednesday of Holy Week simply on the order of his physician who thought it would be good for some minor ailment he had. A constrained spirit would have had to be coaxed for three days before doing this.

But now I want to show you a "sun" that shines more brilliantly than any of these: a really open, detached spirit who holds on to the will of God alone. I've often wondered who was the most mortified of all the saints I know, and after much reflection, I decided it was St. John the Baptist. He went into the desert at the age of five and was aware that our Savior was born in a place very close by, maybe two or three days' journey away. God only knows how much his heart, which had been moved to love his Savior from the time he was still in his mother's womb, would have wanted to enjoy the Lord's sweet presence! Yet he spent twenty-five years in the desert, without once coming to see him; then leaving the desert, he went about catechizing without going to visit the Lord, but waited for the Lord to come to him. Afterward, having baptized him, he didn't follow him but stayed behind to do his appointed work. What mortification! To be so close to his Savior and not see him! To have him so near and not enjoy his presence! Isn't this having one's spirit completely detached, bound to nothing, not even to God, in order to do his will and serve him; to leave God for God, and to not love God so as to love him better? This example overwhelms me with its grandeur.

I forgot to mention that God's will is known, not only by the call of necessity and charity, but also by obedience; so true is this that a person who receives a command should believe that this is the will of God. I hope this isn't too much. My mind is running ahead faster than I would like, carried away by my eagerness to serve you.

In response to your eighth point, remember the feast day of King St. Louis, the day on which you took the crown of the kingdom from your own heart to lay it at the feet of Jesus, your King; the day on which you renewed your youth like the eagle's (cf. Ps. 103:5), plunging into the sea of penance; the day that heralded the eternal day of your soul. Remember that to your great resolution of belonging totally to God — body, heart, and soul — I said "Amen" in the name of the whole church, our Mother; at the same time, the Blessed Virgin and all the angels and saints made heaven resound with their great "Amen" and "Alleluia." Remember that all the past is as nothing and that every day you must say with David: only now have I begun to really love my God (Ps. 77:11). Do much for God, and do nothing without love: refer everything to this love; eat and drink with it in mind (cf. 1 Cor. 10:31).

Have devotion to St. Louis and admire his great constancy. He became king when he was twelve years old, had nine children, was continually at war against either rebels or enemies of the faith, and was king for more than forty years. At the end of it all, after his death, the holy priest who had been his confessor all through his life testified that King Louis had never fallen into mortal sin. Twice he had made voyages overseas; both times he lost his army, and on the last trip he died of the plague. After having devoted much time to visiting, nursing, and healing the plague-stricken men of his army, he himself died, cheerful and calm, a verse from David on his lips. I give you this saint as your special patron for the year; keep him before your eyes, along with the others I named above. Next year, please God, I will give you another saint, after you have profited much in the school of this one.

As to your ninth point, I want you to believe two things about me: first, that God wants you to avail yourself of me, so do not hesitate; and, second, that in what concerns your salvation, God will give me the light I need to serve you. As for my will to serve you, God has already given it to me to such a degree that it couldn't be stronger. I have received the copy of your vows, which I will carefully treasure, looking upon it as a fit instrument of our union, which is totally rooted in God and which will last for all eternity, by the mercy of him who is its author....

In one passage in your letter, you seem to consider it settled that some day we shall be seeing each other again. Please God, my very dear sister, we shall. But for my part, I see nothing ahead to warrant my hoping to find time to get there. I told you the reason in confidence at Saint-Claude. I'm tied up here, hand and foot; and you, dear sister, don't the difficulties of your last journey frighten you? Well, between now and Easter we'll see what God wants from us; may his holy will ever be ours. I ask you to praise God with me for the effects of the trip to Saint-Claude. I can't tell you about them, but they are great. At your first opportunity, write me the story of the gate of Saint-Claude, and please believe that I'm not asking you this out of curiosity.

My mother could not have been more taken with you. I was happy to see that you willingly call Madame du Puits d'Orbe "sister." She has a greatness of soul, if she receives the right help, and God will use her to the glory of his name. Help her and visit her by letter. God will be pleased with you for this.

It looks to me as if I'll never finish this letter, which I've written only with the intention of answering you. Still, I really must finish it now, asking for your prayers, which are a great help. How I need them! I never pray without including you in my petitions; I never greet my own angels without greeting yours. Do the same for me, and get Celse-Bénigne to pray for me also. I always pray for him and all your little family. You may be sure that

I never forget them in my Mass, nor their deceased father, your husband.

May God be your very heart, mind, and soul, my dearest sister. I am, in his merciful love,

> your very devoted servant

... Pray once in a while for the conversion of my poor Geneva.

Several points in the bishop's letter deserve to be noted. First, we become aware that at the heart of his method of spiritual guidance is what has been called the discernment of spirits. He begins by reassuring Jane that her decision to leave her previous director and confide in him is a sound one because it has been conscientiously discerned. It was elaborated upon, outside advice was sought, and it was brought to prayer. The decision did not carry with it agitated, hurried, or violent feelings.

The question of how to discover God's will or, put in a more gracious way, how to align oneself with God's desire for one's life, is a central one in Christian spirituality. Methods for discerning spirits or determining which interior impulses or voices or promptings come from God and which from some other source (collective pressure, a misguided self, or even an evil source) have been outlined for centuries. Particularly clear is Ignatius Loyola's method. This is one with which Francis was familiar. In this method one pays attention to one's feelings or desires on a particular issue and (to oversimplify, for Ignatian discernment is in fact more complex than this in practice) concludes that feelings of peace, completion, and joy represent a Godward movement, while feelings of anxiety, agitation, and disgust represent what is not in the direction of God.

As one continues reading on in the letter, the budding nature of Francis and Jane's friendship begins to appear. As the Genevan bishop explored his feelings about their relationship, he discerned there a joyful, consoling affection that, as the years progressed, did indeed grow and deepen. He would see this particular friendship and the many other bonds he cultivated as part of a larger experience — that of becoming a lover of God. In fact, it was about the time that this 1604 letter was written that Francis began ruminating on a book he would eventually compose. He referred to it in its early stages as his "Book of Holy Charity." Later it would be entitled *Treatise on the Love of God*. It would capture his vision of the intertwining of divine and human love. While his ideas were seeded back in his student days at Padua where he studied the biblical Song of Songs under the Benedictine Génébrard, who interpreted the Song as a mystical treatise, it was no doubt Francis' experience of loving friendship like the one he shared with Madame de Chantal that allowed his ideas to grow and finally bear fruit.

The letter goes on and gives advice to his correspondent about how to deal with her temptations against the faith. It is important to remember that Jane and Francis lived in an era of intense religious divisiveness. Loyalists to the church of Rome were pitted, often to the death, against advocates of the Reformed cause. In our modern age of ecumenism, such advice might well be reconsidered. Or at least one might want to separate the process of resisting "temptations" from the interpretation of what a temptation is. The general process itself is an intriguing one — Francis calls it "slipping out of the gate of your will." In other words, don't get trapped in spinning your wheels in circular arguments. Act or make a decision in a decisive way. The process could have wider application.

But for most or at least many contemporary Christians, doubts are not considered incompatible with authentic faith. Indeed interdominational and interreligious dialogue have made us aware that to encounter a variety of religious perspectives does not necessarily threaten to undermine our own perspective but serves rather to clarify points of variance and affirm common points upon which mutual respect might be founded.

On Jane's fourth point (apparently she had asked her friend about modifying his proposed program of prayers) Francis responds in typically Salesian fashion: Do all through love, nothing through constraint. He emphasizes the necessity for true spiritual liberty, an interior spaciousness that is not turned in upon itself. Throughout his writings de Sales makes much of this "liberty of the children of God." One sees it here especially as applied to prayer. The point of prayer is not to fulfill some particular regime but to facilitate loving, creative relationships with God and others. Whatever enables a person to do this should be pursued. He goes on later in the letter to describe this freedom more fully.

Finally, about the models to which Bishop de Sales appeals, it will be evident to the modern reader that austere heroes who are commended for visiting their brothers' homes and their own gardens only twice, spending twenty-five years in desert solitude, being continually at war with "enemies of the faith" may not be heroes whom twentieth-century Christians would hope to emulate. In our present religious climate we tend to gravitate more toward the humanly fallible sinner-saint or to persons whose lives are heroic in their concerns for justice and advocacy on behalf of the poor. Ideals of holiness have changed considerably over the centuries and in Francis and Jane's day the austere, physically mortified, uncompromising defender of the faith was a primary ideal.

The friendship between Madame de Chantal and Bishop de Sales continued to develop. Early in 1610 he sat once again at his writing desk and penned another letter that gives some glimpse into their developing relationship as well as into his own spirit. Jane's circumstances were considerably different by this time. With Francis' counsel she had gradually begun to discern the outline of her future more grounded in God. She and Francis were to establish (in June of 1610) a new women's community. Jane was to be its first superior. It would be known as the Visitation of Holy Mary. The process through which this discernment had been made was a complex one and it had involved much effort on both their parts.

The overarching vision of this new diocesan foundation was in keeping with the Salesian spirit. During his years of ministry Francis had noted that there was no niche in the institutional structure of the church for women who seemed called to a deep and prayerful intimacy with God yet who were unsuited for life in one of the austere contemplative monastic orders gaining popularity at the time. Women who were frail of health, handicapped, too young or old, or widows who still had some family responsibilities could not qualify for admission into such contemplative orders. Further, married women of spiritual depth had no place of solitude and quiet where they might go for periods of retreat to refresh themselves. The Visitation, Francis and Jane imagined, would be such a place. Founded as a simple congregation (members did not take permanent binding vows), it was open especially to what Francis called "daughters of prayer," women whose love of God was great but who were, in the ecclesial structure of the era, unable to find an environment that could allow them to exercise their gift of prayer because of physical or familial limitations.

The year 1610 was that of the Visitation's founding. When Francis wrote to his friend in January he wrote with enormous anticipation. She would be traveling from Dijon to Annecy, where the community was to be located, with three of her children and her friend Charlotte de Brechard. The latter would be entering the community with her. Her eldest child, Celse-Bénigne, would stay in Dijon to pursue his education. Her three daughters would be coming south with her. Marie Aimée, who had recently been married to Francis' brother Bernard, would be joining her husband at the de Sales' family château. Françoise and Charlotte would live as boarders in the community with their mother. At the time of the letter's composition neither Jane nor Francis knew that little Charlotte would never reach Annecy; she was to die suddenly of a fever just before the trip south began.

January 16, 1610

... In regard to our coming here, do not hurry because of my anticipated trip to Paris, because, having heard nothing more about that beyond what I showed you, I doubt if it will take place; also it seems to me that to take your three little daughters on a trip during Lent would be rather difficult; besides, your nephew told me that your father and your brother had settled on the time immediately after Easter. Your heart may be saying by now, "Look how this man keeps on postponing!" O my daughter, believe that I am waiting for your day of joy with as much longing as you are; but I am forced to act this way for reasons it is not expedient that I write you about. So wait, my very dear sister, "Wait," I say, using words of Scripture, "while you wait" (Ps. 40:1). Now to wait while we wait means not to worry while waiting, for many persons do not really wait while waiting, but are anxious and restless.

So we'll be all right, dear daughter, with God's help. All the little complications and hidden contradictions that come up unexpectedly to disturb my peace actually fill me with an even more serene peace and, it seems to me, are a sign that my soul will soon be settled in God. This really is the greatest and, I believe, the only ambition and passion of my heart. When I say my heart I mean my whole heart, including the person to whom God has united me indissolubly.

While I am on the subject of my soul, I want to give you some good news about it: I am doing and shall continue doing for it all that you asked me to do — have no doubt about this. Thank you for your concern for its welfare, which is undivided from the welfare of your own soul (if we can even use the terms "yours" and "mine" when speaking on this subject). And I'll tell you something else: I am a little happier than usual with my soul in that I no longer see anything in it that keeps it attached to this world, and I find it more in tune with eternal values. How happy I should be if I were as deeply and closely united to God as I am distanced and alienated from the world! And how delighted you would be, my daughter! But I'm speaking of my inner dispositions and my feelings; as for the exterior and, what is worse, my actions, these are full of all kinds of contrary flaws, for "I fail to carry out the good things I want to do" (Rom. 7:15). Yet I know very well, without pretense and without swerving, that I really want to do them. But, my daughter, how can it be that even with such good will, I still see so many imperfections growing in me? Surely, these come neither from my will nor by my will, although they appear to form part of it. It seems to me that they are like mistletoe, which grows and appears on a tree though it is not part of it — on it but not of it. Why am I telling you all this? It's because my heart always expands and pours itself out spontaneously when it is near yours.

Your way of praying is good. Just be very faithful about staying near God, gently and quietly attentive to him in your heart, sleeping in the arms of his providence, peacefully accepting his holy will; for all this pleases him. . . .

I'd like to say more about your prayer, for I reread your letter late last night. Go on doing as you described. Be careful not to intellectualize, because this can be harmful, not only in general, but especially at prayer. Approach the beloved object of your prayer with your affections quite simply and as gently as you can. Naturally, every now and then your intellect will make an effort to apply itself; don't waste time trying to guard against this, for that would only be a distraction. When you notice this happening, be content simply to return to acts of the will.

Staying in God's presence and placing ourselves in God's presence are, to my mind, two different things. In order to place ourselves in his presence we have to withdraw our soul from every other object and make it attentive to that presence at this very moment, as I have explained in the book. But once we are there, we remain there, as long as either our intellect or our will is active in regard to God. We look either at him or at something else for love of him; or, not looking at anything at all, we speak to him; or again, without either looking at him or speaking to him, we just stay there where he has placed us, like a statue in its niche. And if while we are there, we also have some sense that we belong to God and that he is our All, then we must certainly thank him for this.

If a statue that had been placed in a niche in some room had the ability to speak and were asked, "Why are you there?" it would answer, "Because my master, the sculptor, has put me here." "Why don't you move about?" "Because he wants me to be perfectly still." "What use are you there? What do you gain by staying like this?" "I'm not here for my own benefit, but to serve and obey the will of my master." "But you don't see him." "No, but he sees me and is pleased that I am here where he has put me." "But wouldn't you like to be able to move about and to get closer to him?" "No, not unless he ordered me to." "Isn't there anything at all that you want then?" "No, because I am where my master put me, and all my happiness lies in pleasing him."

Dear daughter, what a good way of praying, and what a fine way of staying in God's presence: doing what he wants and accepting what pleases him! It seems to me that Mary Magdalene was a statue in her niche when, without saying a word, without moving, and perhaps even without looking at him, she sat at our Lord's feet and listened to what he was saying. When he spoke, she listened; whenever he paused, she stopped listening; but always, she was right there. A little child who is at its mother's breast when she has fallen asleep is really where it belongs and wants to be, even though neither of them makes a sound.

O my daughter, how I enjoy talking with you about these things! How happy we are when we want to love our Lord! Let's really love him, my daughter, and let's not start examining in detail what we are doing for love of him, as long as we know that we never want to do anything except for love of him. For my part, I think we remain in God's presence even while we are asleep, because we fall asleep in his sight, as he pleases, and according to his will, and he puts us down on our bed like a statue in its niche; when we wake up, we find him still there, close by. He has not moved, nor have we; evidently, we have stayed in his presence, but with our eyes closed in sleep.

Well, your baron [Jane's nephew, Jacques de Neufchèzes] is here, telling me to hurry up. Good night, my dear sister, my daughter. You will have news of me as often as I can write. Believe me that the very first note I wrote you was absolutely true — that God had given me to you. I am more convinced of this in my heart every day. May this great God ever be our All.

I send greetings to my dear little sister [Jane's daughter who had recently married Francis' brother] and all your household. ... Stand fast, dear daughter, and do not doubt: God holds us in his hand and will never abandon us. Glory be to him forever and ever. Amen.

Live Jesus and his most holy mother! Amen. And praise be to our good father, St. Joseph! May God bless you with countless blessings.

Conferences

The friendship between Bishop de Sales and Madame de Chantal bore fruit in the community of the Visitation that they co-founded. On June 6, 1610, Jane and three companions made their way from dinner at Francis' episcopal apartments through the narrow cobblestone streets of Annecy to their new home, the Gallery House, a dwelling deeded to them by a patron. The procession was a festive and triumphal one through the city, for Francis was a beloved figure in his diocese. Jane herself was by now well connected with Annecy's first families through the marriage of Marie Aimée to Francis' brother Bernard. Also accompanying the Baroness de Chantal into her new life was Jacqueline Favre, daughter of one of Annecy's leading citizens, as well as Francis' dear friend Antoine Favre, Charlotte de Brechard, Jane's family friend, and Jacqueline Coste, a lay sister recruited by Francis.

When the little band of women settled in their new home perched on the hillside just above Lake Annecy, they inaugurated an entirely new way of life. They sought to live the devout life in a specific way with other women who felt a deep drawing to the life of prayer but who, because of the limitations of health or family obligations, could not enter one of the formal contemplative orders. The way of the Visitation was to be eminently Salesian. Like the devout life expressed among the laity, the devout life expressed in the Visitation was to be first and foremost an interior reality. To live Jesus was its intent. In fact "Live Jesus!" became the motto of the community.

The asceticism practiced was to be primarily a matter of heart, not of body. The first rule laid out a moderate plan of daily activity including liturgical and private prayer, work (mostly household), and simple recreation. At the center of the life were the little virtues that Francis loved so much and of which he wrote so evocatively in the *Introduction*. The emphasis was to be on creating a community that lived out in a striking way gentleness, simplicity, humility, patience, and the other relationally sensitive virtues.

In 1610, the year of the Visitation's foundation, Francis made it a frequent habit to stop by the Gallery House and visit Jane and the other women. They had one special meeting place, the garden just behind the house where there was a small orchard of pear trees. They fondly named it the "Conference Garden," for it was there that together they spoke about the life they were creating. At other times the bishop held talks on various spiritual themes related to devotion as these women sought to live it. The conversations were later lovingly recorded and compiled in a small book. Of all the conversations, one of the most delightful and typically Salesian is the fourth in the collection, the conference on cordiality.

Obviously the bishop in this conference is directly addressing a community of women dedicated to living a form of what was in his day termed "the life of perfection," a vowed life observing some expression of poverty, chastity, and obedience. Hence his advice is shaped to fit the particularity of their situation. But the conference on cordiality is revealing of Francis' spirituality in a more general way. His vision is profoundly relational. One goes to God not only vertically but horizontally. That is, the spiritual life is carried on not only between an individual and God but between persons as well.

It is in the affectionate (spiritually tempered) relationship between persons that one Lives Jesus! With delightful charm Bishop de Sales describes for Jane de Chantal and the first sisters of the Visitation what a community based on such cordial relational love might look like. He is very aware of the pitfalls that his listeners will inevitably encounter in such an undertaking. He is aware of the danger especially in the life of perfection of making imperfection an occasion for a too self-preoccupied discouragement. The wonderful balance of his spiritual advice is keenly observed in this conference.

Francis took the two great commandments of the New Testament seriously; love of God and love of neighbor were for him the foundations of the Christian life. While he gives some precedence to love of God as the primary source and end of all love, he is among those, certainly a minority in the contemplative tradition, who would especially emphasize love of neighbor. Certainly Christians from earliest times have been counseled to love one another; the persistent tradition of the spiritual and corporal works of mercy vigorously attests to this. But in general, spiritual writers have tended to emphasize love of God so intently that love of neighbor becomes almost an afterthought. Or at least love of neighbor tends to proceed generically and dispassionately as a care for souls out of the one great consuming love of the divine. This was not the case with Bishop de Sales. He argued that a person does not have two hearts, one to love God and one to love others, but only one heart capable of love. Thus all loves are intertwined and, while they are all grounded ultimately in divine love, human love is not necessarily a hindrance to divine love. Rather, directed rightly, human love is essential, for learning to love each other forms us in love, and love is of God.

Thus when the bishop gave his conference on cordiality to the little band of Visitation sisters in the pear garden behind the Gallery House, he was teaching that love of one another should become the basis of an entire way of life. The small, gentle, and attentive relational gesture, the patient bearing with one another, the mutual trust and accountability that he envisioned as hallmarks of Visitandine life are distinctive in the literature for religious houses. The little virtues of affability, cheerfulness, and childlike confidence so prominent here are absent from discussions of virtue in the monastic writings of his day. To Live Jesus! in this community was to make the gentle, humble Jesus of Matthew come to life.

We must then remember that love has its seat in the heart, and that we can never love our neighbor too much, nor exceed the limits of reason in this affection, provided that it dwells in the heart; but as regards the manifestations of this love, we can very easily go wrong by excess, passing beyond the rules of reason. The glorious St. Bernard says that "the measure of loving God is to love him without measure," and that in our love there ought to be no limits, but that we should allow its branches to spread out as far as they possibly can. That which is said of love of God may also be understood to apply to our neighbor, provided, however, that the love of God always keeps the upper hand and holds the first rank. Then, in the next place, we should love our sisters with all the compass of our heart, and not be content with loving them as ourselves, which the commandments of God oblige us to do, but love them more than ourselves, in order to observe the rules of evangelical perfection, which require that of us. Our Lord himself says: "Love one another as I have loved you" (John 13:34). This "love as I have loved you" ought to be well considered, for it means: more than yourselves. And just as our Lord has always preferred us to himself, and does so still as often as we receive him in the Blessed Sacrament, making himself therein our food, so in like manner he wishes us to have such a love for one another that we shall always prefer our neighbor to ourselves. And just as he has done all that he could do for us except condemning himself to hell (which indeed he could not and ought not to do, for he could not sin and it is sin alone that leads to damnation), so he wishes, and the rule of perfection requires, that we should do all that we can do for one another except losing our soul. With that sole exception, our friendship ought to be so firm, cordial, and solid that we should never refuse to do or to suffer anything for our neighbor and our sisters.

Now this cordial love ought to be accompanied by two virtues, one of which may be called affability, and the other cheerfulness. Affability is a virtue that spreads a certain agreeableness over all the business and serious communications that we hold with one another; cheerfulness is that which renders us gracious and agreeable in our recreations and less serious intercourse with one another. All the virtues have, as you know, two contrary vices, which are the extremes of the virtue. The virtue of affability, then, lies between two vices: that of too great gravity and seriousness on the one hand, and on the other of too many demonstrations of affection and using expressions that incline to flattery. Now the virtue of affability holds the golden mean between these two extremes, making use of affectionate terms according to the necessity of those with whom it has to deal, preserving at the same time a gentle gravity according to the requirements of the persons and affairs of which it treats. I say that we must show signs of affection at certain times, for it would not be suitable to carry into a sick room as much gravity of demeanor as we should display elsewhere, not showing more kindness to an invalid than if she were in full health. But we must not make such demonstrations too frequently, or be ready on every occasion to speak honeyed words, throwing whole handfuls of them over the first person we meet. Just as if we put too much sugar on our food it would disgust us, becoming insipid by being too sweet, so in the same way too frequent signs of affection would become repulsive, or at any rate we should cease to value them, knowing that they were given almost mechanically. The food on which salt is scattered in quantities would be disagreeable on account of its tartness, but that into which either salt or sugar is put in proper proportions becomes agreeable to the taste; so also caresses bestowed with measure and discretion are rendered profitable and agreeable to those who receive them.

The virtue of cheerfulness requires that we should contribute to holy and temperate joy and to pleasant conversation, which may serve as a consolation and recreation to our neighbors, so as not to weary and annoy them with our knit brows and melancholy faces, or by refusing to recreate ourselves at the time destined to recreation....

We must, moreover, remark that cordial love is attached to another virtue, which is as it were a consequence of that love, namely, a childlike confidence. When children have, say, a fine feather or something else that they think pretty, they cannot rest until they have found their little companions to show them the feather, and make them share in their joy; and in the same way they want them to share their grief, for if they have but a sore finger they go telling everyone they meet about it, to get pity and have the poor finger breathed upon. Now I do not say that you must be exactly like these children, but I do say that this confidence ought to make you willingly communicate to your sisters all your little satisfactions and consolations, with no fear lest they should remark your imperfection. I do not say that if some extraordinary gift is bestowed upon you by God you must tell everyone about it — no; but as regards your smaller consolations and joys, I wish you not to be so reserved about them and, when the occasion presents itself, to speak of them frankly and simply to one another, not in a spirit of boasting and self-satisfaction, but of childlike confidence. So too as regards your faults, I should wish you not to take so much pain to hide them, for they are none the better for not being outwardly visible. The sisters will not think you have none because they are concealed, and your imperfections will perhaps be more dangerous than if they were detected and caused you the confusion that they do to those who are more ready to let them appear on the surface. You must not, then, be astonished or discouraged when you commit some fault or imperfection before your sisters, but, on the contrary, you must be very glad to be seen as you really are. You may have been guilty of some fault or silliness, it is true; but it was before your sisters, who love you dearly, who can very well bear with you in your faults, and who will feel more compassion for you than indignation against you. Such confidence would greatly strengthen the cheerfulness and calmness of our minds, which are liable to be troubled when we are found out to be faulty in something, however small it may be, as if it were any great wonder that we should be seen to be imperfect!

In conclusion, remember always that if we should sometimes, through inadvertence, fail in gentleness and sweetness of behavior, we must not distress ourselves, or think that we are absolutely devoid of cordiality, for this is not so. An act committed now and then and not frequently does not make people vicious, especially when they have a hearty purpose and will to amend.

Treatise on
the Love of God

In early 1610 Francis had the revised manuscript of his *Introduction to the Devout Life* on his writing desk before him. But this was not the only book he was in the process of writing. Nor was it the first of which he had dreamed. Long before he transformed his memos of advice to Madame de Charmoisy into a publishable piece of writing, Francis had been ruminating on a long-range project that lay very close to his heart. He had dreamed of composing what he originally called "The Book of Holy Charity," a work that would by the time of its publication in 1616 be titled *Treatise on the Love of God.* He had conceived of this work as an exposition on the spiritual life in its entirety, both theory and practice. And he had especially wanted to make such a work available in a small, manageable volume that could be both accessible and portable for the general reader. Where he had addressed the *Introduction* to "Philothea," the feminine form of a name meaning lover of God, he would address the *Treatise* to "Theotimus," a masculine name of the same meaning (with a disclaimer in his preface that asserted that the book was not written primarily for men but for "any human heart anxious to grow in the love of God").

The work had been gestating in the Genevan bishop for many years. During his student years in Paris he had been greatly impressed by the scholarly work of the Benedictine Génébrard, whose lectures on the Song of Songs he had attended. The older scholar had undertaken an exegesis of this scriptural book. Following the medieval interpretive tradition, he had read the Song as a mystical document symbolizing the loving relationship between God and the human heart as well as between Christ and the church. The lectures electrified the young student. From that time on he was unable to conceive of the spiritual life as anything except the most beautiful of love stories between human and divine persons.

The erotic language of the Song of Songs became the lens through which de Sales viewed most of his own and others' religious experience. The actual book about Holy Charity had been growing in him for at least five years by 1610. In February of that year he wrote to his friend Jane de Chantal that he might find time to continue working on the project. The first mention of its existence is discovered in a 1607 letter, also to Jane, in which Francis related to her his excitement that he had drawn up an outline of a book he described as a "biography" of a little known saint, Holy Charity, which was to be twice as long as Teresa of Avila's *Life*, a popular work newly translated from Spanish into French.

No doubt his deep relationship with Jane as well as his other friends nurtured his desire to create this work. Certainly his contact with her and his other spiritual intimates gave him a rich source of reflection and experience to draw upon. We know in fact that a key portion of the *Treatise* (in Book Nine) is a direct reflection of Jane's own prayer experience. Further, the foundation of the Visitation in June of 1610, followed by his frequent visits to the Gallery House, where he lingered in the garden reflecting on the spiritual life with the sisters, fueled his creative spirit. Much of the *Treatise* would be written between then and 1614 when the manuscript's rough draft was completed.

The *Treatise on the Love of God*, which lay as an incomplete manuscript on another part of the bishop's desk, would become his most comprehensive work. The *Introduction* may claim the title of Francis de Sales' most popular piece of writing, but the *Treatise* represents more accurately the breadth and depth of his theological vision. It integrates Catholic dogmatic, moral, scriptural, philosophical, and mystical insights into one overarching narrative.

At root it is the story of a passionate loving God who has created humankind in the divine image and likeness and with the longing to be reciprocally in love with God. The opening sections of the *Treatise* deal with this cosmic vision. It begins by describing the structure of the human soul using the scholastic distinctions of the day and showing how the love of God reigns supreme over all faculties of the person. The entire argument is couched in the luxurious, tactile language of the Song of Songs. The segments included here employ the metaphor of the kiss to depict the intimate relationship of human and divine.

OUR NATURAL TENDENCY TO LOVE GOD MORE THAN ANYTHING

If human beings possessed the original perfection and original justice that Adam knew when God first made him, they would not only have a tendency to love God more than anything; they would be able to achieve it naturally without any other help from God than the ability he gives each creature to perform actions befitting its nature. The Author and Lord of nature lends his powerful hand to fire to shoot upward, to water to flow downward to the sea, to land to sink and settle. In the same way, he planted in the heart of every person a special natural tendency — not only of loving good in general, but of loving in particular and more than anything the goodness of God, better and more lovable than everything else. So God's kindly providence urged him to give humanity all the assistance necessary to realize that tendency. On the one hand, such assistance would be natural, befitting human nature, and leading to the love of God as nature's Author, nature's Lord. On the other hand, it would be supernatural, as befits nature adorned, enriched, and dignified with original justice — a supernatural quality due to a special grace from God. For all that, such love of God more than anything else would still be called natural. Good deeds, after all, are classified according to aim and motive. The object of this love is

God only as he is known by the natural light of reason: Author, Lord, supreme goal of every creature. Consequently, the inclination, the instinct to love him, to put him before anything else, would be natural.

Human nature, as we know it, lacks the original perfection and justice of Adam's creation. It is a badly fallen nature, due to sin; yet the tendency to love God more than anything remains, as does the natural light of reason by which we know that God's supreme goodness is more lovable than all other things. The moment a person seriously reflects on God with nothing but unaided reason as a guide, the heart instinctively leaps with love. The will, aware of its chief good, is captivated and prompted to seek satisfaction in it.

Maternal instinct, or stupidity in not recognizing their own eggs, often drives partridges to steal other partridges' eggs in order to hatch them. Then a strange thing happens, for which there is ample proof.... When the chick first hears the cry of its true mother, it leaves the protecting wing of the thievish partridge and flies to the true one. Some likeness in its nature draws it to the mother bird — a mysterious dormant likeness that only comes to light when the baby partridge is recalled to its first duty. And that, Theotimus, is how it is with the human heart.... Though born and bred amid the material transitory things of earth — beneath the wings of nature, as it were — yet the first glimpse of God, the first awareness of him, fans to flame the hidden spark of its natural instinct for loving God. As this plays on the will, the soul thrills with charity — love at its highest, the love that is due to the first principle and Lord of all.

LOVE SEEKS UNION

Solomon gives a wonderful description of love between God and a devoted soul; so charming, his treatment of it. The work is called the Song of Songs. With the idyllic love of a chaste shepherd and modest shepherdess for his theme, he gently lifts our minds to the spiritual romance between ourselves and God — the response of the human heart to God's inspirations. Solomon

138 ♦ Treatise on the Love of God

gives the first line to the bride suddenly betrayed into an exclamation of love: "A kiss from those lips!" (Song of Songs 1:2).
Notice that the first thing the shepherdess wants — and she represents the human soul, Theotimus — is chaste union with the
bridegroom. It is all she lives for. What else does it reveal, I ask
you? — that initial sigh of hers: "A kiss from those lips!"

Instinctively, it seems, the kiss has always been used as a
symbol of perfect love, of union of hearts — and not without
reason. We express the passions and emotions that we have
in common with the animals by our eyes, eyebrows, forehead,
and other features. "A man's looks betray him" (Ecclus. 19:26)
Scripture tells us; and Aristotle suggests this as a reason for the
custom, in portraits of the great, of almost exclusively depicting
only their faces: "The face," he says, "mirrors the inner self."

Speech and thought, however, which originate in that spiritual part of the soul we call the reason — differentiating us from
the animals — can be conveyed only by words, and so through
the mouth. Speech is simply opening the heart, laying bare the
soul. "Lay the homage of your hearts at God's feet" (Ps. 61:9)
says the psalmist; or, to put it another way, utter the emotions
of your heart in words. So quietly did Samuel's mother say her
prayers, her lips seemed scarcely to be moving, but she was
"unburdening her heart in the Lord's presence" (1 Kings 1:13–
15). In this way, lips meet lips in a kiss, symbolic of that mutual
outpouring of soul for the achievement of perfect unity. That is
why in every age and among the world's greatest saints, the kiss
has been a sign of love and affection. The early Christians always used it for this purpose, as St. Paul shows when he tells
the Romans and Corinthians: "Greet one another with the kiss
of saints" (Rom. 16:16; 1 Cor. 16:20). It has often been pointed
out that Judas pointed out our Lord in this way at the time of
his arrest, since it was the Savior's custom to greet his disciples
with a kiss. Our Lord even gave it to the little children he took
lovingly in his arms, using one of them as a model to impress on
his disciples the love of their neighbor. . . .

Because a kiss so vividly expresses union of hearts, the one
aim of the bride in the Song of Songs is union with her beloved:

"A kiss," she cries, "from those lips!" "So many sighs, so many glances — so tireless is my love! Surely," she seems to say, "they will win my heart's desire. My efforts must surely lead to the prize I am seeking — union heart to heart, soul to soul, with God, my bridegroom and my life. Oh, for the day when I can cast my soul into his heart, when he will pour his heart into my soul! Such blissful unity — a life that knows no parting!"

THE RELATIONSHIP BETWEEN GOD AND HUMANKIND

No sooner do we take the trouble to give even a little thought to the godhead than our heart thrills with pleasure — a sure sign that God is God of the human heart. Nothing delights the mind more than the thought of God. Better to know a little about him than a lot about other things, says Aristotle, prince of philosophers; the smallest sunbeam gives more light than moon and stars together. Let some calamity befall us, we turn at once to God. This goes to show that we recognize, though all other things betray us, that God alone is faithful; that when danger threatens, only our supreme good can keep us safe and sound.

The human heart's natural delight, natural trust in God is due solely to the relationship between soul and God. A close bond it is, but a hidden one; known to all, yet understood by few; undeniable, but unfathomable. Wearing the image and likeness of God — that is how we have been created, and this means that there is the closest of connections between ourselves and God.

The human soul is spiritual, indivisible, immortal; it thinks and wills; it is able freely to make judgments, follow a line of argument, discover facts, possess virtues; in this it is like God. The soul is present in every part of the body, and it is whole in every part of the body, just as God is everywhere within the universe, and whole in each part of it. The soul knows and loves itself — activities of the mind and will; but these activities of two distinct faculties are inseparable from the soul to which the faculties belong. Similarly, in the godhead, the Son proceeds from the Father as the expression of his knowledge, and the Holy Spirit proceeds from Father and Son as the expression of their mutual love. Each of those two persons (Son and Spirit) is distinct from the other and from the Father; yet they are inseparably one in a godhead that is utterly simple, indivisible, unique.

Apart from the bond of likeness, however, a special relationship exists between God and human beings for their mutual perfection. Not that God is completed by human beings in any way; but human beings need the completion that only God can give — so humanity provides God with an outlet for the external expression of his perfection. Human beings need God and are hungry for his favors; God is full of all good things, and longs to give them. Nothing is more timely to the needy than the generosity of wealth, nothing more pleasing to the bountiful than the neediness of the poor. The richer the store of favors, the stronger is the instinct to bestow them; the greater the need in poverty, the more it clamors for relief. How charming it is when wealth and poverty meet! Whose is the greater satisfaction, the bountiful pouring out or the needy drinking in?...We should never know had not our Lord said that "it is more blessed to give than to receive" (Acts 20:35). Now one who knows greater blessedness enjoys greater satisfaction; so God takes more delight in bestowing his graces than we do in receiving them. In the same way, Theotimus, our weakness leaves us needy, in want of all God has to give; but God's fullness has no need of our emptiness, save as the overflow of his goodness. God's perfect goodness knows no improvement by being shared; it does not gain by overflowing — it gives. Humanity's poverty, on the other hand, would hold us sunk in destitution, in wretchedness, unless God's fullness came to our aid.

We find no perfect contentment here; nothing this world offers can satisfy our desires. The mind ever wants to know more; the will never comes to the end of its search for goodness to love. Surely we can recognize that it is not for this world we were made! A supreme good attracts us, some infinite Craftsman who has fashioned us with an endless longing for knowledge, with a hunger for good that knows no appeasement. That is why we must turn and reach out toward God —

whose creatures we are — and seek for union with his goodness. Such is the relationship in which we stand to God.

Language of the Heart

For Francis de Sales the world is a world of hearts and of desire, divine desire graciously inclining toward creation and human desire reaching to God. His theological vision has been deemed optimistic in the sense that he affirmed the intrinsic goodness of the person and the human capacity to respond out of that goodness. Not that he ignored human limitation or what the tradition calls the legacy of original sin. He treats this topic at length in the *Treatise*. But he did have a positive view of human reason and potential and he emphasized the crucial role of human choice in all decisions. All this he would describe as being ultimately constellated in the heart, which he conceived as the dynamic core of the person where God-directedness was located.

The human heart mirrors the heart of God, which "breathes" in and out, creating out of love and calling back all creation into itself through love. Like its divine counterpart the heart of a person contracts and expands in a motion both receptive and active, drawing God's life into itself through inspiration and pouring out its aspiration through praise and service. The activity of the heart is at the center of the spiritual or devout life as de Sales imaged it.

For centuries the language of the heart had been one of the primary ways that the mystical life was given expression. Francis continued and considerably nuanced that tradition, expanding the metaphor beyond the human-divine relationship to describe the loving relationship of human hearts that, at the level of their deepest desire, long together to return home to God. Thus friendship, community, and human interactions of all kinds — including preaching, teaching, ministering, and caretaking — were potentially modes of encouraging the shared desire of hearts to become more intimate with the divine lover.

The *Treatise on the Love of God* therefore dealt not only with the

theoretical vision of God's love for creation and creation's reciprocal enamorment of God; it also concerned itself with the means
by which love of God might be enhanced or obstructed. In his
characteristically concrete and vivid manner, Francis enumerated
the ways in which charity was to be practiced. One of the chief
ways this was to be accomplished was by prayer.

The entirety of Books Six and Seven of the *Treatise* (there are
twelve altogether) is concerned with prayer. In a masterly exposition the Genevan bishop synthesized centuries of wisdom
from the church's contemplative tradition and gave it a twist
of his own. His description begins with a classically formulated
comparison between meditation and contemplation. It might be
worthwhile to keep in mind that this clear-cut distinction, which
dominated reflection on prayer and the spiritual life up until the
middle of the twentieth century, was one that Francis inherited
from mystical writers of the centuries just before him. It was not
a distinction that was so clearly made earlier in the Christian
tradition. Moreover, meditation (described as a primarily me-
thodical process of imaging or thinking about the mysteries of
faith of which all are capable) as compared to contemplation (described as a nondiscursive enjoyment of the presence of God that
is available only to a few select souls) is not normative throughout the entire tradition. Be that as it may, Francis provides his
readers with wonderfully colorful depictions of these ways of
prayer. He begins by observing that prayer is only one of the
two chief ways people show their love for God; the other way is
through service. He calls these ways affective and effective love.

MYSTICAL THEOLOGY — ANOTHER NAME FOR PRAYER

We express our love for God chiefly in two ways — spontaneously (affectively), and deliberately (effectively, or, as St. Bernard puts it, actively). In the first of these ways we grow fond
of God, of what he likes; in the second we serve God, do what
he enjoins. The first way unites us with God's goodness; the second urges us to carry out his will. The first way gives us our fill
of gratification, of benevolence, of spiritual yearnings, desires,

aspirations, fervor, leading us to commune heart to heart with God; the second way brings to birth in us the firm resolve, steadfast courage, and absolute obedience necessary for carrying out whatever God's will ordains, and also for suffering, accepting, approving, and welcoming all that he permits. In the first we find God pleasing; in the second he is pleased with us. By the first we become pregnant with virtue; through the second we give birth to it. In the first way we clasp God to our hearts in loving embrace; in the second we carry him in our arms by the practice of virtue.

We love God in the first of these ways principally by prayer. So many internal impulses are involved in this, it is impossible to put them all into words, not only because of their number, but also on account of their nature, their characteristics. Being spiritual, they are inevitably subtle, almost beyond the reach of the human mind. Often the cleverest, best-trained hounds are put off the scent by the cunning of stags, which double back on their tracks or use other wiles to escape the pack. Just as frequently we lose our way when it comes to our emotions; they twist and turn so deftly, so unexpectedly, we cannot keep track of them.

God alone, through his infinite knowledge, can know, fathom, and see through the ins and outs of the human mind. He reads our "thoughts from far away" (Ps. 138:3-5); he keeps track of all our twists and turns. Such wonderful wisdom is far beyond our reach; no thoughts of ours can attain it. Most assuredly, to turn the mind in upon itself by introspection, by reflection, would be to enter a maze out of which we should almost certainly never find our way. To think of what we are thinking, to reflect on our reflections, to be conscious of our spiritual insights, to know that we are knowing, to remember that we are remembering — all this would demand an attention we cannot give, would so entangle us that we should find it impossible to break free. That is why this is a difficult book, especially for one who is not deeply prayerful.

I am not taking the word "prayer" in this context merely in the sense of "petition" or "the request for some benefit that the faithful express in God's presence," as St. Basil describes it. I mean what St. Bonaventure meant when he said that prayer, widely speaking, embraces the whole of contemplative activity; what St. Gregory of Nyssa meant when he taught that "prayer is an interview or conversation between the soul and God"; also what St. [John] Chrysostom had in mind when he asserted that "prayer is talking to God"; and finally, what St. Augustine and St. [John] Damascene meant when they said that prayer is "an ascent, or uplifting of the mind toward God." If prayer is a talk or conversation between the soul and God, then in prayer we talk to God and God also speaks to us; we aspire to him and he inspires us; we are alive to him and he lives in us.

But what do we talk about in prayer? What is our topic of conversation? God, Theotimus, nothing else. After all, what does a lover talk about but his beloved? Prayer and mystical theology, therefore, are identical. Prayer is called theology, because it deals with God as speculative theology does; only there are three differences.... First of all, speculative theology deals with God as the supreme being — the divinity of the supreme goodness; mystical theology deals with him as supremely lovable — the supreme goodness of the divinity. Secondly, speculative theology is concerned with God and human beings, mystical theology with God alone. Thirdly, speculative theology leads to knowledge of God — turning its pupils into learned scholars and theologians; mystical theology leads to love of God — turning out intensely affectionate lovers (now a Philothea, now a Theophilus, according to sex).

Prayer is called mystical because of the hidden nature of the conversation: God and the individual speak heart to heart, and what passes between them can be shared with no one else. So personal is lovers' talk, it has no meaning outside the two who engage in it. "I lie asleep," said the mystic bride, "but oh, my heart is wakeful!" That is because "my true love's voice is calling me" (Song of Songs 5:2). Who would have guessed it? — a sleeping bride, yet all the while deep in conversation with her bridegroom. No need, however, in the realms of love for the spoken word, for appeal to the senses, when lovers share their thoughts. After all, prayer, or mystical theology, is simply a loving talk between the soul and God where the topic of conversation is the attraction of God's goodness and how to achieve union with him.

Prayer is manna, since those who feed on it never come to the end of love's delight, of charms beyond price; but it is hidden too, falling upon the mind's solitude — before knowledge ever dawns — where the soul is alone with its God. "Who is this," we could ask, "that makes her way up by the desert road, erect as a column of smoke, all myrrh and incense, and those sweet scents the perfumer knows?" (Song of Songs 3:6). For it was the desire for intimacy that prompted her to beg the bridegroom: "Come with me, my true love; for us the country ways, the cottage roof for shelter" (Song of Songs 7:11). That is why the loving soul is called a turtle-dove, a bird that seeks its haunts amid shade and solitude, where the female sings for her one mate alone — wooing him in life, or mourning his death. So in the Song of Songs the spiritual bride and the heavenly bridegroom betray their love for each other by a continual conversation. The occasional interjections of their friends are merely asides, in no way interruptions. That is why the saintly Mother Teresa of Jesus, taking her first steps in the spiritual life, used to find it more helpful to think of our Lord in those incidents of his earthly life where he was most a lone figure — in the Garden of Olives, for example, or waiting for the Samaritan woman. Since he was by himself, she used to imagine, he would promptly let her come close to him.

Love craves privacy; even when lovers have no secrets to keep, they still prefer to talk in private. For one thing, if I am not mistaken, they feel that intimacy is lost when their conversation can be overheard; for another, their love for each other invests even ordinary topics with a new meaning, a different atmosphere. Although the language of love consists of a vocabulary in common use, its intonation is so personal as to be intelligible to no one but the lovers themselves. A friend's name spoken in public has no special significance; murmured intimately, in private, it is charged with wonder. The greater the intimacy, the more delightful it sounds. What a language they speak, those ancient lovers of God — Ignatius, Cyprian, Chrysostom, Augustine, Hilary, Ephrem, Gregory, Bernard — so different from theologians whose love for God is not so great! We use the same words as they did: Coming from them, however, those words held warmth and charm; coming from us, they are cold and stilted.

Love is not limited to lips alone for its expression; eyes, facial movements, sighs also have a part to play; even silence and reserve can substitute for words. "True to my heart's promise, I have eyes only for thee; I long, Lord, for thy presence" (Ps. 26:8). "Keeping watch for the fulfillment of your promise, my eyes languish for comfort still delayed" (Ps. 118:82). "Listen, Lord, to my prayer, let my cry reach thy hearing, and my tears win answer" (Ps. 38:13). "Day and night, Sion, let thy tears stream down," cried out to Jerusalem the distressed hearts of its inhabitants; "never rest thou, never let that eye weary of its task" (Lam. 2:18). The silence of saddened lovers was vocal through tear-filled eyes. Obviously the chief activity of mystical theology is to talk to God and to listen to him as he speaks deep down in the heart. Since this dialogue consists of hidden aspirations and inspirations, we call it silent speech. Eyes speak to eyes, heart to heart, and none but those blessed lovers understands what passes between them.

THE SECOND WAY IN WHICH MEDITATION AND CONTEMPLATION DIFFER

Meditation is a reflection in great detail, point by point, on those things that are capable of touching our hearts; contemplation, however, takes a single concentrated look at what we love — concentrated reflection that has greater energy, greater power to move the will. There are two ways of admiring the beauty of a costly crown: Either you can look at each of its jewels and precious stones in succession, or, after noting all the different pieces, you can take in the whole brilliant work at a glance. The first way resembles meditation — when we reflect, for instance, on the expressions of God's mercy in order to quicken our love for him; but the second way is similar to contemplation — when we reflect, with one fixed gaze of the mind, on the diversity of those expressions, as though we were looking at a single object of beauty. In meditation we tell over to ourselves, as it were, each of God's several perfections that we see in any given mystery; but in contemplation we add them all together and view them as one.

The bride's companions in the Song of Songs asked her how they should recognize her sweetheart. She gave them their answer in a wonderful description of his perfect beauty, detail by detail:

> My beloved is all radiant and ruddy,
>   distinguished among ten thousand.
> His head is the finest gold, his locks wavy,
>   black as a raven.
> His eyes are like doves beside springs of water,
>   bathed in milk, fitly set.
> His cheeks are like beds of spices, yielding fragrance.
> His lips are lilies, distilling liquid myrrh.
> His arms are rounded gold, set with jewels.
> His body is ivory work, encrusted with sapphires.
> His legs are alabaster columns,
>   set upon bases of gold....
>   (Song of Songs 5:10–15)

So she goes on, meditating on the details of his superlative beauty, until at length she finishes by contemplating all his perfections at once: "Nothing of him but awakes desire. Such is my true love; such is my companion" (Song of Songs 5:16).

Meditation is like smelling first a carnation, then a rose, then rosemary, thyme, jasmine, orange-flower, each one separately; contemplation is equivalent to smelling the scented liquid distilled from all those flowers put together. Undoubtedly the combined scents in the liquid are sweeter, finer, than the separate scents of each flower. That is why the heavenly bridegroom sets such store by the fact that his true love looks at him "with one glance of an eye," that her hair was dressed so as to give the impression of "one ringlet straying on her neck" (Song of Songs 4:9). One glance simply implies a single concentrated gaze, without looking again and again; and curled hair indicates a single idea undivided by various reflections.

Blessed are those who reduce all their motives for loving God to one, who gather all the thoughts of their meditation into one conclusion, who engage their minds in the unity of contemplation.... When we have aroused a number of pious emotions through the numerous reflections that go to make up a meditation, we concentrate them until we produce a quintessence — an emotion that has greater rigor, more power, than all the other emotions from which it springs. In this single emotion are contained all the characteristics of each of the others; and we call it contemplation.

Discerning the Will of God

Books Eight and Nine, along with Books Six and Seven on prayer in its various manifestations (including mystical phenomena), form the nucleus of the *Treatise on the Love of God*. Book Eight bears the title "Love Compliant" (sometimes translated as "Love of Conformity"). Book Nine is referred to as "Love Submissive" (or "Love of Submission"). Together the books provide in extended discourse the Salesian answer to the question, "How do you know the will of God?" The books take us down a number of lengthy and intricate pathways of thought on the topic, so perhaps it might be best to summarize, in contemporary terms, the gist of de Sales' answer to the question that has occupied Christian thinkers from earliest times down to the present day.

Basically he taught that there are "two wills" of God or, rather, since God's own will in essence is unknowable from a human point of view, God's unified will is apprehended by persons in two distinct modes. The first he calls the signified will of God or, in the translation used here, the declared will of God. The second is referred to alternately as the will of God's good pleasure or as God's permissive will. What these refer to are, first, "God's will to be done," known through what God says, directs, and inspires. The individual, carefully discerning in his or her own heart and carried in the arms of the church community with its store of traditional wisdom, seeks to discover this signified will for his or her own life. The person makes choices based upon judgment sifted through the sources at one's disposal: Scripture, church teaching, devotional literature, private and corporate prayer, spiritual direction. Then he or she aligns with that "signified" will by observing and loving the indications received. This volitional response the bishop terms "compliant love."

Second is "God's will done," the events, facts, and existing realities of one's immediate situation. This permissive will of God is independent of human control. Where one finds oneself as well as where one feels one ought to be is revelatory of God's will. Especially difficult situations or events — both inner and outer — fall into this category. To follow the will of God in these instances is to exercise the "love of submission" by aligning oneself graciously to whatever is and trusting that God's gracious providence is ultimately at work. What "living between the two wills" means is that the totality of the will of God is not to be found either in individual discernment or in the factual, limiting situations that seem often to thwart that discernment. It is not that one is God's will and the other isn't, but that the human task is to live *between* those "two wills." To find the will of God is to maintain a creative tension that refuses to limit God to one expression or another. To follow God's will in this way is to live into the immensity and mystery of a God whose fullness cannot be contained in any one aspect of creation.

To grasp the subtlety and beauty of what seems to be the germ of de Sales' teaching can be a bit of a task when confronted by some of the texts of the *Treatise*. There are moments, in discussing God's permissive will especially, when he seems to be saying that the permissive will of God boils down to punishment for the individual sins of humankind. So if suffering is encountered, it is because someone has sinned and God is punishing him or her. However, the very title given to this expression of God's will, permissive, would belie that reading of the text. Being a seventeenth-century figure whose understanding of political, social, medical, and scientific theory was definitely not the same as ours, Francis would have seen poverty or hunger as part of God's providence, or as part of the human condition which is marred by the taint of original sin. Thus it is "God's will" that these conditions exist only to the extent that God allowed free human choice and, in the Fall, that choice was exercised and thus became part of what is encountered in the human condition from that time forward. But in reading the text one might get the impression that God punishes individual persons for specific sins by sending sorrow and misery their way. A more charitable and expansive reading of the text is required, for in our day the question of evil and suffering is differently posed. We tend to ask why bad things happen to good people. And we tend to assume that, with more sophisticated technology and more just economic and political structures in place, the evil and suffering that plague humanity would be reduced.

While it is well beyond the scope of this discussion fully to engage these issues in their contemporary form, I think the Salesian voice can be an edifying contribution to the general dialogue. What Francis is concerned with here is balancing human choice, creativity, and activity with the inevitable limits that constantly arise. We find ourselves between the immense reaches of our deepest dreams and hopes, which we rightly connect with God's own dreaming and hoping, and all that seems to negate, crush, or reverse them. What Francis seems to be saying is that God's gracious loving presence is *in all* of it, somehow accompanying us, somehow sustaining us. God is found in our well-laid plans and heroic undertakings as well as in disappointment, resistance, and seemingly random losses. The point of Books Eight and Nine is to explore the human response to both these wills. We must be willing to marshall all our faculties to respond energetically to God's signified will, and willing also to surrender graciously to the permissive will of God.

Love Compliant:
Union of the Will with God's Declared Will

Initially, de Sales wrestles with the nature of discernment, especially the various "inspirations" that feed into one's ultimate decision-making process as well as the freedom with which the process of conscientious discernment should be undertaken.

HOW TO COMPLY WITH GOD'S WILL DECLARED BY INSPIRATIONS; THEIR VARIOUS KINDS

The sun's rays give both light and warmth together. Inspiration is a ray of grace bringing light and warmth to our hearts: light to show us what is good; warmth to give us energy to go after it. All living things in this world are numbed by winter's cold; with the return of spring's warmth they come to life again. Animals move more swiftly, birds fly higher with livelier song, plants gaily bud and blossom. Without inspiration the life of the soul is sluggish, impotent, useless. Once the rays of God's inspirations strike it, however, we are aware of light and life . . . our minds are enlightened, our wills inflamed and quickened with strength to intend and fulfil whatever may lead to our salvation.

After God had formed Adam "from the clay of the ground," as Moses describes it, he "breathed into his nostrils the breath of life, and made of him a living person" (Gen. 2:7) — in other words, a soul that gave life, movement, and activity to Adam's body. The same eternal God breathes, infuses into our souls the inspirations of the spiritual life, so that (in the words of St. Paul) they become "living souls," in other words, souls that give life, movement, feeling, and activity to the operations of grace. He who gives us being, gives us power of functioning too. The human breath warms the things it enters. Witness the Shunammite woman's boy, on whom the prophet Elisha lay "mouth to mouth, till the boy's flesh grew warm" (2 Kings 4:34). As regards God's breath, however, it not merely warms, but enlightens to perfection. The Holy Spirit is infinite light; he is the living breath we call inspiration. Through his Spirit God breathes into us, inspires us with the desires or intentions of his heart.

The ways he has of inspiring us are past all counting. St. Anthony, St. Francis of Assisi, St. Anselm, and many others often received inspirations while looking at creatures. Preaching, however, is the usual way; but occasionally those who are not helped by hearing the word are taught by trials. As the prophet said: "The very alarm of it will make you understand the revelation at last" (Isa. 28:19) — in other words, those who fail to amend their lives after hearing God's threats to the wicked will be taught the truth by the effects of some untoward event; the experience of misfortune will gain them wisdom. St. Mary of Egypt was inspired by seeing a picture of our Lady; St. Anthony by hearing the gospel read at Mass; St. Augustine by listening to a life of St. Anthony; the Duke of Gandia [St. Francis Borgia] by the sight of an empress's corpse; St. Pachomius by noticing an act of charity; the saintly Ignatius of Loyola by reading the lives of the saints. St. Cyprian (not the bishop of Carthage, but a layman who was a glorious martyr) was touched at the sight of the devil admitting his impotence against those who trust in God.

A SHORT WAY OF KNOWING GOD'S WILL

God's will is made known to us, says St. Basil, by what he disposes, what he commands. This calls for no deliberation on our part; we simply carry out God's orders. In everything else, however, we are perfectly free to make our own choice of what seems good — though it is not a question of doing everything that is permissible, but only such things as are suitable. To discover exactly what is appropriate, St. Basil concludes, we are to take the advice of a prudent spiritual director.

However, I have a warning for you, Theotimus. Souls who long to come as near as possible to God's will in everything often meet with a troublesome temptation. No matter what they are about, the devil raises doubts as to whether God wants them to do one thing rather than another. Is it God's will, for instance, to dine with a friend or not; to wear black or grey; to fast on a Friday or a Saturday; to enjoy oneself or not? Much time is lost in this way. While they busy or worry themselves trying to discover which is better, they miss the opportunity of doing much that is good. Deeds give God far more glory than any amount of time wasted in trying to discriminate between good and better.

We are not given to weighing tiny coins, only large ones. Trade would be troublesome and eat up too much time if we had to weigh farthings and halfpennies. Neither are we to weigh every tiny action to see if it is better than another; in that way lies superstition. What good does it do to rack our brains over whether it is better to hear Mass in this church rather than that; whether to knit or sew; whether to give alms to a man or to a woman? To spend as much time reflecting on our duty as doing it is not the ideal way to serve a master. We must proportion our attention to the importance of the task at hand. To take as much trouble over making up our minds about going a short journey as about traveling a thousand miles or more would be conscientiousness run riot.

Choosing a vocation, planning something that is important, time-consuming, or costly, moving house, making friends — things of that kind deserve serious reflection to see where God's will chiefly lies. In tiny daily activities, however, where even a mistake is neither important nor irreparable, what need is there to make a fuss about them, or give them too much thought, or get in other people's way by seeking advice about them? What is the point of troubling myself to find out which God would prefer me to say — the rosary or the Little Office of our Lady? The difference between them is too slight for all that investigation. Should I visit the sick in the hospital or go to vespers? Should I listen to a sermon rather than visit a church where I could gain an indulgence?... There is nothing, normally, to show that one thing is so evidently superior to the other as to call for the making of great decisions. We are to go ahead simply and sincerely on such occasions, choosing what we think is good (as St. Basil says), without giving ourselves a headache, wasting our time, or laying ourselves open to the dangers of worry, scruples, or superstition — always on the understanding, of course, that there is no great disparity between one thing and another or no special considerations involved.

Even in spiritual matters we are to be very humble, and we are not to imagine that we can discover God's will by prying or by clever reasoning. First we must ask for light from the Holy Spirit, then concentrate on discovering God's permissive will, take the advice of our spiritual director and (if necessary) of two or three others, make up our minds, and come to a decision in God's name.

Afterward we are not to question our choice, but devotedly, calmly, steadfastly keep it up, carry it through. Although difficulties, temptations, and many different things may beset our path, to make us wonder if we have done right, we are to remain resolute and take no notice. Remember: Had we made another choice, we might probably have found things a hundred times worse — to say nothing of the fact that we are in the dark as to whether God wishes us to experience comfort or trials, peace or war. Once our decision has been made with God's help, we need never fear but that God will aid us to carry it through; as long as it does not depend on us, it cannot fail. To act in any other way is proof of excessive self-love, or of childishness, want of character, and sheer stupidity.

Love Submissive:
Union of the Human Will with God's Permissive Will

Francis treats in this ninth book of the unwanted and unbidden events that cross one's path in life and of how he sees them as part of God's gracious will. He extends his discussion beyond exterior events to include interior difficulties as well. Always he suggests a flexible, nonattached attitude willing to plumb the depths and diversity of experience to find there the traces of God's love.

UNION OF HUMAN WILL
WITH THE DIVINE PERMISSIVE WILL

Sin excepted, nothing happens but by God's will — by a positive or permissive will that no one can obstruct, which is known only by its results. These events, when they occur, show us that God has willed and planned them.

If we reflect here and now on everything that was, is, or ever will be, we shall be lost in wonderment, forced to echo the psalmist's cry: "Lord, I praise you for my wondrous fashioning, for all the wonders of your creation. Of my soul you have full knowledge... such wisdom as yours is far beyond my reach, no thought of mine can attain it" (Ps. 138:14, 6). From that we pass to gratification, to delight that God is infinite in wisdom, power, and goodness. The universe is but a tiny sample, a showcase, as it were, of these three divine attributes.

Think of human beings and angels, of the many-sidedness of natures, qualities, states, faculties, emotions, passions, graces, and privileges that supreme providence has bestowed on that countless host of heavenly intelligences and human beings in whom God's justice and his mercy find a wondrous scope.... We shall know a joyous awe, a loving fear, unable to restrain ourselves from bursting into song. "Of mercy and justice my song shall be; a psalm in your honor, Lord, from one that would guide his steps more perfectly" (Ps. 100:1). We are to experience extreme gratification as we watch God's mercy at work in the manifold graces bestowed upon angels and upon human beings, as we see his justice active in an unending variety of penalties and punishments. God's justice and mercy have equal claim upon our love, are an equal source of wonder; both are good, because both are God.

Since we find the working of God's justice sharp and distressing, he always tempers it with mercy — preserving a twig of olive under the flood of his wrath where the devoted soul, like Noah's dove, can find it at last... if such a soul is prepared for loving reflection, however, as is the way with murmuring doves. Thus death, distress, sickness, toil, which fill our lives, which God's justice lays down as the penalties of sin, are also — through his gentle mercy — ladders leading up to heaven, means of growing in grace, merits for gaining glory. Blessed are poverty, hunger, thirst, grief, sickness, death, persecution; punishments to fit the crime of our sins, they are also tempered with God's loving-kindness, with his clemency, until their bitterness becomes a joy.

TRIALS ARE THE CHIEF SOURCE OF UNION
BETWEEN THE HUMAN WILL AND GOD'S PERMISSIVE WILL

There is nothing attractive about trials in themselves; only when seen as coming from providence, enjoined by God's will, are they infinitely lovable. On the ground Moses' staff was a frightful serpent; in his hand it was a miraculous wand. Trials in themselves are dreadful; seen as part of God's will, they are attractive, delightful. Nothing is commoner than to experience reluctance at taking remedies prescribed and administered by a doctor; yet, were they to come from someone we love, we should take them gladly — love conquering disgust. Love either rids work of its disagreeableness or renders our experience of it pleasant; that is certain. They tell of a river in Boeotia where the fish seem to be golden; take them out of their native element, they are like any other fish. So it is with things that distress us: If we divorce them from God's will, they are naturally unpleasant; if we see them as part of God's eternal permissive will, they are perfectly golden, lovable, unspeakably precious.

UNION OF OUR WILLS WITH GOD'S PERMISSIVE WILL
IN THE DIFFICULTIES OF THE SPIRITUAL LIFE — BY DEFERENCE

Love of the cross leads us to go out of our way to meet unpleasant things — fasting, vigils, hair shirts, and other bodily mortifications; it makes us give up pleasures, honors, riches. God finds the love behind these practices most attractive. Still, such love is even more pleasing when we accept toil, trouble, trials patiently, calmly, gracefully, because God means them to befall us. Love is at its highest, however, when we go further than calmly, patiently accepting trials, that is, when we welcome them, love them, clasp them, because they come to us through God's positive or permissive will.

The highest, purest test of love is undoubtedly inward assent to the trials of the spiritual life. The saintly Angela of Foligno gives a wonderful description of the inner anguish she sometimes felt. Her soul suffered, she says, "like a man bound hand and foot hanging by the neck, half strangled, between life and death, all hope of rescue lost" — unable to put foot to ground, use his hands, cry for help, scarcely able to breathe or moan. That is how it is, Theotimus. There are times when our souls are harassed to such an extent by inward trials that all their powers and faculties are deadened through being deprived of all possible relief, through being aware and afraid of all possible discouragement. After our Savior's example, we begin to grow dismayed and distressed like a man in his last moments, until we can truthfully echo our Lord's cry: "My soul ready to die with sorrow" (Mark 14:33–34). Deep down inside ourselves we are led to wish, to plead "that if it were possible, this chalice might pass us by." The soul's very peak, its apex, alone remains riveted to God's love, to his permissive will, in simple submission: Eternal Father, "only as thy will, not as mine is" (Matt. 26:37–39).

What is important is that we make this act of deference to God's will in the face of so much difficulty, so many obstacles, so much reluctance, that we are scarcely aware of making it. At least it seems so cold and lifeless as to be made grudgingly, unbecomingly. Doing God's will, at times like these, not only lacks all pleasure, all contentment, but it goes against all our inclinations, all our self-satisfaction. Love lets the heart lament (where lament it must), lets it rehearse all the lamentations that fell from the lips of Job or Jeremiah—on condition, however, that the virtue of submission be practiced deep in the soul, at its apex, its noblest and highest part.

There is nothing loving or peaceful about such submission; genuine, steady, indomitable, and heartfelt though it is, it can be scarcely felt. It seems to withdraw to the very core of the soul, the center of the citadel, where it stands its ground, though all around is unrest, unhappiness. The more such circumstances deprive love of all encouragement, cut short all assistance to the soul's powers and faculties, the more credit it deserves for remaining so staunchly faithful.

Such union, such compliance with God's permissive will, is achieved either by the virtue of deference or by the more perfect virtue of disinterestedness. The practice of deference involves effort, submission. Life is preferable to death, for instance; but we defer to death because God permits it. We would rather live, if that met with God's approval; in fact we turn to him for length of life. We may be ready to die, but we have a much greater readiness to live; we may depart this world submissively enough, but we would be much happier to remain. Job, in his troubles, practiced deference: "What, should we accept the good fortune God sends us, and not the ill?" (Job 2:10). Note that he speaks of accepting, of enduring or putting up with something. "Nothing is here befallen but what was the Lord's will; blessed be the name of the Lord" (Job 1:21) — that is deference, that is acceptance speaking, patience under suffering.

UNION OF OUR WILLS WITH GOD'S PERMISSIVE WILL — BY DISINTERESTED LOVE

Deference means that we prefer God's will to all else, though we know a great attraction to many other things. Disinterestedness is a stage higher; it means that we are lovingly attracted to a thing only because we see God's will in it; nothing else interests the unencumbered heart when God's will makes itself felt.

Of course even the least committed heart can find itself in the grip of some emotion when it has no clear idea in which direction the will of God lies. Eliezer, for instance, when he reached Haran's fountain, looked at the virgin Rebecca; he was well aware that here "was a maid most beautiful, fair of face" (Gen. 24:16–22). He did not commit himself, however, until he knew from the sign he had asked God to give — that she was the destined bride of his master's son; only then did he present her with golden earrings and bracelets.

Jacob, on the contrary, if he had loved Rachel because she was Laban's daughter, would have loved Lia too; marriage to either would have fulfilled his father's wishes, would have united him with Laban's stock. However, he wanted something else, a wife to his own liking; won by Rachel's grace and beauty, he hated being married to Lia, but he was forced to accept what he could not undo.

The disinterested man is not at all like that. He recognizes the worst misfortune, ill-favored as Lia, to be the offspring of God's permissive will; for this reason he has the same love for it as for consolation, which he finds more pleasing. In fact he knows an even greater love for misfortune; the only attraction he finds there is the expression of God's will. If all I want is a drink of water, do I mind whether it is in a golden goblet or a plain glass? Does it really matter, then, how God's will is presented to me, since it is equally present in misfortune or consolation? I should probably prefer the plain glass, to see the water.... God's will is never clearer than when there is no distracting beauty about the way it comes.

Calvary is the Mount of Lovers

Frances de Sales closes his lengthy manuscript by returning to the theme of hearts that so dominated the book's earlier segments. In fact, the transformation of the human heart by the heart of the divine has been the underlying subject of the entire work. He returns too, although implicitly, to a theme repeated explicitly in the *Introduction to the Devout Life*, the cry of "Live Jesus!" Francis ends this exposition on the "birth, progress, decay, operations, properties, advantages, and excellence" of divine love by taking us to Mount Calvary where Jesus died, the mount of lovers, as he calls it. It is there that the heart of Jesus is discerned, that heart into which all human hearts must be formed in order for God's fullest love to be apprehended. For Jesus' heart is the mediator between divine and human hearts. Gentle and humble, yet radically God-directed, that heart as fully human was utterly responsive and compliant to its divine lover. So too must all other hearts be.

CALVARY—LOVE'S APPRENTICESHIP

And now, to end my book at last.... Our Lord's passion and death form the sweetest, strongest motive capable of quickening our hearts in this life. Samson found that bees had made a comb of honey in the lion he had slain; we shall find that the mystics achieved the perfection of charity in the wounds of "the Lion that comes from the tribe of Judah" (Rev. 5:5), who was slain, broken, and reviled on Mount Calvary. Like Samson too the children of the cross are proud of their wonderful riddle, for which the world can find no meaning: Out of death, eater of all things, comes the food of solace; out of death, strongest of all things, comes the honey of love. Your death claims my love, Jesus my Savior, for it gave your love supreme expression.

In heaven too, next to the vision of God's essential goodness, our Savior's death will be the most potent source of rapture for the saints. This was revealed in the transfiguration, a foretaste of heaven, when Moses and Elijah spoke with our Lord "of the death which he was to achieve at Jerusalem" (Luke 9:31)—the death by which the world's lover was robbed of life, to give it to those he loved. And I can imagine the incessant repetition of this paean in the eternal song of heaven:

> All for Jesus! In whose latest breath
> Love was stronger still than death.

Calvary is the mount of lovers. Love that does not spring from the Savior's passion is a perilous plaything. Heaven help the deathbed devoid of Christ's love; and heaven help that love which has no reference to Christ's death! In our Lord's passion love and death blend so inextricably that no heart can contain one without the other. No life without love on Calvary; no love without the Redeemer's death. Beyond that, only two ways lie open — eternal death or eternal love; and the essence of Christian wisdom lies in making the right choice. To help you there, Theotimus, I have written this book.

> One path alone our feet must tread
> While this life lasts, and God holds sway:
> Eternal love, or death — the choice;
> And God has left no middle way.

Eternal love — my soul demands it; my choice is made! Yes, come Holy Spirit, fill the hearts of your faithful and kindle in them the fire of your love. Love or death! Death *and* love! Death to all other loves, to live for love of Jesus, to escape eternal death. Living in your eternal love, Savior of our souls, let this be our song forever: "All for Jesus! I love Jesus! All for Jesus, my love! I love Jesus living and reigning forever and ever. Amen."

•

And so I bring this long treatise to a close in words that echo St. Augustine's, when, before an eminent congregation, he concluded a wonderful sermon on charity.... Charity inspired and penned these pages for you, dear Theotimus. May their contents find a lasting place in your heart, where charity can practice rather than praise my preaching. So be it. Blessed be God!

Epilogue

In 1610 Francis moved his belongings out of the episcopal apartments in the Maison Lambert into the townhouse belonging to his dear friend Antoine Favre. The latter had recently been named president of the Senate in Savoy and was quitting Annecy for Chambery. As he did so he insisted that Francis take over his spacious dwelling, reported to be the most beautiful in the city. The young bishop hesitated, unsure whether a priest dedicated to the service of the poor man Jesus should live in such elegant surroundings. There were, however, a number of good reasons why he might make such a move, so he decided in favor of the relocation; but he made one striking provision. For his own office and bedroom he chose a tiny garret apartment so that, to paraphrase his own words, after he had paraded around all day in those great salons and hallways like the most powerful men of the age, at night he could retire to his four walls and single bed reminding himself that he was just a man and a miserable one at that. If he could walk around as the bishop of Geneva by day, at night he could be merely Francis de Sales.

So for the rest of his episcopate until his death in 1622 at the age of fifty-five, Francis de Sales worked out of his garret apartment at the Hôtel Favre. He accomplished an enormous amount during his relatively short lifetime. Besides his writing projects, which were in fact secondary in occupying his attention, although he loved finding the spare moment to give to them, he was constantly occupied with the business of his diocese, spiritual direction, and the greater concerns of the church. He continued the evangelization among the Protestants that he had begun as coadjutor to the former bishop. He was actively involved in reforming monastic communities and pilgrimage sites within his jurisdiction. His preaching and pastoral duties consumed the better part of each day. A firm believer that a bishop should genuinely preside over his own flock, Francis also found time to travel with the courts of various royal houses, attending to the pastoral needs of princes, priests, religious, merchants, scholars, and commoners equally. He oversaw the flowering of the Visitation community, which in 1615 moved beyond the borders of Savoy into France, where it quickly became transformed into a formal contemplative order. By the time of his death there were over twenty houses of the Visitation in existence. In the midst of all this activity he managed to correspond with hundreds of persons. Over two thousand of his letters are still extant and attest to his attentiveness, sensitivity, and creativity as director and advisor of people in all walks of life.

When he died (on the road, in Lyon of an apoplectic stroke) on December 28, 1622, he had just given a conference to a group of Visitation sisters. Three days previously he had preached through the night at the three festive Christmas Masses at court. Only nineteen days before he had seen his friend and co-founder, Jane de Chantal, for the last time as they discussed for three hours the concerns of their growing community.

Besides the vivid memory of his presence that lingered long among his contemporaries, Francis de Sales left two major works, The *Introduction to the Devout Life* and the *Treatise on the Love of God*, as well as a host of smaller treatises and letters of correspondence. It is through these written works that his spirit is primarily available to Christians today. It is, in my view, well worth the trouble to seek out his writings, for he is one of those who has gone before us who has struggled to learn what it means to live the Christian life in its vitality and integrity. We might well learn from him.

Further Reading

English Translations of Francis de Sales' Own Works:

Francis de Sales, St. *Introduction to the Devout Life*. Translated by John K. Ryan. New York: Doubleday, 1982.

———. *Introduction to the Devout Life*. Translated and edited by Fr. Armind Nazareth, M.S.F.S., Fr. Antony Mookenthottam, M.S.F.S., Fr. Antony Kolencherry M.S.F.S.. Malleswaram, Bangalore, India: S.F.S. Publications, 1990.

———. *Treatise on the Love of God*. Translated and revised by Vincent Kerns, M.S.F.S. Westminster, Md.: Newman Press, 1962.

Francis de Sales and Jane de Chantal. *Letters of Spiritual Direction*. Classics of Western Spirituality. Translated by Peronne Marie Thibert, V.H.M. Selected and introduced by Wendy M. Wright and Joseph F. Power, O.S.F.S. Mahwah, N.J.: Paulist Press, 1988.

Library of St. Francis de Sales. Translated and edited by H. B. Mackey. London, 1873–1910. Vol. 1: *Letters to Persons in the World*; vol. 2: *Treatise on the Love of God*; vol. 3: *The Catholic Controversy*; vol. 4: *Letters to Persons in Religion*; vol. 5: *Spiritual Conferences*; vol. 6: *Mystical Explanation of the Canticle of Canticles* and *Depositions of Ste. Jeanne de Chantal*; vol. 7: *The Spirit of St. Francis de Sales*, by his friend Jean Pierre Camus, Bishop of Belley.

On the Preacher and Preaching: A Letter by Francis de Sales. Translated by John K. Ryan. Chicago: Henry Regnery Co., 1964.

St. Francis de Sales in His Letters. Edited by the Sisters of the Visitation, Harrow-on-the-Hill. St. Louis: B. Herder Book Co., 1933.

St. Francis de Sales. Selected Letters. Translated by Elisabeth Stopp. New York: Harper and Bros., 1960.

The Spiritual Conferences of St. Francis de Sales. Translated by Abbot Gasquet and the late Canon Mackey. Westminster, Md.: Newman Bookshop, 1943.

The Sermons of St. Francis de Sales. Translated by Nuns of the Visitation, edited by Lewis S. Fiorelli, O.S.F.S. Rockford, Ill.: TAN Books and Publishers, 1985– . Vol. 1: *On Prayer;* vol. 2: *On Our Lady;* vol. 3: *Lent;* vol. 4: *Advent and Christmas.*

St. Francis de Sales: A Testimony by St. Chantal. Translated by Elisabeth Stopp. Hyattsville, Md.: Institute of Salesian Studies, 1967.

Books about Francis de Sales in English:

Abruzzese, John A. *The Theology of Hearts in the Writings of St. Francis de Sales.* Rome: Pontifical University of St. Thomas Aquinas, 1985.

Bedoyere, Michael de la. *François de Sales.* New York: Harper, 1960.

Bremond, Henri. *A Literary History of Religious Thought in France from the Wars of Religion Down to Our Own Times.* 3 vols. New York: Macmillan Co., 1930.

Camus, Jean Pierre (Bishop of Belley). *The Spirit of St. François de Sales.* Translated by C. F. Kelley. New York: Harper and Bros., 1952.

Henry-Coüannier, Maurice. *Saint Francis de Sales and His Friends.* Translated by Veronica Morrow. Staten Island, N.Y.: Alba House, 1964.

Lajeunie, E. M. *Saint Francis de Sales: The Man, the Thinker, His Influence.* 2 vols. Bangalore, India: S.F.S. Publications, 1986, 1987.

Muller, Michael. *St. Francis de Sales.* New York: Sheed and Ward, 1937; reprint, Bangalore, India: S.F.S. Publications, 1984.

Ravier, André, S.J. *Francis de Sales, Sage and Saint.* San Francisco: Ignatius Press, 1980.

Wright, Wendy M. *Bond of Perfection: Jeanne de Chantal and François de Sales.* New York: Paulist Press, 1985.

Sunshine at the Comfort Food Café

Debbie Johnson is an award-winning author who lives and works in Liverpool, where she divides her time between writing, caring for a small tribe of children and animals, and not doing the housework. She writes romance, fantasy and crime, which is as confusing as it sounds!

Her best-selling books for HarperCollins include *The Birthday That Changed Everything*, *Summer at the Comfort Food Café*, *Christmas at the Comfort Food Café*, *Cold Feet at Christmas*, *Pippa's Cornish Dream* and *Never Kiss a Man in a Christmas Jumper*.

You can find her supernatural crime thriller, *Fear No Evil*, featuring Liverpool PI Jayne McCartney, on Amazon, published by Maze/Avon Books.

Debbie also writes urban fantasy, set in modern day Liverpool. *Dark Vision* and the follow-up *Dark Touch* are published by Del Rey UK, and earned her the title 'a Liverpudlian Charlaine Harris' from the *Guardian*.

🐦 @debbiemjohnson
📘 www.facebook.com/debbiejohnsonauthor
www.debbiejohnsonauthor.com

Also by Debbie Johnson

Cold Feet at Christmas
Pippa's Cornish Dream
Never Kiss a Man in a Christmas Jumper
The Birthday That Changed Everything
Summer at the Comfort Food Café
Christmas at the Comfort Food Café
The A-Z of Everything
Coming Home to the Comfort Food Café

Debbie
JOHNSON
Sunshine
at the
Comfort
Food Café

HarperCollins*Publishers*

HarperCollins*Publishers*
The News Building
1 London Bridge Street
London SE1 9GF

www.harpercollins.co.uk

This paperback edition 2018

First published in Great Britain in ebook format by
HarperCollins*Publishers* 2018

A catalogue record for this book is available from the British Library

ISBN: 9780008263737

This novel is entirely a work of fiction.
The names, characters and incidents portrayed in it are
the work of the author's imagination. Any resemblance to
actual persons, living or dead, events or localities is
entirely coincidental.

Set in Birka by Palimpsest Book Production Limited,
Falkirk, Stirlingshire

Printed and bound in the United States of America
by LSC Communications

For more information visit: www.harpercollins.co.uk/green

18 19 20 21 22 LSC 10 9 8 7 6 5 4 3 2 1

encouraged all of us to pursue – a life of freedom and discovery and fulfilment. They've just been missing from the events of the last two years. Missing at the time when everything changed.

I don't think I'd realised how much Angel's rejection had hurt me. Not just his rejection of me, but his rejection of Mum, the way she can sometimes be now, and his rejection of being part of our lives. It had been an awful day, only a couple of months post-diagnosis, after the brain scans and the interviews and the sympathetic meetings with neurologists. Just about classed as early-onset, it had started small, as I'm told it often does.

Car keys would go missing and turn up at the bottom of the bread bin. She'd come home from the shops with nothing apart from the list she left with, because she got confused in the supermarket aisles, blaming the store manager for rearranging things without consulting her first.

She'd forget my name, and point at me as though it was my fault for being deliberately mysterious. She tried calling her parents, and couldn't understand why the number now belonged to someone else, phoning the poor people back three times and eventually accusing them of locking her mum and dad in the cellar.

All of this was spread out over months, so random that it had probably been going on for a lot longer than that. My mother isn't the most conventional of people to start off with, and we have a generous approach to eccentricity in our home. I'd see her trying to find words, and piece

147

together information, looking confused and scared, until eventually she'd shake her head and say something like, 'I give up! I must be getting old, my memory's not what it used to be.'

I think the fact that she was so physically fit and active helped to shield it, and it was only when Cherie started to notice the difference that I accepted there might be a problem. Getting my mum to accept there might be a problem was an altogether different matter though, and I think she was still angry about it the day Angel came.

To start with, she'd been up all night, looking for a book she was reading –a book she'd finished ages ago, and had already taken to the charity shop. Then, on the morning he arrived, she decided that Bella was Pickle – one of her predecessors in the long line of Border Terriers who've owned us at various times.

All of this was building up and up, and when he finally arrived, she didn't recognise him. To be fair, neither did I – he'd shaved off all his blonde curls and the wispy beard he had the last time we'd seen him, and he was dressed like . . . well, like a biology teacher. Mum thought he was someone from the hospital – she was feeling quite irrationally resentful of anyone from the hospital at that stage – and sat in the corner of the room with her arms folded, glaring at him like he was about to whip out a straitjacket and pile her into the back of a white van.

He couldn't cope and left quickly, with promises to come back, and to send money. The money materialised – but the return visit never did. He emails me occasionally asking about her, but it's not quite the same. Angel was never the strongest of characters – he was squashed between Van and Auburn, who were both alpha dogs, and me, a scrappy little terrier. Despite not being the youngest, he still managed to be the runt of the litter.

He was a quiet kid with no real sense of self although, perhaps ironically, he might actually have had the strongest sense of self of all of us. He just needed to find a new self, with a new name, and a new lifestyle.

After that, I vowed I wouldn't reach out for help again. That I'd cope. That *we'd* cope. She's not your typical mother, Lynnie – she wasn't pining away for her babies, or hoping for grandchildren and a multi-generational trip to Center Parcs. She'd always wanted us to be independent, and that's what she got, except for me.

I was significantly younger than the others, and was at home on my own for longer. I was only twelve when Van left, and the other two followed within a couple of years. Maybe that's why I stayed – Mum and I became close after that. I liked Budbury, and loved being out in nature, and was content to stay at home. I tried college for a few weeks – some weird course involving creative writing, as it was the only thing I was ever any good with at school – but it didn't take. I missed the coast. I missed the open spaces. I missed my mum.

The sad thing is, I still miss my mum – sometimes even when she's in the same room as me.

Now, I have to decide whether to take the risk again – to reach out to Auburn and Van, and open us both up to change. Change that could be potentially heart-breaking or, I tell myself, absolutely brilliant. There's no use hiding away from the facts; things are only going to head in one direction.

I've seen some of the other people at the clinic, and I've read the leaflets. I know what might be down the road – more confusion, more memory loss, physical problems, trouble with eating and washing. Less lucid spells, more challenges. She'll become less and less her old self, and more her new self. It'll be my job to love her and look after her – but I have to be realistic about how much of that I can do on my own.

Admitting I need help doesn't come easily to me, especially when it comes to my siblings. My family role as the pup at the bottom of the heap has left me guarded and defensive. There are only so many times you can get the chair pulled out from beneath you at dinner, or have your diary stolen and read out loud on the school bus, or be goaded into bursting into a haunted room, before you decide enough is enough.

I loved them all, and I know they loved me – but we were never friends. Van used to make me feel safe and protected, until he decided it was more fun to make me feel freaked out and jittery. And Auburn . . . well, Auburn and I always had a confrontational vibe. When she left home I was thirteen, and I celebrated with a tea party in the bedroom that was now mine, all mine. I still get a childish thrill at not having to share my space after all these years.

They've all come home at various times, regaling us with stories of their travels and adventures and in Angel's case, teacher training college. Mum lapped it all up – well, the travels bit anyway. Van headed straight for the back-packing trail; Auburn started university but dropped out after a year and followed him on a similar path. They'd turn up now and then, filthy and hungry, their hair in tangles and feet coated in foreign soil, full of stories and plans.

Mum occasionally mentions them, but not in a 'where are my children, why have they forsaken me?' way – more as though they're on some kind of spirit quest, living in ashrams with ancient yogis, which makes her proud and content.

She once even gently suggested it might be about time I followed suit, and set off on a spirit quest of my own – which might have been more convincing if she hadn't been calling me Joanna at the time. I still have no idea who Joanna is, but I'm sure she totally rocks.

I'm still turning all of this over in my mind when Cherie bangs the doors to the café open with one bountiful hip, and ambles towards me bearing a tray of goodness. Her hair is up in a messy bun, and she's kicked off her Birkenstock sandals so she can feel the grass beneath her toes. The toes in question are painted bright turquoise. Old hippy chic.

She places the tray down on the table, and I automatic-ally hold it steady. The ground is sloping so much in parts of the garden that a strong breeze can whisk a cafétière down the side of the cliff in seconds. It might bop someone on the head as they sunbathe, which would prove once and for all that coffee can be bad for your health.

I inspect the contents of the tray approvingly: a long, tall mocha topped with whipped cream and grated Galaxy, and a slice of the raspberry and white chocolate cheesecake that Laura's had chilling in the big fridge ready for tomorrow.

Cherie lowers herself onto the bench, propping her feet up in front of her so she can catch the now-fading sun. She closes her eyes, and turns her face to the sky, sighing with satisfaction. I leave her to bliss out, and use my spoon to scoop up the cream and chocolate. Better eat it quick before one of the raucous seagulls wheeling and turning overhead decides to dive-bomb us.

'Gorgeous . . .' says Cherie, once she's absorbed a few minutes' worth of warmth. 'So – what's going on with you, Willow? And don't say "nothing", because I can tell something's wrong. Come on. Tell your Auntie Cherie all about it. You know you want to.'

I pause for a moment, licking the spoon clean, while I try and formulate a sentence that describes a very complex situation in very simple terms.

'I'm trying to decide whether to get back in touch with Van and Auburn,' I say, frowning. It actually sounds pretty simple when I say it out loud.

'I thought you didn't know where they were?' she replies, obviously confused.

'I didn't, but thanks to Tom, I now do. And now I know, I can't really carry on ignoring it . . . which I'd kind of been planning to do for a bit longer.'

'Ah. So as well as having to make that decision, you're also maybe a bit annoyed with Tom, even though you know you shouldn't be? Because he's forced you to think about something you were happier not thinking about?'

'Exactly! I knew I wasn't going mad! Tom was only being kind – I know that. And it's not like it was even difficult. Apparently he managed it with this amazing new thing called Google. And it's also not like he's invited them over to eat pizza and watch telly with me or anything – all he's done is find them, tell me where they are, and in Auburn's case, come up with a phone number. So I shouldn't be annoyed . . .'

'No, you shouldn't,' she says gently, smiling at me like she totally understands. 'But I see that you are, even though you hate yourself for it. Do you know what I think is going on?'

'Is there anything I could do, short of severing your vocal cords, that would stop you telling me?'

'Of course not. Even then I'd do it with sign language. Look . . . it's been you and your mum against the world for so long, Willow, that whenever someone gets too close, you feel a bit invaded. You're like that with us sometimes, without even noticing it.

'The difference is, we know you well enough to ignore you and do whatever it is that needs doing anyway. We

153

respect your independence, but try and support you by stealth. Now there's someone new on the scene – someone you sort of like, which even by itself is a bit worrying for you. You work so hard, love, and you're such a strong girl, but I know you're clinging on by your fingertips sometimes, and change can be scary when your grip on life feels so fragile.'

I am horrified at the fact that her words immediately bring the sting of tears behind my eyelids, and I screw them away. I don't even know why I'm crying. It's like I have the world's worst case of PMT, my emotions are all over the place.

'Ignore me,' I say, swiping at my face. 'I think I have something in my eye.'

'You do. They're called tears,' she says, reaching out to cover my hand with hers and gently squeezing my fingers.

'Tom doing this for you, sweetheart,' she continues, 'isn't going to suddenly erode all your superpowers and leave you as a puny human. It's not a sign that he sees you as weak.'

'Well, what is it a sign of, then?' I ask, mashing my cake up mercilessly. Die, cheesecake, die.

'It's a sign that he's a decent human being,' she replies. 'That he's a friend. That he cares what happens to you. That he wants to find a way to help you.'

'Oh . . . what a bastard.'

'I know – we should tar and feather him!' she says, laughing at me. I don't mind. It's a nice laugh, one that says 'you're a dick but I love you anyway', not one that says 'I am mocking you for the fool you so clearly are.'

'And as for Van and Auburn, well . . . life's too short for keeping loved ones at arm's length, my love. I should know. Me and my sister Brenda lost most of our adult lives to that sort of nonsense, and we only have Laura to thank for us being in touch now. It's been such a joy to me, getting to know her again, and all those nieces and nephews I never knew I had. If Laura had asked my permission first, I'd have said no – it felt too big, too scary. So I'm forever grateful that I had a friend who knew me well enough to do it anyway.'

'So you think I should call Auburn?' I ask, desperate by this stage for someone to simply tell me what to do.

'I can't make that decision for you, Willow. I barely know them – I have vague memories of them as wild teenagers, that's all. I wasn't as much a part of life here back then. But I will say that maybe you should go upstairs to my flat, take half an hour on your own, and think about it. There's a phone up there, you know. Maybe it'll come in handy. And if not, help yourself to the orange truffle flavoured Baileys . . .'

Chapter 13

Today is April 1st. My name is Willow Longville. I am twenty-six years old. I live in a village called Budbury, with my mum Lynnie. I work as a waitress at the Comfort Food Café, and I run my own cleaning business called Will-o'-the-Wash. I have a dog called Bella Swan, and I love my life. In the last twenty-four hours, the following things have happened . . .

1. I kicked over a whole bin full of dog poo.
2. I changed the scarecrow's name from Wurzel to Superwurzel.
3. I dreamed about Girls Aloud coming into the café and all of them ordering milkshakes.
4. I found my mum's bedroom completely covered in yellow Post-it notes – she seems to be taking a pre-emptive strike against forgetting the words for 'wardrobe' and 'knicker drawer'.
5. I held Little Edie while Becca nipped to the loo, and

I swear the baby looked right into my soul – she immediately giggled and sicked up some milk.

6. I decided to wear an entire dress made out of shiny silver material, because I was in a reflective mood.

7. I saw Cal and Zoe snogging in the bookshop, and felt happy for them and also sad for me – I haven't had a snog in a very long time.

8. I realised how lucky I am to have all these friends who help me by stealth – Katie, who refuses to let me pay her for spending time with my mum; Frank, who hasn't put the rent up on the cottage for donkey's years; Cherie, who pays me well over the odds for being a weird waitress; Laura, who always packs up food for me to warm up later; all the millions of little ways people's kindness makes my life better. I am lucky, and I am grateful.

9. I spoke to my sister Auburn for the first time in almost three years – she isn't living on an opium farm or anything; she's living in London, where she's qualified as a pharmacist. She has a real job in a Boots near Charing Cross, and says she'll come home to see Mum soon, and was actually quite nice to me.

10. I noticed what today's date is and am now wondering if it has all been a joke. I mean, how can Auburn have a real job? And why was she nice to me? Maybe she's been abducted by aliens?

Chapter 14

The next morning, I know I need to make amends. I didn't leave things badly with Tom – there was no exchange of cross words, no storming off, no slamming of van doors. But there was some silence, some obvious surprise, and a less than ecstatic response on my part. Things have been so natural between us since we first met that anything less than easy banter felt almost as bad as me slapping him across the face and calling him a ball-bag.

I didn't mean to hurt him, but I suspect I did, and he doesn't deserve that. He's uncertain of himself in social situations already, without me making it any worse.

I have decided to make amends via the gift of a Baby Groot – one of those things with wibbly-wobbly arms and a smiley face made of crochet and pipe cleaners, bouncing around in his own tiny plant pot. When I arrived at the day centre yesterday to collect my mum, they were in the middle of a craft activity, which she always loves.

She was always the kind of woman who was knitting or crocheting or creating, and we grew up doing the same.

Even Van is a dab hand with an embroidery needle, or at least he was until he decided it wasn't something Kurt Cobain would do and dumped it.

Mum was sitting at a table, showing some of the others how to make crocheted flowers to put in tiny plant pots. She's patient and kind and, when she's focused, really good at this stuff. Of course, that's not always the case – sometimes the connections don't quite click and she gets frustrated.

Yesterday, she seemed to be on form. In fact, she appeared to be holding the class, rather than taking it. Carole, bless her, often lets her do this kind of thing and it's one of the main reasons she enjoys going to the centre. We're lucky to have it, even if it seems to live under constant threat of closure due to budget cuts.

At first I wasn't sure how she'd take to it, as most of the other clients are much older than her, and many of them are in different stages of dementia conditions. But Carole's a smart cookie, and by letting my mum help out rather than be helped, she gets to feel useful and valued rather than dumped in a room full of strangers.

That day had clearly been a good day, and Mum seemed serene. I sat down with them all, and joined in. I fully appreciate the charms of crochet – you need to concentrate enough that your mind can't wander too far, but not so much that it becomes stressful. I decided against the flowers, and instead started to fashion little Groot, taking him home to finish him off that same night.

He's a beautiful creature, with shiny dark eyes and a zig-zaggy head and a big grin. The perfect peace offering for a man who speaks Klingon.

Mum is at home now with Jackie, one of the carers social services introduced us to, and Bella, who wasn't at all keen on Baby Groot. She was giving him that look she gets when she's thinking 'I'd like to tear you apart and see what's on the inside.'

Successfully rescued from a potentially lethal terrier experience, Groot is now with me at Briarwood, on a quick visit before my shift at the café starts.

I get out of the van, and see that a small parallel universe of building supplies has arrived. No workmen as yet, but it won't be long before the place is filled with clomping steel-toed boots, flasks of strong tea and the smell of sawdust.

The weather is weird today – really warm, but slightly unreal. As though Mother Nature is toying with us, and will unleash an insane rainstorm later on to keep us on our toes.

The trees are hanging lush and green as I make my way down the path at the side of the building, heavy boughs rich with blossom holding hands over my head to create a fragrant arch, the low-level humming of insects all around me. I can hear the joyful chirruping of finches and nuthatches, the slightly more sinister screech of jays, and even the distant drumming of a woodpecker. It's like a bird orchestra.

The path beneath my feet becomes softer as I walk deeper into the woods, cushioned by a springy layer of leaves and moss, my boots padding on natural carpet as I make my way down to the pond. It feels sticky and moist out here, as though I'm wading through the jungles of Brazil rather than ancient woodland in a quiet corner of England.

I emerge into the clearing, planning to skirt around the edge of the pond and head to Tom's camper van, where I will present him with Baby Groot, and all will be well with the galaxy.

Except Tom isn't in the camper van. Tom is in the pond. And yet again, he isn't wearing any clothes – at least not that I can see. Maybe he has old-fashioned Victorian bloomers on beneath the water level, I don't know.

I freeze, hidden behind the gnarled trunks of the oaks and the broad, swishing leaves of the clumps of fern. I remember my mum telling us a folk legend about the fern – that anyone carrying it could be rendered invisible. I consider swooping up a branch and hoping for the best.

I tell myself that I should just start whistling, or cough loudly, or start stomping around and snapping twigs, perhaps while singing Girls Aloud – anything to let him know that I'm there. That I'm not actually skulking around behind trees, holding a crocheted film character in a plant pot, stalking him.

I know that's what I should do – but somehow, my body

just doesn't want to cooperate. My feet feel rooted to the earth, and my breath is stuck midway down my chest.

The first time I saw him like this, dappled and shining in the sunlit water, my mind leapt immediately to Edward Cullen, my teenage crush. Now, Edward Cullen is nowhere – all I see is Tom.

Tom, my friend, who speaks Klingon. Who goes to the gym a lot, and looks damn fine on it. Who is bare-chested and bare-shouldered. Who has tiny droplets of water sprinkled across his skin, and pouring from the short, thick coat of his hair.

He's splashing and diving, swooshing his head in and out of the water, shaking himself like a wet dog every time he emerges. Rick Grimes is in there with him, paddling around and grinning as he snaps at enemy twigs. Rick Grimes also looks like a wet dog, but it's less troubling on him.

Tom is laughing, alive with the sheer joy of the day. He is doing what he set out to do – loosening up.

I don't know how he'd feel if he knew I was lurking in the background, watching. Creeped out, possibly. Maybe just embarrassed. I don't really know – but I do know how I feel.

I feel like kicking off my boots, stripping naked, and jumping in there with him. I feel like reaching out to touch all that bare skin, and stroking that wet head, and wrapping all my limbs around his body. In short, I feel like a woman who has just noticed her libido switch click firmly into the 'on' position.

I place a hand on one of the oak trees as though I'm earthing myself – not quite able to turn away, not quite able to move forward. The old me might have done the impulsive thing, and run straight in yelling 'Geronimo'. But the new me? She has a lot more to think about than her own needs. Even if Tom didn't recoil with horror – even if he felt the same – it couldn't possibly end well.

I know all of this, but I still can't quite make myself leave. I'm enjoying the view too much. And when the rain finally starts, lashing down in warm torrents, it gets even better.

Tom stands still in the water, and turns his face up to the sky. He closes his eyes, smiles at the world, and holds out his arms in welcome. He grins as rivulets run across his skin, around his jaw, fat drops splashing on his shoulders and chest. He lets out a whoop of sheer happiness, and Rick Grimes joins in with a deep, resonant woof that echoes around the clearing.

The rain might be contributing to the erotic mirage playing out in front of me – but it is also, at least, helping to shake me out of it. The downpour is one of those fast, sudden storms that pass as quickly as they start. Within what feels like seconds, I'm drenched, and I fear for Baby Groot's wellbeing. He is made of wool, after all.

I shove him into my pocket, and ever so quietly, start to retrace my steps. Running away is the best thing for both me and Tom, I know. I'm only flesh and blood, and I might have ravaged him if I'd stayed there any longer.

Now Tom can carry on swimming like nobody's watching, and I can retain my super-cool image. The one that's so subtle, only I can see it.

I walk stealthily back to the place where the footpaths meet at a small, green junction, and pause. I am quite literally at a crossroads, and wonder if the devil might leap out at any moment and offer to buy my soul for a handful of beans or the ability to play Flamenco guitar.

I glance back down the way I came. That way lies Tom, in all his man-bodied glory. I glance down the other path, which leads back around Briarwood and on to the camper van via a longer route. That way lies sanity.

In a move my teenaged self would never have believed, I choose sanity, and head away from the Pond of Much Temptation. I clomp through the woods, knocking branches and shrubs out of my way with an edge of anger – or more accurately, frustration. Everything feels very complicated, and a bit unfair, so I take it out on the green stuff.

By the time I reach the clearing where Tom has his van, the rain has passed – and I have cooled down. I've talked it all over with Groot and that has helped. He's a good listener, and I am almost at the point where I can laugh at myself.

This is becoming a bad habit, spying on Tom in the pond. The poor bloke would be mortified if he knew. He might get a restraining order out, and then where would we be?

I tell myself not to take it all so seriously, and Groot

agrees. I need to give myself a break. I'm a human being – I have needs. The fact that I've resigned myself to ignoring them doesn't mean they don't exist. And as chastity fails go, it wasn't that bad – I looked, but I didn't touch. I have the feeling that if I give in and let myself touch, something will snap and the carefully constructed house of cards that is my life will scatter around me in a flurry of jacks and hearts.

At the camper van, one of the chairs is set up outside, next to a small folding table. There's an empty coffee mug sitting there, next to a book called *The Martian*, which is now a bit soggy. He definitely must be loosening up if he's reached the stage where he's recklessly abandoning soiled crockery in public.

I place Baby Groot on the table next to the book, giving his head a little pat before I leave. I wonder, as I walk away, if Tom will assume that alien life forces have snuck in and invaded his tiny patch of paradise.

Chapter 15

It's Saturday night. And that means it's ballroom night.

The café is packed for the occasion, with all of the usual suspects along with a gaggle of Edie's nieces, nephews, and their children. Her fiancé is conspicuously absent, obviously, due to the fact that he is sadly deceased.

Laura's laid on a table full of sandwiches and cupcakes, and there are many open bottles of wine scattered around the room. It feels a bit like a party already, even though this is only actually a practice run.

Edie is presiding over events at a table with Becca, looking so excited I fear for her health. Little Edie is somehow managing to sleep her way through the chatter and bustle, snugly tucked up in her buggy, one podgy bare foot poking out from beneath a blanket decorated with baby ducks.

The teenagers are all here, set up on a Base Camp at the back of the room, tables covered in textbooks and highlighter pens and notepads. Lizzie has GCSEs coming up, and Josh and Martha have exams on the first year of their A-levels. Nate is winding them up with his carefree schedule, playing Pokémon on his DS instead. It's only a matter of time before someone punches him in his Pikachu.

My mum is sitting with Katie and Saul, colouring books and pens and craft materials in front of them. We've left Bella with Midegbo for the night, so they can keep each other company at Laura's house at the Rockery. Putting a young Labrador in a room full of novice ballroom dancers seemed like a foolish idea. He also has a bad track record of counter-surfing, so I don't think the cupcakes would have survived for long.

We also wanted Tom to be able to bring Rick Grimes with him – if nothing else, it will make him feel less over-whelmed, and give him a good excuse to go outside every now and then.

Right now, Tom is sitting with Matt, Frank, Sam and Cal, drinking the home-made cider that Scrumpy Joe has brought with him. I check in on him every now and then, but start to feel like I'm his mum, and back off. He'll be fine. We're back on normal terms, Baby Groot having worked his magic, and I need to let him get to know everyone without hovering like a helicopter parent.

Matt, our local vet and Laura's other half, isn't a million miles away from Tom's personality type anyway. He comes alive when he's around Laura and the kids, or anything with four legs, but other than that is definitely on the quiet side.

He fell completely in love with Rick the minute they walked into the room, and that was a good ice-breaker.

'What is he? German Shepherd and Rottweiler?' he asked, kneeling down and plunging his hands into Rick's ruffled neck mane.

'Probably,' replied Tom, one hand proudly on his dog's huge head. 'Maybe some Retriever or Chow, looking at that fur?'

'Could be. Laura tells me he's not keen on other dogs?'

'He is keen on other dogs – for dinner. It's . . . well, it's a real shame, he's such a gentle giant with people, but a bit of a psycho with other canines.'

Matt nodded and stood up, not quite making eye contact with Tom. That's a habit of Matt's – he gazes off into the distance slightly while he talks to you. He didn't need to bother with Tom, as he was doing exactly the same thing. In fact, it looked quite weird, the two of them chatting but busily looking in other directions.

'Is he a rescue?' asked Matt, staring at the bookcase.

'He is, though I've had him for over a year. He was a stray, and in the shelter for a long time – he was too ugly-looking for most people, and his size put them off, so he ended up as a long-term resident,' said Tom, watching the fridge.

'Right. Well, that might explain some of it – he's protecting you, and his role in your pack, and he doesn't want to let any other dogs near in case they threaten that. He might also have had bad experiences with other dogs in his previous life that have left him scared. Dogs often react aggressively when they're scared. There are a few things we can try, if you're interested? No miracle cures, but it might help.'

Matt is a dog whisperer of great renown, and I see Tom's face light up at the thought of being able to solve some of Rick's behavioural issues. He even looks right at Matt, and smiles. Matt is looking at the floor by that stage though, so it's wasted.

Almost against his will, Tom was scuttled off to sit with the Menfolk, and he's currently trying to look anything less than uncomfortable while the others discuss their excitement about our new ballroom teachers, who are due any minute.

All Cherie's told us is that she's arranged for two tutors to come for the next few weeks, to give us the basics we'll need to make Edie's party go with a swing. Edie can already dance – she's of that generation that learned from a young age – as can Frank. Sam and Becca mastered a rumba for their performance in our Christmas talent show, and I know my own mother is a salsa demon. The rest of us, as far as I know, are absolute beginners – so this could be very amusing indeed.

'I reckon,' says Cal, big and blonde and wearing his usual cowboy hat, his Australian accent pronounced after a couple of drinks, 'that we're in for a treat. I've watched that *Strictly* show – and those dancers are hotties.'

Surfer Sam raises his cider in salute of that concept, and nods.

'I'll drink to that!' he says, quickly glancing to check if

Becca's listening. She is, of course, and shoots him a mock scowl.

'I mean,' he adds, lamely, 'I'll drink to a celebration of the beauty of the human form . . . not to hotties. I have no interest at all in hotties. Apart from my gorgeous girl-friend, of course.'

She gives him a thumbs up, and goes back to chatting to Edie instead.

'And there are two of them! One is bound to be a leggy blonde!' Sam says, much more quietly now. He sounds way too excited for a grown man; more like a kid anticipating a new Xbox under the Christmas tree – he doesn't get out much these days.

I glance at Cherie, and see that she is looking highly amused. She, of course, has the advantage over all of us – she already knows who's coming, and what level of hotness they'll bring with them. Laura is shaking her head as the men continue to anticipate the sheer gorgeousness of our flimsily-dressed mega-babe dance teachers, and Zoe wanders over to me, bearing wine.

'I think', she whispers so they don't hear her, 'that they're overlooking something quite important.'

'What?' I ask, accepting the glass with a nod of thanks. 'That you ladies are going to kill them if they carry on?'

'No,' she replies, grinning. 'The fact that Cherie is highly unlikely to have booked two female dance teachers, when half of us are women. It's pretty simply logic, but as ever, logic seems to desert men as soon as they start thinking with their cha-cha-chas . . .'

Ah. She has a point, I think, looking across at their table. Even Frank looks a little giddy at the prospect, and he really should know better. Has age taught him nothing?

By the time the dancers actually arrive, anticipation is at a fever pitch. Wine has been consumed, cupcakes have been fondled, and a hundred theories about our mystery guests have been put forward. Cherie has refused to be drawn on the subject, but I can tell from her expression that it won't end up with two Ukrainian supermodels tangoing through the doors to the Comfort Food Café.

The reality, when it arrives, is definitely not one that the men had considered – and it leaves everyone in the room biting back laughter. Well, when I say everyone, I mean everyone with boobs – because Cherie has really outdone herself.

There are indeed two teachers – one male, and one female. The lady teacher is approximately five foot tall, and not much less across. She has one of those incredibly solid builds where it looks like she needs scaffolding instead of a bra, and is dressed in a pair of skin-tight jeggings and a cold-shoulder top that shows a lot of shoulder. She has dyed black hair frosted solid with spray, a ferocious expression, and is approximately 700 years old. She looks like the Yoda of ballroom dancing.

The male teacher, however . . . well, he's a little different. He's long and lean and Latin-looking, with slicked back hair and a widow's peak. He's in his twenties, dressed all in black, and comes across as a bit of a sexy Dracula. He's eyed up every woman in the room within seconds, and manages to give off the vibe that he'd cope with us all if he had to.

'Oh my!' squeaks Edie, gazing at him over the top of her specs. 'I'm looking forward to seeing his hip action!'

That breaks the silence, and everyone burst into laughter. Or at least the female half of the room does. The men . . . well, they look a bit scared. Their teacher is brandishing a cane, and she looks like she knows how to use it.

'Serves them right,' says Zoe, pointing at Cal and grinning. 'Sexist pigs!'

Cherie bustles to the front of the room, and introduces the teachers as Zelda and Mateo. Zelda nods and waves her cane at us all, and Mateo gives a low bow from the waist. Both of them are provided with drinks, and after a few minutes of small talk, the serious business begins.

Matt has rigged up the speakers, and Zelda has brought the music. She separates us into groups arranged in lines as she begins to demonstrate the basic steps of the waltz. She might be sturdy, but she's nimble, and soon we're all gazing at her with admiration as Mateo whips her around the room. My mum is smiling as she watches, and I can see her tapping the one-two-three rhythm on the table top as they go. She's so entranced she doesn't notice that Saul is busily drawing all over his face with red felt tip.

We all practise the steps in lines, before our teachers

demonstrate the correct hold positions. After that, basically all hell breaks loose. If someone had had the foresight to rig up a ceiling camera, it would have looked like a roomful of people all spontaneously being possessed by demons.

The next hour is spent bumping into tables, colliding with each other, tripping over our own feet, and in the case of the giants, occasionally getting whacked on the head by the mobiles hanging from the ceiling. Zelda raps various people's ankles with her cane, and Mateo spreads his charm around the room to make up for it.

Frank and Edie glide majestically at a pace that belies their combined age, but the rest of us have no dignity at all. It's absolutely hilarious, and I seem to spend a lot of time wiping tears of mirth from my eyes as we all unleash our inner Fred and Gingers. If Fred and Ginger had been drunk, and on acid. And getting electrocuted.

Katie is the surprise of the evening, turning out to be one of those women who had ballet lessons as a child and never lost her grace; Cal gives it a good go despite his rough-and-tumble Aussie exterior, and Laura and Matt spend so much time laughing they barely get any steps right at all.

We're all partnered up with various people as the lesson wears on, Zelda casting a stern assessing eye over our efforts, barely breaking a sweat while the rest of us huff and puff our way in and out of hold.

By the time I end up with Tom, we're both red-faced and tired. He's actually limping after a close encounter with

Cherie's rise and fall, and I'm glad I wore Docs for my box step with Joe.

'I feel like I've been in a combat zone . . .' he murmurs, as Zelda points at us with her Cane of Justice.

'I know,' I mumble back. 'And she's our sergeant major . . . come on then! Put your arms around me, I won't break!'

He accepts the challenge, and swoops me into his arms with a flourish, bending me backwards and then whirling me back up to my feet so suddenly I end up lolling against his chest. That'll teach me.

Once we've stopped laughing, we assume the correct position – his hand on my back, my hand on his shoulder, the other two clasped and raised – and begin to dance.

It's actually reached the stage of the night where at least some of the repetition has started to sink in, and we manage a pretty decent attempt. Maybe it's also because he's actually so much taller than me, but I even start to feel a bit girly – letting him lead me around the way I should, and the way I've found impossible all evening.

Zelda notes this, and nods approvingly as we swirl past, a slight smile creasing her foundation. She's not the only person who notices we're partnered up, and Laura gives me a sneaky thumbs up as we flit by her and Cal treading on each other's toes. Within seconds, the lighting has dimmed low enough to make this feel like the slow dance at the end of the school disco, and I know exactly who's responsible.

'Don't panic,' I say to Tom, as I feel him tense slightly.

'It's not a zombie invasion. It's just Laura, trying to make it more romantic – she's trying to pair us off. In Laura's universe, life only makes sense if there's a happy ending.'

'Ah,' he replies, surprising me by tugging me in even closer. 'I see. And would that be a disaster? A happy ending?'

'No,' I answer, forcing myself to relax into his body. 'But it would be a bit of a surprise . . .'

We're dancing to Aretha, belting out 'You Make Me Feel Like A Natural Woman', and I'm hoping that she'll stop very soon. I'm enjoying this way too much, and can't quite shake the image of Tom, bare-chested in the pond, laughing at the rain.

The combination of the music, the lighting, and, just possibly, this man holding me close against him is quite intoxicating. If I close my eyes, and trust him to guide me, his hand firm on my back, I can almost imagine I'm someone else. That I'm not in a crowded café; that I'm not a born-again virgin; that I'm not going to eventually have to leave his arms, and go back to reality.

That it would be perfectly okay to turn my face upwards. To meet his eyes. To let him kiss me. To ignore everything that's wrong, for just a few minutes, and concentrate on what's right.

The song comes to a close. We stop dancing. We stay in each other's arms. I look up, and wonder what might happen next.

'Hello Auburn!' shouts my mum, waving a crepe paper daffodil in the air.

Chapter 16

At first I assume she's talking to Zoe, but soon realise that the focus of the room has shifted slightly, an uncharacteristic silence hovering over the crowd as the music pauses between tracks. As Seal's 'Kiss From A Rose' kicks in, I twist around to see what everyone, including Tom, is staring at.

I turn, pulling free from his embrace, but notice that he keeps one hand on my shoulder, as though he's reassuring me. Standing by the doorway, a glass of wine already in her hand, is Auburn. My big sister. The girl who tormented me throughout my childhood, and who I haven't seen for years.

Nobody else knows who she is, of course – but they do know she's a stranger, and the café isn't the sort of place you pass by accident at night.

The lighting is still dim, but I can see the ways she's changed. She's tall and slim, like me, but that's where the similarity ends. Her hair, which she hated as a kid and kept chopped in a bob, is now long and gleaming, hanging in a straight, glossy curtain over her shoulders. Where Zoe is ginger – bright, fiery red – Auburn is definitely . . . well, auburn.

She's wearing skinny jeans and a leather jacket, and looks a bit like she might have come straight from a glamorous rock festival in the Alps. Her clunky biker-style boots add to the image, as does the backpack she has balanced at her feet.

I see her wave at Mum, and then she grins at me. I suddenly feel hot and bothered and tense, as though I've just been noticed by one of those velociraptors in *Jurassic Park*. This is obviously unfair and silly, but is a deeply ingrained response, honed by years of sibling rivalry, stolen hairbrushes, mutilated Justin Timberlake posters and catfights over territory.

I give Tom a quick smile to show I'm okay, and make my way towards her. I try and keep the smile on my face for her as well, but it's a little strained, I suspect. This is change. This is chaos. This is hard to handle, even if I know it's for the best.

'Hello, stranger!' she says, reaching out to give me a quick hug. I notice now I'm closer that she's still tanned despite living in London – it's like her travels in exotic locations have left a permanent mark. It suits her, I have to admit. She's not one of those pale gingers who burn at the first ray of sunlight, Auburn – she has the kind of skin tone that turns to chocolate, and big hazel eyes to match the concoction.

'Hello back,' I reply, wishing I didn't have to drive, so I could drink more wine as well. 'Do you want to go outside? I'm boiling to be honest . . .'

She shrugs, and I follow her through the doors. I'm perfectly aware of the fact that every eye in the room has followed us, and I turn to face them all as I reach the doorway. I raise my eyebrows and give them a stern look, and they all unfreeze, like someone's just pressed the play button in a game of musical statues. Cherie, at the far side of the room, blows me a kiss.

Outside, the air is blessedly cool compared to the oven of our makeshift ballroom. It's well after eight, and the sky is a clear, deep indigo, dotted with stars and washed with an almost-full moon. Even over the hum of the music from inside, I can still hear the waves murmuring in down at the bay, the gentle hiss of water sucking sand.

The garden is lit with fairy lights, and always looks mysterious at night-time, its winding path curving around the hillside, the wrought-iron archway glinting beneath the moon. In winter, we set up big patio heaters, so people can still sit outside with their hot chocolates. This was the place Frank and Cherie got married, and where Laura and Matt properly got together, and where Cherie first laid eyes on her sister Brenda again after decades apart. This little garden, perched on the side of a cliff, has a lot of history – and now I can add a little bit of my own to that.

Auburn has plonked herself down on one of the benches, feet stretched out in front of her, biker boots propped up and ankles crossed. She has a glass of wine in one hand, and a lit cigarette in the other.

'Are you sure you're a healthcare professional?' I ask, watching as she sips and puffs. She never used to smoke.

'What can I say?' she replies, shrugging unapologetically. 'I'm a pharmacist, not a saint. But . . . yeah. Bad habit. I keep meaning to quit, but every time I do, something stresses me out and I start again. How are you, anyway, sis?'

Good question, I think. How am I? I'm hot. I'm a bit worried. And I'm feeling strangely disconnected from my body. Like I could be floating above us looking down, rather than sitting here talking.

'And what's with the hair?' she continues, reaching out to flick a lock of neon pink with her fingers. 'When did that happen?'

'I just woke up one day and my hair had gone pink,' I reply, smoothing it back down. 'It was the weirdest thing.'

She snorts a small laugh at that one, and gazes back inside the café. Everyone is dancing again now, I'm glad to see.

'This place has changed,' she says, quietly. 'Grown. What was the name of the lady that bought it, all those years ago?'

'Cherie,' I reply, 'Cherie Moon. She's the one who looks like a plus-size Pocahontas. She married Farmer Frank.'

'Oh! Right. The guy who owns the cottage . . . wasn't he already married?'

'He was. She died a few years ago. You might have been away, but life goes on.'

She nods, and drops the cigarette butt to the floor, grinding it out with her boot heel. I'm glad to see her pick it up, and slip it into her pocket.

'Who was that guy you were smooching?' she asks, teeth shining in the moonlight as she grins at me. She looks ever so slightly predatory, like a fox that's been turned into a human. 'Is he your *boyfriend*?'

She manages to give the B-word exactly the same inflection she used when we were kids, and she was winding me up about some boy in my class. These little exchanges often ended in her holding my head while I tried to punch her, my shorter arms windmilling as she kept me just far enough away for it to be funny. Every now and then, though, I'd get one in. Call me Slugger.

'No, he's not my *boyfriend*,' I reply, giving it the same intonation. 'He's just a boy who's a friend.'

'Okay. He's hot, though, in case you hadn't noticed – though I'm not sure about that *Firefly* T-shirt . . . who was the blonde guy? Good-looking, tall?'

'Good-looking, blonde and wearing a cowboy hat?'

'Yeah – that's the one.'

'That's Cal. He's taken.'

'Oh. What about the other good-looking blonde one, surfer dude?'

'That's Sam. He's taken.'

She chews her lip, and looks thoughtful.

'All right. Brawny one, a bit on the Harrison Ford side of the spectrum?'

'Matt. Very much taken . . . look, what's this all about? Have you come here to film a reality dating show or to see your mother?'

She doesn't seem to hear me, and instead is staring through the steamed-up café windows again.

'Well, if Firefly's not your boyfriend, maybe I'll have a crack at him . . .'

I slam my hand down on the table to get her attention, and her head whirls round to face me.

'Auburn, you've been home for fifteen minutes, and I already want to kill you.'

She puffs out a breath and tucks a stray lock of silky hair behind her ear, before she gives me a sheepish grin.

'The joys of family life, eh? I'm sorry, Will. I'm . . . well, I think I'm nervous, to be honest.'

This is something of a revelation to me. I have never – as far as I've known – ever seen Auburn anything less than full-on, confrontational, and oozing confidence.

'You? Nervous?' I say, incredulously. 'You're Auburn Longville. Toughest girl in the west. You're never nervous!'

'Well I am now, okay? So give me a break.'

She grabs another cigarette from the pack on the table, and lights it with hands that do, in fact, seem to be trembling. Huh. She *is* nervous. It must bring out her lecherous side.

'Where've you been then?' I ask, gently. I'm nervous too,

and I don't want our mutual nerves to engage in some kind of stand-off and escalate until they're weapons of mass destruction. 'And why didn't you tell us you were back?'

She taps her fingertips on the cigarette pack, drumming them against the photo of a man with a diseased lung, which doesn't seem to be putting her off at all.

'Well, I was in Peru for a while, wasn't I?'

'On the cannabis farm?'

She grins, and blows out a cloud of smoke, tilting her head to try and avoid hitting me in the face with it. Obviously, the breeze automatically adjusts and gusts it towards me anyway.

'Sorry, first rule of smoking,' she says, making wafting gestures with her hands. 'Wherever the non-smoker sits, the wind will blow. Anyway. It wasn't actually a cannabis farm – I'd forgotten I said that! Bizarrely, I think I was just trying to impress Mum. I know most mums would be horrified, but ours always likes a bit of spice, doesn't she? And Van was doing his Tibet thing, and I always felt so competitive around him . . .'

Around everyone, I add silently.

'So. It wasn't a cannabis farm. It was a kind of ranch that ran tours for backpackers. And after that, I moved around South America, and then spent some time in South East Asia before heading back to Europe. Bit of a stay in Barcelona, and then . . . well. Long story. Let's just say I decided it was time to grow up a bit, so I signed up for the pharmacy course. I'd got some credits from the first year of my degree, and my A-levels were good, so I managed it in two years.'

I nod, and think that over. She's been in the UK for over two years, and we've not heard a word from her. Two very tough years back here at home.

'And why didn't you tell us you were here? We assumed you were still running drugs in Columbia.'

'I never ran drugs in Columbia – though to be entirely fair, I did *do* some drugs in Columbia. Oh look, I don't know, okay? We've never exactly been the kind of family that lived in each other's pockets, have we? And, cards on the table? I thought Mum might be disappointed in me.'

'Disappointed? You thought she'd be disappointed in your training to be a pharmacist?'

'I know! It's messed up! And I'm sure she wouldn't have been – but it all felt a bit boring. You know how upset she got about Angel.'

'That wasn't because of his job,' I reply, frowning at her. 'She was happy he'd found something he was passionate about. It was because he changed his name – that felt like a rejection to her.'

Auburn nods, and drops the cigarette, and chews her lips viciously. She really does seem quite strung out.

'Yeah. I know. I was also . . . well, I wasn't sure if I'd stick it out. I don't have the best track record with that sort of thing – sticking it out. I've always moved around, kept mobile. I wasn't a hundred percent convinced I'd be able to hack staying in the city for long enough – there was always a part of me that thought I might jack it all in and book a midnight train to Georgia. It was something I just needed to do alone. Anyway – enough about me. How's Mum? I was relieved she even recognised me, I didn't expect that from what you said on the phone.'

'Don't flatter yourself,' I snap back reflexively. 'She calls everyone with red hair Auburn.'

As soon as the words are out, I regret them. By my sister's standards, she's being super-conciliatory here, and me sniping at her won't help either of us.

'I'm sorry,' I add straight away, reaching out to touch her hand. It's still shaking. 'That was mean. But . . . also true. She's always convinced that Zoe, who runs the book-shop over there, is you. I'm often someone called Joanna. She thinks her parents are alive and well and being kept in a cellar, and she still runs yoga classes at the Community Centre. She sometimes tries to get to the café at night, and I've even found her halfway up the road to Briarwood.'

'That old house on the hill? That's still there?'

'Very much so. In fact, Tom, the boy who's a friend – the one you may definitely not have a crack at, by the way – has bought it. Turns out, he's . . . well. Another long story. I'm not even sure how much time we have – are you staying for a bit?'

She nods, and tucks the lighter back inside the pack with the cigarettes. She starts glugging her wine instead, and I realise she simply can't sit still without fiddling with something.

'I took two weeks' leave for family reasons. God, I'm sorry it's like this, Will – I know this can't have been easy for you. I would have come, really, if I'd known. And Van would, too. Angel . . . well, maybe he'll have a change of heart.'

I remember the look on his face as he all but ran towards his car, and suspect he won't. No use worrying about that now – not when I have a real-life sibling sitting right here in front of me, peeling away the skin around her fingernails.

'What's Van up to, anyway? I thought he was in Tibet, but Tom says he's in Tanzania.'

'Yep. He's running a school there. He's hard to get hold of, but I managed to get an email to the charity he works for, explaining what was going on and asking him to contact us. He moved a few years ago – we met up for a weekend in Phuket. Didn't you get the postcard? We sent you one, honest. Even tried Skype, but we couldn't find you.'

'Um . . . no. No postcard. No phone calls. We've not heard anything from him for ages. Mum occasionally talks about him, her proud spirit warrior – but no contact. With either of you. For. Ages.'

I sound resentful, and hate myself for it. But her being here – it's a bit like it's popped some kind of bubble I've been using to keep myself content. A bubble full of bitch-iness and pain, all of which now wants to spill out.

Reacting in the way I traditionally associate with my sister, she picks up her cigarette packet, and lobs it at my head.

'We didn't know, all right?' she says. 'I realise you've been coping on your own, and that sucks – but don't blame me for not being here when you never even took the time to tell me about it. I might not have been in touch, but I wasn't hiding – Tom found me easily enough. I get that you're angry, and probably exhausted, and you're entitled to that, but give me a break. I only found out about Mum a few days ago, and I came as soon as I could. So put your big girl pants on and let's figure out how I can help!'

I rub the side of my head, saying 'ouch' and pretending it's hurting a lot more than it is. In reality, it's not my head that's hurting, it's my sense of fair play. She has a point, after all. I told her, and she came. Time to stop bleating, and pull up those big girl pants.

'Okay. Fine. Where are you staying?' I say, throwing the cigarettes back at her. She easily catches them, and shoves them back into her bag.

'Well, I thought I'd stay in my childhood home, with my mother and sister and dog, if that's all right with you?'

'I suppose so,' I say grudgingly, standing up to go back inside. 'But if you think you're getting your bloody room back, you're deluded.'

Chapter 17

By the time we get home, everyone is tired, and in Auburn's case possibly a bit tipsy.

Mum has accepted her presence here as completely normal, which is both lovely and a little confounding. A petty part of me feels like my nose has been put out of joint: I'm the one who stayed, but Auburn gets to waltz back in here and resume business as usual.

I give myself a telling off for that, because it's not a noble thought. The most important thing is that Mum seems happy. She's had an enjoyable night out in company. She played with Saul, and created a whole florist's shop of crepe paper flowers, which she drapes around the cottage like exotic decorations.

She kisses us both, sings us a song about the sandman, and takes herself off to visit him.

Auburn automatically heads for what she clearly thinks of as still her room – but I notice her do a quick course-correct and push open the door to the boys' room instead. I still think of it as that – the Boys' Room – even though the boys in question haven't set foot in there for a while.

We were planning on redecorating it, but Mum's diagnosis overtook us, and it remains much as it was back in the day. There are still two single beds, still two blue duvet covers, still a thick line in yellow duct tape down the middle of the room where Van and Angel demarcated their turf. Van's side is draped with tatty-edged posters of grunge bands from Seattle, and Angel's with his Cameron Diaz shrine. I'm not sure it's possible that it still smells of sweaty socks and puberty, but somehow it seems to.

I walk into the kitchen, and make each of us a mug of tea. Auburn follows me through, boots off, revealing feet clad in Little Miss Naughty socks.

'I swear it still pongs in that room . . .' she says, wrinkling her nose. A-ha. It's not just me.

She wanders around the cottage, holding her tea, investigating. I realise this must be very odd for her as well – being back here after so long. I don't think much has changed – there's just a lot less clutter. She stares at the framed family photos on the walls, smiles at Mum's paper flower arrangements, and inspects our DVD collection.

'This is weird.Since when did you guys become such big fans of Hannah Montana?'

I shrug, and sip my tea.

'She finds them relaxing,' I say, glancing at our stacks of boxed sets. 'What did you expect? That we sat at home watching *Still Alice* on repeat every night?'

'I don't know what I expected, Willow, and it wasn't a criticism, okay? This isn't going to work if you're so bloody defensive all the time. I'm going outside to blacken my lungs. Come if you like.'

It's hard to storm off when you're wearing Little Miss socks, but she does her best. I follow her through into the garden, and sit next to her on the bench.

That almost-full moon is hanging low and yellow, casting an eerie glow over the vegetable patch and Frank's fields beyond. Superwurzel is looking fine though, and I know he'll keep us safe.

'Sorry,' I say eventually, as she smokes. 'You're right. I am defensive. But old habits die hard, and I'm used to needing to defend myself. It's not like we had a dream relationship as kids, is it?'

'No,' she replies, tapping ash into the saucer she's brought out with her. 'I was a grade A bitch. But we're not kids any more, are we? So maybe I can try being less of a bitch, and you can try not to snap into combat mode every time I open my mouth. How does that sound? And why *have* you got pink hair now? It looks weird as shit in the moonlight, and I'm actually a bit scared of you right now.'

I pull a horror-movie face, and let out a villainous cackle. A small one, though, because I don't want to risk waking Mum up.

Auburn's still waiting for an answer on the hair front, and I suppose it's as good a time as any to start being the caring, sharing sister I ought to be. It's a harmless enough story, but for some reason I've never told anybody.

The day I walked into the café with neon pink hair, Cherie simply looked at me, nodded, and said: 'Suits you, love – get some nice new lipstick to match.' I suppose between the nose ring and the boots and my generally random wardrobe choices, people weren't at all surprised when I changed my hair from its usual light brown. For sure, nobody asked me why.

'It's for Mum,' I tell Auburn, as I watch the glowing red tip of her cigarette move around in the darkness. 'So she knows who I am.'

'What do you mean? Explain further,' she instructs. 'And in simple words, as it's possible that I'm slightly drunk.'

I think she might be – she definitely drank enough wine in the café, once we'd rejoined the curious hordes – but she hides it well. I wonder how much practice she's had at that, and it makes me sad for her.

'Okay – well, I'm guessing you know something about Alzheimer's from your training and your work?'

She nods.

'Then you know it's very unpredictable. Some people struggle with physical coordination. Some have problems with speech. Pretty much everyone has issues with memory – sometimes just words, or actions, or finding their way around. With Mum, she tends to remember things from the past really vividly – but her timeframes get messed up. She'll remember me as a little girl, but sometimes not know who I am as an adult. That's not nice for me, but it can be terrifying for her – sharing her life with a person who can be a stranger to her.

'So we've tried various techniques. Her nurse and psychologist have been really good, and suggested things to use. She has a notepad, and fills it with pictures and keepsakes and her life story. And in the notepad, she also fills in important stuff – addresses, phone numbers, that kind of thing.

'One of the ways she seems to locate people in her brain is by association. Like, she sees a small child with curly blonde hair, and she thinks it's Angel. Or people with red hair, she thinks they're you. So I thought perhaps I'd try and use that to our advantage, by giving myself hair that nobody else has. In the front of all her notepads, she always writes 'Willow is my daughter. Willow is the girl with the pink hair'. So when she looks at me, eventually, she'll figure it out.'

Auburn is silent for a while, as she thinks it through.

'Does it work?' she asks, eventually.

'Not all the time, no. If she doesn't look in her notepad, for instance. Or if she thinks I'm Joanna. But a lot of the time, yeah, it does. She knows I'm the one with the pink hair. It makes me different from everyone else, and that helps. I did make a bit of an error a while back, where I gave Cherie and Laura some pink tips, but luckily that didn't result in her thinking a woman in her seventies was her daughter – that would have been confusing for us all.'

Auburn sips her tea, and stubs out her cigarette, and nudges me with her shoulder.

'That,' she says, firmly, 'is pure genius. And anyway – it really suits you. I think you should always have pink hair. Now, sis, I'm going to bed. I'll probably dream of Cameron Diaz singing "Smells Like Teen Spirit", so wake me up if I start screaming . . .'

Chapter 18

I am sitting in a pub. Drinking a pint of lager. With my friends.

This might not seem overly exciting, but for me, it's something of a revelation. I mean, I get out every now and then, but usually I have Mum with me, or I'm dashing around watching the clock.

Tonight, I am not watching the clock. Well, I am – but only so I can keep track of when it might be last orders, so I don't miss my chance for another pint. I seem to have turned into an alcoholic after two hours of freedom.

This newfound freedom is one of the very nice side effects of my new circumstances. Auburn has been here for four days now, and we've started to settle into each other's company. When I say settle, I mean we've reduced the bickering, and been at least partially united in our common goal – Mum.

It's not been easy for my big sister, and I'll say this for her – she's grown up a heck of a lot in the last few years. Way more than anyone should. I'm guessing some stuff

Debbie Johnson

has happened to her, some stuff she doesn't want to talk
about, and that's fine by me. For the time being, we're
focusing on Lynnie, and life as it evolves. Maybe there'll
be time to catch up properly at some point but for now,
it's one day at a time, sweet Jesus.

She's been introduced to Carole and the team at the day
centre, and even agreed to join in with their frantic fund-
raising activities; she's met Jackie, the carer we sometimes
use, and she's talked to Katie in some foreign health-speak
language I suspect they were making up to prove that
nurses and pharmacists are special snowflakes.

Mum, as usual, has had her up days and her down days.
There was an almighty battle of wills over her medication,
which she declared was poison – she even drew a skull
and crossbones on the pill box.

That one was eventually only won when Auburn
persuaded her they were homeopathic, putting them in a
new pill box and spritzing it with lavender oil. I felt bad
about that – about lying to her, about manipulating her,
about treating her like a child having a tantrum. She's my
mum and it doesn't feel respectful, but she needs to take
the tablets. Auburn knows more about what they do than
me, and she's insistent they will be helping.

Mum also lost her notepad briefly, which sent her into
a downward spiral for hours while we turned the house
upside down searching for it. She was convinced 'that boy
from the caravan' had broken in and stolen it. We have no
idea who the boy from the caravan is but to her, he's very

real, and obviously based on either a genuine memory or a jumble of snippets of memories. We found the notepad under her yoga mat, where she'd hidden it the day before.

On the plus side, today had been a very good day. She spoke to us both completely lucidly at breakfast, asking about our plans for the day and laughing at our surprised expressions when she voluntarily walked up to her pill box, chose the right day, and took the right tablets. I did feel a twinge of guilt when she sniffed it appreciatively though.

'Don't worry, girls,' she said, scribbling away on her pad of Post-it notes. 'I'm feeling groovy today. Living the sweet life – like Zack and Cody. That's spelled S-U-I-T-E, you know, because they live in a hotel and get up to all kinds of shenanigans! Anyway – here's my little reminders all sorted.'

With that, she leaned over the table, and slapped a Post-it note each on both our foreheads. I stared at Auburn, and she stared at me, and for a moment it felt like one of those weird party games where you have to ask each other questions to figure out what's written on your face.

'Am I male or female?' asked Auburn, obviously thinking the same thing as me.

'Yours says "Daughter Number One – Auburn". What does mine say?'

She screwed up her eyes, as though trying to decipher the writing, and replied: 'Yours says "Daughter Number Two – Willow – the Inferior One".'

'It doesn't say that, does it?' I asked, flicking a spoonful of muesli at her face and watching it splatter on her nose.

The day continued in a similar vein – quite a lot of fun, in other words. Auburn and Mum came with me to the café, but then went off to spend the day together, strolling the cliff pathways and doing some shopping and even going on one of Sam's nature walks down on the beach.

By the time I got home, they were both crashed out on the sofa, bare-footed, in various stages of snooze with an episode of *Shameless* playing on the TV. Definitely not Disney. Must be the Auburn effect.

I crept around in the kitchen unpacking the leftovers that Laura sent me home with, making myself some tea and clearing up. Having Auburn here was strange – good in many ways, unnerving in others. It had also massively increased the amount of tidying up I have to do, as the woman seems incapable of putting milk back in the fridge or washing a mug.

I try not to focus on such trivialities, because life is way too short to argue over housework, and because, I tell myself, she'll be gone again soon, back to London, and her real life. This is just a visit, so there's no point getting upset about what's wrong – or relying too much on what's right.

I was drinking my tea, and reading a message from Tom on my phone when Auburn walked into the room, stretching her arms over her head and yawning loudly. Her shiny hair was tied up in a pony tail, and I reached out to swish it from side to side.

'Your pony tail actually looks like it belongs on a pony,' I said, closing my screen down. 'A nice shiny chestnut. One of those ponies that shits a lot and bites people's hands when they offer them apples.'

'Yep, that's me,' she answered, baring her teeth and whinnying. 'Who was on the phone?'

'Nobody was on the phone. Somebody was on the text.'

'Oooh. I bet it was Tom. If it was anybody else, you'd have said who. You'd have been, like "oh, it was Laura", or "oh, it was Cherie", or "oh, it was Brad Pitt". You always go a bit moony-eyed and mysterious when it's *Tom*.'

I glared at her, and started wiping down the surfaces, giving some real consideration to slapping her across the smug chops with the soggy cloth. Mainly because she was right.

'What did he want?' she persisted, actually putting the milk away in the fridge. Probably just to annoy me.

'He wanted to know if I was going to the pub tonight. Some of the others are and they invited him, but he probably won't go if I don't.'

'Is he shy?'

'Yeah, he is, actually. Do you have a problem with that?'

'No,' she'd replied, picking my phone up from the counter and running away with it. 'But I do have a problem with you moping around the kitchen cleaning when you could be getting hammered with sexy geek boy . . .'

I chased her through the kitchen, into the hallway, and out through the back door, Bella following us, tail wagging as she sensed a game afoot. We played a small instalment of dodge-the-scarecrow, and I almost caught her when she tripped over a potted lavender bush by the patio, but she was too nimble for me to get her in time. It was always the same when we were kids.

After dashing around the garden shrieking and laughing, she finally came to a standstill, hands on hips, out of puff. She passed the phone back and said: 'Wow. I'm knackered after that. I really need to pack in the ciggies. There – all sorted. You'll meet them all there at eight. I'll stay in with Mum. You're welcome!'

I snatched the phone back, and quickly flicked through to my messages. She'd tried to keep it simple, but I suspected had blown it with a giant row of alternating kisses, smiley faces and winky devil emojis at the end. Sure enough, a reply landed immediately: 'Is this actually you Willow?'

That was the perfect moment to back out, of course. All I needed to do was answer, 'no, my sister stole my phone, sorry I can't make it tonight.'

My fingers were hovering over the keypad when Auburn spoke. 'Don't. Don't cancel. Go to the pub for goodness' sake. You deserve a night out, Willow, and we'll be fine here. I know it doesn't come naturally, but try and trust me – if there are any problems, I'll call you straightaway. Go on. Have a shower, put some nice smellies on, treat yourself to your favourite Docs. I'll hold down the fort, I promise.'

I think it was the thought of the smellies that did it. I

couldn't remember the last time I'd had a really long, luscious soak. With bubbles and oil and maybe even one of those bath bombs that sheds fragrant petals in the water. These days I'm usually more of a quick shower kind of girl, always keeping an ear out for what's going on in the rest of the house.

But with Mum dozing, and Auburn here, I could actually make a bit of time for myself. Maybe even – drum roll please – shave my legs. The weather's hotting up, and I didn't want people to mistake me for a St Bernard when I wear skirts.

So, fully buffed, polished, exfoliated and coated in lovely shea butter body cream, I was waiting for Tom to collect me at 8 p.m. at the end of the lane. We'd changed the arrangement to that because he wanted to show me his new car, which he'd bought to avoid cramming the camper van around narrow country lanes.

I'd asked him to collect me away from the cottage to avoid Mum and Auburn looking at us out of the window, and my sister running outside singing 'Willow and Tommy, sitting in a tree, K-I-S-S-I-N-G . . .'

Tom's new car was a shiny red Fiat 500, and he looked frankly ridiculous driving it. He could barely squeeze his head in beneath the roof space.

'Hello Noddy!' I said, as I climbed in. 'Busy day in Toytown?'

'Very busy, thank you Big Ears,' he replied, sniffing and staring at me as I fastened my seatbelt.

'What's that smell?' he asked.

'It's the smell of clean woman. You're probably not used to it.'

'It's lovely. I feel a bit giddy. I'm not sure I'll be able to drive.'

'Man up, Mulligan – I am in need of beer.'

He'd given me a little salute, and done as he was told. Now, two hours later, I am on my fourth drink, and feeling decidedly tipsy. I don't drink very much, to be honest – at parties, and every now and then at the café if we're all feeling sociable, but not at home, and rarely in the pub.

I find that I'm enjoying the novelty. Enjoying being here, in the Horse and Rider, surrounded by chatter and warmth and the hustle and bustle of human companionship. The village pub is packed, as usual, its long wooden-topped bar surrounded by men in cords and plaid shirts perched on stools; its various nooks and crannies filled with tables of locals and tourists.

Our own corner of the room is especially convivial. Cal and Zoe are squashed together, holding hands and celebrating the fact that Martha's teachers have suggested she should apply for Oxford. This is quite a turnaround for Martha, who until only quite recently was bunking off school and skulking around Bristol with squatters. Understandably, the two of them are pleased – and in Cal's case, amazed. He's a clever bloke – one of those men who can build sheds and fix engines and, as we saw with Becca last year, actually deliver babies.

He's not, however, 'book' clever, as he puts it. Martha's mum, who died before they moved here, was by all accounts book clever enough for both of them – and they're thrilled that Martha seems to be following suit. Or, as Zoe said, 'doing anything at all that doesn't involve me being on first-name terms with the local police'.

Laura and Matt are here, and Matt has been talking to Tom about Rick Grimes. He thinks the issues with other dogs will be helped by neutering, which makes all the other men at the table gulp down some of their ale and look uncomfortable.

He's also going to try some obedience classes, so that Rick will respond more readily to 'sit', 'heel' and 'down', even when another dog is around. He even has a plan to borrow some very calm, non-aggressive dogs from a friend, and do sessions where Rick is given a treat and encouragement every time he sees them, so he starts to associate other dogs with good things that taste of bacon, rather than bad things that need destroying.

'It won't happen overnight,' he warns Tom. 'And you'll probably always need to be cautious with him – he's a big, powerful dog. But hopefully some of this will help. If you get more relaxed, he will. At the moment, you probably tense every time another dog is around, because you're worried about what might happen. He picks up on that, and it makes him tense as well so he associates the other dog with you feeling unhappy. Does that make sense?'

'Perfect sense,' replies Tom, nodding. I can see him

turning it all over in his mind, processing the logic of it, and formulating his response. He'll probably have invented a Crazy Dog Taming Machine by the end of the night.

Frank and Cherie are here too, sharing their plans for a round-the-world cruise. We all nod, and pretend to believe them – but as Laura and I have learned, it'll probably never happen. They're both semi-retired now, but neither of them seems able to completely give up work. Probably because it's not work to them, it's a way of life. They're happy to have given the bulk of the responsibility to Cal at the farm and Laura at the café, but they're always chipping in and helping.

'You'll never go on a world cruise,' I eventually say, pointing at them accusingly. 'You're both too nosy to be away for that long – you might miss something.'

Edie – who has popped over 'for a quick sherry' – bursts out laughing at this, giggling so hard her perm wobbles.

'You're so right, dear!' she says, once she's recovered. 'If I were a betting woman, I'd take any odds on them never making it past Southampton. In fact, I might open a book on it – who's in?'

Becca immediately whips a notepad and pen out of her bag, and starts jotting down our bids. Cherie and Frank ignore us with great dignity, and carry on muttering about the wonders of Bali as if to prove us wrong.

Becca and Sam are doing shifts with us – they live across the road from the pub, and Sam got the first half of the night. Now Becca's here instead, even though he claimed it was wasted on her as she doesn't drink. He's probably back at home telling Little Edie about his plans to open a bar in Tenerife one day.

'What about you, Tom?' Cherie says, once the gambling fever has died down. 'Have you travelled?'

Tom, who has been quiet but in an I'm-still-enjoying-myself way, looks momentarily shocked to be the centre of attention. I let my hand lie on his thigh beneath the table, and he holds onto it.

'A bit,' he replies. 'With my parents, before they died. Then later, for work – I spent some time in Hong Kong. That was interesting. Not as interesting as Budbury, but close.'

'How old were you, Tom?' asks Laura, who I can tell has been dying to know more about him. 'When you moved to Briarwood?'

'I was twelve. My parents died in a car crash.'

He leaves it at that, and there are sympathetic sighs around the table.

'That's a tough break, mate,' says Cal, who can be weirdly sensitive given the fact that he looks like he'd rather be lassoing cattle than talking about emotions. He offers Tom a salt and vinegar crisp in manly solidarity.

'It was,' says Tom, accepting the offer. 'But here I am. Back again. All grown up and doing okay.'

'More than okay,' says Cherie, reaching across the table to pat his hand. 'Doing brilliantly. Nobody can change their past, but I'd say you're doing a pretty good job with your present, my love. Willow's told me what you're doing with Briarwood, and it's fantastic. You just let us know if you need any help at all, and we'll be there.'

I can see that Tom is touched by this, and perhaps that's why he says what he says next.

'I will. And maybe . . . well, I was thinking that it's about time you all came out and saw it anyway. The roof's been sorted, and the damp-proofing. Some building work as well. Things are going to start changing, and I thought you'd all like to come and see what's going on? It's part of your community, after all. I was even thinking of gathering some information about its history, putting it on the website eventually . . .'

This is a major step forward for Tom – actively inviting strangers into his territory. Maybe Rick Grimes isn't the only one benefiting from training, maybe the treats Tom always receives at the café are conditioning him to respond differently to people as well.

'Oh, that would be marvellous!' says Edie, clasping her tiny wrinkled hands together. 'Will you take me, Becca? I'd love to see it again. It was very different, you know, years ago – there were balls and parties and it was the social centre of the whole village. Then during the war, it was used as a base for some very glamorous American airmen who always had chewing gum and nylons . . . I know the war was a terrible thing, but I have some very happy memories of that time as well. My fiancé and I went to quite a few dances up there at Briarwood, you know.'

We all nod at this, treading carefully, as we always do when Edie's fiancé is mentioned. She's already tucked a bottle of what she calls 'stout' in her handbag to take home for him later.

'Aye, I remember some of that,' chips in Frank, nodding. 'I was just a kid during the war, but I remember the airmen. They were like film stars to us. And the evacuees, Edie, remember them? Poor little kids from London, with their suitcases and strange accents.'

'Of course I remember! I was just a young girl myself, back then. We all tried to make them feel welcome, but they must have been terrified, the mites. I was in the Timber Corps in those days, you know.'

She says this last part with great pride, and I try not to look clueless.

Frank notes our confused expressions, and fills in the gaps: 'You'll all have heard of the land girls, but there was also a women's timber corps. We didn't have enough timber, see, because of Norway being invaded by the Germans . . .'

He goes a little misty-eyed when he says this and, like Edie, I suspect he also has some fond memories of what was undoubtedly a terrible time.

'Yes,' says Edie, sipping her last drop of sherry. 'I was a lumber jill. Had a nifty little uniform and everything. Anyway! I must be going. Can't be a dirty stop-out – what would the neighbours say? Tom, I would love to come and see Briarwood, so please don't forget about me.'

'I could never forget about you, Edie,' he replies,

standing up like a gentleman and helping her through the crowd of seats. 'In fact, I think you could be the star of my website.'

She pauses, and strikes a giddy pose, hands under her chin like a Hollywood starlet.

'I always knew I'd make it big one day! I'll be insta-famous, like that Kim Kar-do-dah one – I'll break the internet!' she replies, before cackling in amusement at the idea.

'I'll walk you over,' says Becca, climbing nimbly over the assembled feet and bags. 'There's only so much Diet Coke a girl can take. Plus, Sam is probably making cheese on toast by now and I need to stop him burning the house down.'

Once those two have gone, waving goodbye to half the pub as they leave, linked arm in arm, the party slowly but surely starts to break up. Zoe and Cal make some excuse about needing to go home and check on Martha, and I see Laura and Cherie exchange significant glances across their G&T glasses. Both of them yawn, as though choreo-graphed, and make 'time for bed' noises. Laura is the world's worst actress – it's official.

I can't help but grin as they drag their obviously confused menfolk away with them, Matt looking yearn-ingly at the half-pint of Guinness he's forced to leave behind. Frank is quicker on the uptake, and gives us a salute as he and Cherie wind their way towards the door to a chorus of village farewells.

'What just happened?' asks Tom, frowning and looking around at the now-deserted seats and orphaned glasses. There are crumpled crisp packets and randomly scattered peanuts, and Laura has left behind her umbrella, which I collect to pass on the next day. It's not been raining, but she's one of those women, Laura – always prepared.

'What just happened,' I reply, laughing, 'is Laura and Cherie giving us some time alone. You know – so we can fall in love and plan our wedding and choose names for our babies?'

'Oh. Right. Well, in that case, I'd better finish my pint. Celeste and Starbuck.'

'What?'

'The babies. Celeste for the girl, and Starbuck for the boy. After my favourite character in the original *Battlestar Galactica*.'

'Hmm . . . well, I can live with Celeste,' I reply, giving it some thought while I drain my glass. 'That's actually really pretty. But I have to use my fictional parent veto power on Starbuck. Everyone would think he was named after a coffee shop. And even worse, they might think we were like the Beckhams, and naming him after the place where he was conceived . . .'

'You're right,' he says, tidying up the table litter as he speaks. Of course. 'That's not classy. I didn't think of that. What do you suggest?'

'I suggest we make a move,' I answer, standing up and gathering my things. 'And that we give some consideration to naming our son Idris Elba. Everyone would think that was cool.'

I lead Tom out of the pub, shouting goodbye to the bar staff, and we get into his Noddy car for the drive home. We debate the coolness of Idris Elba for a while – undeniable, we both agree – but ultimately decide that it might make him the target of much schoolyard mockery. Settling on a shortlist of Bill Murray, Indiana Jones and Sirius Black takes up a good proportion of the drive back to the cottage, and somehow distracts me from the fact that I'm actually quite drunk.

I notice this more as we approach the road that leads home, and ask him to park a short walk away. I need the air.

'They might still be up,' I say, explaining the other reason as I clamber out of the car, just about stopping myself from toppling into a hedgerow that suddenly leaps out in front of me. 'And I don't want them to have any wind-up material.'

'You're probably right,' Tom replies, getting out next to me, and placing a steadying hand on my back. 'We'd be best keeping it quiet until we've narrowed down that shortlist. But I will of course be a gentleman, and walk you the whole ninety seconds home.'

'Good idea,' I answer, smiling up at him. It's dark out here – there are no streetlights, and the only illumination comes from a cloudy moon and the silver scattering of stars. 'Just in case any more hedgerows get frisky with me. How are you handling the quiet now?'

He pauses, and pretends to listen, cupping one hand around his ear.

'It's not that quiet, is it?' he says. 'Not once you know what you're hearing. Owls. Foxes. Occasionally cows. The sea, if you're close enough to the bay. It's just a different lullaby to the one I'm used to, and I'm growing to like it. In fact, I'm growing to like most things around here.'

'I noticed that,' I reply. 'It was nice, inviting them all out to see Briarwood. Can I stroke your head again? It looks all dark and fuzzy.'

He leans down obligingly, and I run my fingers over the thick fuzz. Lovely – like a velvety carpet.

As we make our way slowly along the lane, he takes my hand in his, and I let it rest there. Maybe it's the starlight. Maybe it's the velvety head. Maybe it's the lager. I don't know, and I don't care – because it feels like the most natural thing in the world, and I'm not going to spoil it with too much thinking. Thinking is the enemy of happiness.

We near the end of my driveway, and I glance over the gate at the lights shining from the cottage windows, casting a welcoming yellow glow over the garden. I make a 'shhh' gesture with my fingers, not wanting to wake Mum or Auburn up, and we stand silently together, breathing in the warm night air and listening to the solitary hoot of the tawny owls that live in the woods nearby.

'This is funny, isn't it?' I whisper, reluctant to say goodnight. 'Sneaking around like this. Does it remind you of being a teenager?'

'Not so much,' he whispers back, smiling sadly. 'I was living in Briarwood, and hiding in my room most of the time, wishing I was Starbuck.'

I reach up, and stroke the side of his face, feeling suddenly sad for him. What a lonely childhood he must have had.

'I'm sorry,' I say, letting my hand come to rest on his shoulder.

'Don't be,' he answers, pulling me closer towards him, so our hips meet and our faces are inches apart. 'Don't be sorry, because everything in life leads on to everything else, doesn't it? Like the great George Michael once said . . .'

'Turn a different corner and we never would have met?'

'That's the one. And right now? I get the feeling I've turned the corners I needed to turn. I get the feeling I'm exactly where I'm supposed to be, at exactly the time I'm supposed to be there, and with exactly the right person.'

I know the kiss is coming. I see the light reflected in the deep brown liquid of his eyes, and feel his fingers tilt up my chin, and sigh as his hand tangles up into my hair.

I know the kiss is coming – but I don't know how good it's going to be.

I am expecting a drunken fumble, maybe something we'll giggle over tomorrow – an awkward battle of the noses, maybe, or an accidental clash of foreheads. The usual first kiss hilarity.

What I actually get, though . . . well, what I actually get is quite simply the best kiss I've ever had in my entire life. Gentle but confident; slow and easy; starting warm and building to hot, it's a kiss that takes its time. A kiss that knows its business. A kiss that tells me Tom might be unsure of himself in many ways, but this isn't one of them.

I hold onto his shoulders, feeling the solid bulk of the man beneath the jersey of his T-shirt, and give myself over to it, letting myself sway into him, his arm holding me steady as he slowly and surely reduces me to a trembling mess of girl.

When we eventually pull apart, he sweeps my ruffled hair away, holds my face between both his hands, and lays a soft kiss on the end of my nose. He breaks out the lopsided grin, and gives me a wink as he finally moves away. I lean against the fence post, and relearn how to breathe.

'See you tomorrow,' he says, as he retreats down the pathway. 'Sweet dreams, Willow . . .'

I stand there for a few minutes, watching until he disappears into the shadows, listening until I hear his car door close, and the noise of his engine starting up. I hear the Fiat move off, and I hear the tawny owl whistling – I swear it sounds impressed – and I can even hear my own heart thudding in my chest. At least that's what it feels like.

I shake my head to clear my thoughts, and walk towards the cottage. I say walk, it's more of a float, really. I'm shaken and stirred and completely manboozled, as my mother might say. My feet crunch on the gravel, my head's in the clouds, and I feel like every nerve ending in my body is tingling. My lips feel tender, and I touch them with my own fingers, already replaying the whole scene in my mind.

I unlock the doors, glad that Auburn remembered the security precautions, and drift through the cottage. The living room is empty and the TV has been left on, but I don't care. The kitchen is peppered with dirty plates and leftover pizza, but I don't care. The milk is out, as is the butter, but guess what? I really don't care.

I dump my bag on the kitchen table, and walk down the corridor towards my mum's room. I peek my head through the partially open door to do my usual late-night check, and see that her bed is empty. That, I do care about, and I bite down on a surge of panic as I trot towards the Boys' Room.

I open the door as quietly as I can, and my mind is immediately put at rest. Auburn is out for the count on one single bed, dark red hair cascading over the pillow, legs twitching slightly, not even fully at rest in her sleep. Mum is in the other bed, curled up and peaceful, wearing a zebra-print onesie. Between the two of them, on the bedside table, a CD player is still issuing low-level whale sounds, and a stick of incense has burned down to its floppy ash remnants. All is well with the world.

I smile, taking a mental photo of the two of them, and pad down to my own room. I fling off my clothes, still feeling a bit wobbly from both my night out and a very fine kissing, and curl up beneath the duvet. Bella has been waiting for me, and contorts herself into a very small ball next to my head. She raises one whiskery eyebrow at me, and I know she's asking a question.

'I did have a very good night, yes, thank you, Bella,' I say, reaching out to stroke her ears, unable to get what I know must be a very silly grin off my face. 'And right now? I'm exactly where I'm supposed to be, at exactly the time I'm supposed to be there, and with exactly the right dog.'

Chapter 19

I wake up with the silly grin still on my face, and spend a few luxurious moments stretching out under the covers, wriggling my toes and losing myself in the memory of the night before.

I feel like a fifteen-year-old who's just been passed a note in class from the boy of her dreams. I know it's daft, and it doesn't fit into my real life, and it's all going to get complicated – but for a few minutes, I ignore all of that. I just let myself wallow in that magical feeling – that feeling of liking someone and knowing they like you back. The feeling of potential, and wonder, and hope.

Before long, I'm glad I let myself have those few self-indulgent minutes, because life outside my own room isn't shaping up so well.

I find Auburn in the kitchen, clutching a mug of coffee and biting her lip so hard I know she must be tasting blood. She's staring out of the window, and when I follow her gaze, I see Mum out there. She's still in her zebra print onesie, and she's glaring in at us, waving a trowel and muttering under her breath.

Auburn glances over to me, and tries a smile that isn't even half-hearted – more like an eighth.

'She doesn't know who I am,' she says simply, those quiet words laden with all the sadness I've become used to over the last two years. 'She keeps asking where she is, and who I am, and when she can go home. I don't even know where home is to her right now.'

I nod, and take the coffee mug from her hands. It's empty, so I make a fresh brew for both of us. I wave at Mum through the window, looking as friendly and non-threatening as I can, and try to gauge the level of her agitation. She's holding the trowel, which isn't a good sign, but she's looking at me uncertainly, which might be – it could be that my hair has triggered a feeling of safety, and that she'll start to calm down. Could be that she'll lob a giant rock through the window at any moment, though.

'It's okay,' I say to Auburn, seeing how upset she is. 'It'll be all right.'

She looks at me, frowning, and takes the coffee gratefully. She's still in her PJs, her hair is insane, and she's clearly not keeping up with the rapidly changing landscape of life with someone suffering from Alzheimer's. I can't blame her – she's coming late to this party and she doesn't understand the etiquette.

'I don't know what I've done wrong,' she says, staring out of the window, eyes wide and shining with tears I know

215

she'll refuse to shed. 'She seemed really good yesterday, and we had a nice night. Then this morning, she's completely different . . .'

'You didn't do anything wrong,' I reply, quickly. 'It's not your fault. It's not hers either. It just . . . is. Someone once described it to me as being like a radio station – sometimes it's tuned in really clearly, other times the signal isn't as clear, and everything sounds fuzzy and distorted. And sometimes it bounces around between the two. It's unpredictable, and that makes it hard, I know.'

'But how do you stay so calm?' she asks. 'I've not seen you stressed about it once since I got here. Are you sneaking diazepam behind my back?'

'Not yet, but I won't rule anything out. And I'm not that calm, honestly – it's a duck-on-the-surface situation with me. Auburn, I've had a lot more experience with it, so I know more about what to expect and how to cope. I think maybe it was waking up in a different bed that might have done it – you know how that happens? If you've ended up sleeping somewhere else and when you wake up, you're not quite sure where you are for a minute?'

'Oh yes,' she replies heartily, managing a genuine smile at that one. 'That's happened to me way too many times . . .'

'Well, imagine that feeling – but not being able to shake it. With us, we'd take a moment to remind ourselves of where we are and why we're there, to catch up. We might have a few regrets and a bit of a hangover, but we'd be fine.

With her, perhaps she wasn't able to do that – catch up. Then she feels scared and anxious, and it all starts to escalate. We have to stay calm, because she isn't – and I know this is tough for us, but imagine what it's like for her, trapped in a place where she feels confused and threatened.'

Auburn nods, and we both look on as Mum finally puts down the trowel, and sits cautiously on the bench. It's sunny outside, but there's still an early morning chill in the air, so I'm glad she's sensibly dressed at least. If you can call a zebra onesie sensible. She crosses her arms in front of her chest, and keeps a close eye on us both, in case we make any sudden movements.

'I know. I understand the science of it, and I can see the logic, but . . . well, it's horrible, isn't it? Seeing her like this. It's so bloody hard. I can literally feel my heart cracking. I don't know how you cope.'

I feel the ringing of an alarm bell go off when she says that, and realise that my first instinct is to go on the offensive. Tell her if it's too hard, she can bugger off back to London and take her cracking heart with her. Tell her we were coping fine before she came along, and we'll carry on coping fine after she's gone. That isn't necessarily true, but it makes me aware of how much I'm treading on eggshells here.

Having Auburn around has been a big help, I can't deny that. But I also can't deny the fact that letting myself rely on her too much might be bad for my mental health. Quite frankly, she's a bit of a flake, and has always had a well-developed selfish streak.

She also knows exactly what I'm thinking right now. She looks at me over the steam of her coffee, and narrows her eyes.

'I'm just saying it's hard,' she adds. 'Not that it's *too* hard. I'm here, and I want to be here. I spoke to my boss yesterday, and he says it's fine if I want to extend my leave – his own mum had dementia and he gets it. I can make it a month . . . if that's what you want.'

I distract myself from having to look at her by making Mum a cup of chamomile tea. Kettle. Mug. Tea bag. Water. Simple actions that buy me a bit of time. Do I want her to stay? Part of me does, yes – it's opened up all kinds of possibilities for me. I've been to the pub, and had a kiss on the walk home, and felt so much less stressed about time-keeping since she's been here.

I've been less lonely, too, I have to acknowledge. I mean, I have great friends, and potentially something more in Tom, but I have been lonely. Living here with Mum has felt solitary and sad sometimes. Having Auburn around the house . . . well, she's never boring, my sister, I have to give her that.

But I have some doubts. I'm not sure how reliable she is. I'm not sure I can trust her. I'm not entirely sure I even like her all the time – though that's probably a throwback to the days when she made my childhood an entertaining tapestry of torment. Somehow, she's managing to both disrupt my life, and improve it.

I don't answer her – I concentrate on making the tea, and on singing 'Bare Necessities' out loud. For some reason, that song always helps me forget about my worries and my strife. I'm also, frankly, not used to having to consider other people's feelings this much – I'm used to being on my own with my mum. Now I need to weigh my words, and strike a balance between what I'm thinking and what I'm saying, and it's all very tiring.

'I snogged Tom last night,' I say instead, in a shameless distraction technique.

It totally works. Her eyes pop wide, her mouth forms a perfect 'O', and she lets out a huge wolf whistle as I plonk the tea bag in the bin.

She does a little dance around the room, the kind you see people do on American chat shows when they're celebrating something, and chants: 'Go sister! Go sister!' as she bumps and grinds her way around the room. She ends up next to me, shouting 'whoop whoop!' and holding her hand up for a high five.

It's quite a performance, and I slap her palm in response. Her 'Willow's getting some' dance was definitely worthy of some skin.

'Tell me everything!' she says, looking excited. I grin at her, and it feels good. Good to have someone to share with, someone to high five with, someone to do a victory dance around the kitchen with. Maybe I'm worrying too much about her staying or not staying – maybe I should just enjoy the good parts.

'I will – just let me pop out and see Mum. You stay here for now, while I see how the land lies.'

She nods, but I see a flicker of sadness cross her face. This is all some crazy shit to adapt to, I know.

I walk outside with the chamomile tea, stopping off on the way to get Mum's notepad and pen from her room. I sit down next to her, and pass over the mug. She looks at me a little suspiciously, but accepts it. Her grey hair is fuzzing all over the place, but her skin and eyes are clear and gorgeous. She's still my beautiful mother – she just needs a bit of help remembering that.

'Hi Mum,' I say, casually passing her the notepad. 'It's a lovely morning to sit out in the garden, isn't it? I brought you your notepad. I thought you might want to look at it.'

She has a brief internal debate, then turns the first page. I see her scan the lines, and stay quietly at her side. It is a lovely morning – bright blue sky, the warmth of the spring sunlight starting to take the edge off the fresh temperatures, the whole place bathed in birdsong.

'Willow,' she says, eventually, glancing from the notebook to my hair and back again. I nod, and let that settle for a minute.

'And there's Auburn,' I add, pointing at the kitchen window, where my big sister is pretending to look uninterested. Mum's face breaks out into a genuine smile, and she waves at her.

'She needs to run a brush through her hair,' Mum says, which is ironic given the state of her bird's nest.

'Where are the others?' she asks, sounding vaguely puzzled. 'The . . . boys?'

She frowns as she says this, and I can tell she's struggling with their names and trying to cover it.

'Van is still away on his adventures, and Angel is living in Scotland – you remember, he's a teacher now?'

'Of course I remember!' she says quickly, sounding slightly insulted. Silly me. She sips her tea, the notepad still open on her knees, and looks around the garden.

'I think I'll do some work out here today,' she decides. 'That vegetable patch needs a bit of weeding. Is that all right?'

'Of course it is,' I answer. 'I'll come and help you later.'

'And Auburn?'

'And Auburn,' I nod, laughing inside. Gardening is right up there on my sister's list of Top Ten Things She Never Wants To Do – she always hated it, even as a kid, and I can't imagine anything has changed. She'll just have to suck it up today. I'm supposed to be going in to the café this morning, and was due to meet with the estate agent about a new cleaning job later, but both can be rearranged. I think Mum needs a day with us all to herself – she's calm now, but I know from past experience that if she wakes up in a bad state, it can bubble up again later in the day.

I give Mum a hug, and go back inside the cottage. I'm really starting to feel the need for my own coffee now, as my body has realised it has a bit of a hangover, and this was a less than ideal start to the day. I'm a lightweight, what can I say?

'That looked . . . okay?' says Auburn as I mooch back into the kitchen. 'Is she all right?'

'She will be. She's drinking her tea, and reading her notepad. Need to keep an eye on her today though, just in case. I volunteered you for gardening duty. I know how much you love gardening.'

She pulls a face, but doesn't argue, accepting her fate bravely. For some reason this makes me feel very tender towards her, and I give her a hug as well. I am a hug machine today.

'So,' she says, sitting down at the kitchen table while I root out some cake. I always have cake in the house – Laura is a feeder. Today's special is blueberry muffins, which I plate up with some halved strawberries and a handful of almonds. What I really need is a bacon butty, but I can't face cooking just yet.

'So,' I echo, sitting down next to her and putting the plate in between us. I know she'll steal some anyway, I might as well pre-empt it.

'So . . . you kissed a nerd and you liked it?' she sings, in a terrible Katy Perry impression. I suspect she's been waiting to do that ever since I told her.

'Did he taste of cherry chap stick?' she continues, popping a strawberry into her mouth and raising her eyebrows at me.

I lean back, and can't help but smile. It's weird how fast

this has all happened – sitting here in my kitchen, talking about boys to my sister. I actually don't think we've ever done that before, even when we were younger. Our relationship was too combative back then. It's also weird that there's even a boy to talk about.

'He tasted of cider actually,' I reply. 'Possibly a hint of salt and vinegar crisps. And . . . good things. He tasted of good things.'

'You've gone a bit cross-eyed,' Auburn says, throwing an almond at my head to bring me back to earth. 'It must have been good. Was it just a kiss then? No over-the-bra action? Or even under-the-bra action?'

'Nope. Just one long, luscious, glorious kiss. Which to be honest is the most action of any kind I've seen for a very long time.'

She glances out of the kitchen window into the garden, where Mum is sitting quite serenely now, cross-legged on the bench in the sunshine.

'I can imagine. I suppose things haven't exactly been conducive to romance . . . but I'm here now. For a bit at least. Maybe there'll be time? If you wanted there to be? Do you want there to be? How do you feel about it all?'

I recoil slightly from all the questions, because I'm really not used to this kind of thing. Especially in the morning, at home, with a mild hangover.

'I haven't got a clue,' I reply simply, breaking off a chunk of blueberry muffin with my fingers. 'When I first met him, I did . . . well, like him, I suppose. But I convinced

223

myself that nothing would ever happen between us, that I just couldn't let it. Everything felt too hectic. Too fragile. I don't have space in my life for worrying about whether a boy is going to call me, or checking texts, or finding matching underwear. Some days I barely have time to brush my bloody teeth.'

'What about now?' she asks, looking at me intently. 'Now that I'm here?'

'You really want me to answer that?' I reply.

She nods, so I do.

'Well, in some ways I'm really enjoying it. More than I used to enjoy living with you, anyway. And I can't deny that it's good to have some help. But part of me is still resisting it – this is new to you, and it might wear you down. You've had your own life for a long time, and there's nothing wrong with that. But what happens if I get used to you being here, and start to rely on you, and then you decide you can't hack it? Or that you need to go off backpacking around Guatemala or something? Then I'm back at square one, or even worse – because I'll miss you. She'll miss you. And then it'll all be even harder.'

I say this as gently as I can, because the intention isn't to hurt her – it's just to be honest. I can't afford to live in some fantasy land where my big sister rides to the rescue, and I escape into the arms of a handsome knight.

I see her react by chewing her lip again, and know that the old Auburn would probably have dumped her coffee on my head, or slapped me around the face before going into my wardrobe and stealing my favourite top.

The new Auburn probably wants to do some of those things as well – but she controls it. I can see it takes an effort, but she breathes deeply, finishes her muffin, and waits for a while before she responds.

'Fair enough,' she says, staring out of the window again. 'I can see where you're coming from. And I'm not going to make any big promises – all I can say is that I'll do my best. I'll stay, for as long as you need me. I can find work nearer here, or just come down at the weekends. I can be as involved as you want me to be. I have no plans to back-pack around Guatemala, but it's not like I've ever been particularly steady or reliable. I know that. But I've changed, like we all have, and I will do my best.'

Chapter 20

Auburn's best turns out to be pretty darn good, at least for the time being.

She arranges to initially stay for a month, and she even draws up a rota – the days Mum is at the centre; the days Katie is around; the days Jackie is available; the days when my work allows me to take her with me; appointments with nursing staff and her healthcare team at the hospital; trips out she's booked to go on with Carole and the centre staff; local events we can join in with.

I've always had to be organised, obviously, and keep a detailed diary – but I've never needed a rota as such, because it's always been me doing it all. Now, Auburn has colour-coded us to within an inch of our lives – and even added in some new ideas such as places we could all go to together, restaurants we should try, and art galleries and museums that Mum might like.

Some of it seems overly ambitious; I'm not convinced a trip to the V&A will be possible, but I may be wrong. Some of it is really imaginative and helpful – like getting all three of us to join a quilting club an hour's drive away. A lot of it is stuff I've been meaning to do myself but never found the time to do, like taking Mum to the craft centre to stock up on knitting and crochet supplies.

Auburn programmes all the relevant numbers into her phone, and meets Mum's care team to do a drug review of all her medications, looking at ways it might be tweaked or experimented with. She spends time at the café getting to know the others, and manages to barely flirt with any of the men. She hits it off with Becca especially, which I could have predicted – they share the same sense of humour, a combination of silliness and snark.

She still smokes too much, and drinks more than I think she even notices, and doesn't put the milk away - but nobody's perfect, and she is at least trying to use her endless reservoir of disturbingly nervous energy in a positive way, as though she's trying to make up for lost time.

I accept her help, gratefully, but part of me remains ever so slightly cynical like I'm waiting for the bubble to burst. I keep that to myself, though – I don't want to be the one who bursts it.

Possibly the best thing to come out of the whole scheduling process is the fact that her colour coding includes a whole section shaded in bright red. The bright red – 'because it's sexy', she says – signifies Willow's Special Time. WST for short.

WST is a revelation to me. WST can be a morning, an afternoon or an evening, all to myself. So far, WST has featured long luxurious baths, a walk on the beach, and even a sneaky solitary visit to the cinema, where I paid for a premium seat, gorged on popcorn and ate two whole Magnums. One Classic, and one Almond.

WST has not, as yet, included any of Auburn's other name for it – Willow's Getting Laid Time. Not that it's an unpleasant prospect but I need to be careful not to lose my balance.

One kiss, I told myself, does not a fairy tale make. It might have been a one-off. It might have been us caught in a fleeting moment on a beautiful spring night. It might never happen again – and I have to be okay with that. Because really, honestly and truly, I'm finding the whole thing a bit frightening.

The day after the kiss was spent with my mother, and the one after that was spent at the café. For a couple of days after that, Tom was meeting with building contractors and nipping back to London for a night. Our lifestyles conspired to keep us apart, and maybe that wasn't an altogether bad thing. Like one of those cooling off periods you get when you book something online.

He texted me, and we talked on the phone, but neither of us mentioned what had happened – me because I was still building myself some wriggle room. Him because . . . well, who knows? Perhaps he regrets it. Perhaps he's letting me make the next move. Perhaps he's been kidnapped by mind-control aliens. Perhaps he'd been kidnapped by mind control aliens the night he kissed me, and it was actually a clone, and now he doesn't remember anything about it.

It's exactly this kind of brain-drivel that concerns me – even after one kiss I've started to turn into a stereotypical chick who gazes into space trying to figure out what a man is thinking. And that, I've seen over the years, is pointless – women seem to spend hours of their lives wondering what significance a certain glance had, or what he meant when he said he 'just wanted a night in to watch the match'.

Most of the time the bloke just means he wants a night in to watch the match – but women can translate this into a thousand different languages, meaning anything from 'he's seeing another girl' to 'he's fed up of me' to 'the magic's gone, I'm signing up to match.com.'

I'm not hugely experienced with relationships, but I am hugely experienced with myself – and more than anything I value my peace of mind. I don't like going to sleep with knots in my stomach, or ruining the present by worrying about the future. In a life that is pretty complicated, I like to keep my own head space as simple as possible.

Working is good for that, so I'm happy to have spent time on my new cleaning job, and today, a full shift at the café. The last paying customers leave at around 4 p.m., and we spend the next hour or so clearing up and getting ready for tonight's ballroom dancing session. It's the third one, but I missed the one in the middle, and will probably be bottom of the class and get my legs whacked by Madam Zelda.

Now I'm outside, gathering the extremely annoying kids' lunchboxes, and Lizzie, Laura's daughter, is helping me. She's been quiet, which is unlike her, and she's now voluntarily going into the doggie crèche field to do a poo patrol. As I know myself, this is the last resort of a tortured mind, so I follow her in to lend a hand.

'Everything okay?' I say, holding open a bin bag while she plonks smaller bags inside it. Her blonde hair is tied up in a messy pony tail, and her eyeliner is slightly smeared. This, for Lizzie, is a major signifier that all is not perfect in the universe.

'Yeah,' she replies, kicking her scuffed DM boots into the grass so hard a small divot flies up. 'I s'pose.'

'Come on – out with it,' I say, following her around as she scoops and bags, every movement sulky and resentful. 'My superpowers tell me there's a problem. And as you've not talked to your mum about it, I'm guessing it's to do with something that would embarrass you. Which means it's Josh.'

Lizzie and Josh have been together for ages now – at least ages in teenager world. Actually, now I come to think of it, they've been together longer than I've ever managed with a man, so maybe I'm not the best person to be having this conversation with. I keep quiet on that one. The teenagers all think I'm super cool because I have pink hair and a nose stud and tattoos – best not show any weakness and blow my cover.

Lizzie looks up at me, and frowns.

'Kind of. A bit. Sort of,' she says.

'Well, that's very specific. What's going on?'

Josh is a nice kid, and from what I've seen he thinks the world of Lizzie, but they are only kids – and even nice kids do shitty things.

'It's nothing really. I'm just being a knob.'

'Okay. I accept that you're being a knob – we all are sometimes. But what's bothering you? A problem shared is—'

'A problem you can then go and tell my mum about?'

I put the bag down, and employ my best serious face.

'No. Not unless it was something I thought put you in danger, like you've developed a magic mushroom addiction. Or you have gangrene in your brain. Or you've joined a cult run by people who think the key to eternal life is dressing like Kermit the Frog and singing Barry Manilow songs.'

This does the trick, and there is a glimmer of a smile, hastily hidden.

'Nah. Though that last one does sound cool. It's silly, really . . . it's just that Martha and Josh are looking at universities together. It feels like it's all they talk about. And I get it – it's exciting, and I'm dead happy for them. They've got all these prospectuses, and they're planning trips to open days, and Martha has the Oxford thing, and . . .'

'And you feel a bit left out. Not because they're being mean and trying to exclude you, but because their lives

231

are about to change, and you're wondering exactly where you're going to fit into all of that?'

'Yes! Exactly! And I don't feel like I can say anything, 'cause that makes me sound like even more of a knob, and I don't even think they've noticed I'm upset, which makes me even more upset, and the whole thing is just . . . crap. Really crap. I mean, I know they're going – but what's it going to be like here when they do? I'll lose my boyfriend and my best mate at the same time, and they'll be off in Oxford or wherever Josh goes, and I'll be stuck here. With you lot.'

She realises as she says that last line that maybe it wasn't very polite, and looks up at from behind her fringe apologetically. Poor kid. She's tangled up in blue.

'That is tough,' I reply, leading us away to the exit from the doggie field. We've both handled enough shit for one day. 'And there isn't an easy answer. You're only a year behind them, but I know it's scary. Change always is. My big brothers and sister all left to go off and have adventures, and I was left at home. Though to be fair, I didn't actually mind, so that was different – all I can say is that you need to have a bit of faith.'

'What do you mean, faith? Like, go to church or say my prayers or something?'

'If it helps, yeah – but what I mean is have a bit of belief. In Josh and Martha. Their lives might change but they won't forget about you. You and Josh might be together when you're Edie's age, or you might not. Most importantly,

I suppose, have a bit of faith in yourself – you'll be absolutely fine, Lizzie. I know this sounds like a rubbish
grown-ups thing to say, but it will work out. And if all else
fails, I'll be your best mate for a bit.'

She ponders this for a while, and seems to decide she
likes it.

'Okay,' she says, giving me a cheeky grin. 'Sounds like
a plan. I can get a fake ID and we can go and see gigs, and
go clubbing, and maybe join that Muppets cult . . .'

'All of the above, yes. Now do me a favour, and go back
inside. Sit with Josh and Martha, and try not to sulk. Tell
them you're feeling a bit nervous, and I bet they'll be great
about it. If not, let me know, and I'll come and dump all
this dog poo on their heads. Deal?'

'Deal!' she says, slapping me a high five and scampering
off back to her friends. Girls her age are weird, aren't they?
One minute they're all serious and angsty and 'my-life-
has-no-meaning-and-I'll-never-get-to-see-The-Doors-in-
concert', and the next they're playful and fun and look
about ten years old. Trapped between girl-child and
woman.

I put the bag in the bin, and follow her into the café.
Cherie and Laura have set the trestles up, and will have
them full of food and drink before our guests arrive. Cal
and Sam are on dance floor duty, hefting the tables and
chairs off to the side to create the space where the magic
will happen. Or at least the space where we will all trip
over and laugh a lot.

Debbie Johnson

Laura calls me over and I join her at the counter, where she's currently perched on a high stool, pouring us mugs of coffee and slicing up lemon drizzle cake.

'Nice talk with Lizzie?' she says, gesturing over to the corner where the teens are holed up, pretending to work but actually showing each other videos on their phones. I nod, but don't say anything – I have a pledge to uphold. What happens in the dog poo field stays in the dog poo field. It's like a really smelly version of Vegas.

'She's worried about Josh and Martha leaving for university,' she says, smiling sadly. 'Thinks it's the end of the world, obviously. Also thinks I have no clue about it.'

I refrain from asking how she does know – because Laura is the uber-mama. The mother of dragons. One mum to rule them all.

'Yeah . . . well, I can understand that, can't you?' I ask, tucking into the cake.

'Of course I can. To be honest I've been a bit worried about what will happen with her and Josh ever since they got together. Heartbreak is an inevitable part of growing up, I suppose, but I still don't want to see her going through it. I never did myself – I suppose it'll have to be another one of those What-Would-Becca-Do situations. She had enough teenaged angst for both of us.'

'You never had your heart broken?' I ask, interested. I mean, neither have I – but there was that time Calvin McKenna dumped me on the night of the school disco, which I thought at the time was the end of the known

234

universe. Most girls go through that at some time or another – but apparently not Laura.

'Nope,' she says, in between sips of her coffee. 'Not at that age, anyway. I was with David from when we were in primary school, and we got married when we weren't much older than the gang in the corner. We were really happy together, and I never went through that phase. Skipped it entirely. Of course, I made up for it later, when he died so young – that was real heartbreak. The kind I never thought I'd recover from, to be honest.'

She looks thoughtful as she says this, twirling one of her curls around her fingers, gazing at her kids. One of the many weird and wonderful things about this place – these people – is how much sadness they've endured. Laura lost David; both Cherie and Frank lost their partners; Zoe lost her best friend, Martha's mother Kate. Becca went through something, though I don't know the full story. Everyone has suffered – but everyone has survived. Not just survived, they've gone on to thrive.

'But look at you now,' I say, reaching out to touch her hand. 'A whole new life, here, with the kids, and us, and Matt.'

'And Midgebo! Don't forget Midgebo! I know. I'm so lucky. It's incredible really. If someone had told me it would all work out like this, I wouldn't have believed them. I never thought I could love another man after David, but . . . well, I was wrong, wasn't I? It wasn't easy to let myself, but I'm so glad I did.'

'What do you mean?' I ask, curious. 'What wasn't easy?'

She smiles at me, and I feel the full power of her mama-wisdom aimed in my direction.

'I mean it wasn't easy to surrender to it. To let myself fall in love again. I was scared witless, to be honest – the pain I'd gone through losing David was so extreme it felt like I had died as well.

'When Matt came along, I was convinced it wasn't worth the risk. Especially after Jimbo died – losing the dog almost completely put the stoppers on it all. Because it opened up all those old wounds, you see. It made me realise how much of a risk I was taking, letting myself care so much about someone again. We're all risk averse creatures, aren't we? Like turtles, hiding in our little shells, trying to protect ourselves – never quite realising that we're protecting ourselves from the good stuff as well as the bad.'

There's a look in her eyes as she makes this speech that somehow lets me know she's not just talking about herself. That the message was intended for me as well. I feel a bit like I've been hit by a whammy of life advice from a village elder, and I'm not quite sure how to react. She is, of course, right – but she is, of course, also not me.

'You're not-so-subtly referring to me and Tom, aren't you?' I ask, pointing my spoon at her accusingly.

'What? Me? Never!' she replies, waving her hands in mock horror and surprise. 'But if the lecture fits . . .'

'Hmmm. I'm not sure it does. I'm not sure of anything right now. It's all very confusing. Having Auburn here

236

means I have more time, and that's not always a good thing. It's so weird – I keep finding myself thinking about him, you know? Like, I'll be doing something completely different, like hoovering or working or reading, and he's just there, at the back of my mind. Like a pop-up ad in the brain.'

'Is he looking gorgeous when he pops up?'

'Yes, he's looking gorgeous. Sometimes he's also naked, in a pond, in the rain . . . long story. But sometimes not even that. Sometimes I'll just remember a funny thing he said, or think about how he'd react to the book I'm reading, or I'll want to tell him some weird random thought I had that I know he'll understand. And, like, even a minute after I've talked to him, I feel like I miss him. I mean, I barely know the man – what the heck is all that about?'

Laura actually bursts out laughing at that one. A big, loud, hearty laugh that makes all her curls bob around, and attracts curious glances from everyone else in the room. Probably they'll just assume I told an awesome joke.

She reaches out and gives me a big hug – one that's almost as good as a Cherie hug, although she lacks her physical advantages.

'Oh Willow,' she says, as she finally lets me go. 'You've really never been in love before, have you?'

Chapter 21

I am very unnerved by that question, and spend the rest of the night in a state of high stress. The tension flows through me like liquid, which makes learning a quickstep especially difficult – particularly after I see Tom quietly sneak into the room.

He's obviously been hard at work all day, and is wearing a battered old T-shirt and even more battered old Levis. There's a smear of something dark on the side of his face that he hasn't noticed, and his thick layer of buzz-cut hair is dotted with flecks of something lighter – maybe plaster, or sawdust.

My brain immediately starts to play a show reel of Tom the Builder, accessorising him with power tools in a slow-mo montage, which does very little for my sense of coordination – or to dispel the uneasiness that my conversation with Laura caused.

I react to my own tension by avoiding him as best as I can, which I know makes no sense and isn't fair, and won't even work for the whole night – but I'm all discombobulated and don't know what to do. I need to get my mind affairs in order, and until then, I'm ashamed to admit that I play Cowardly Lion.

This involves dancing with everyone else, and hiding in the toilets whenever it looks like Tom might be coming into rotation anywhere near me. Or hiding behind the counter. On one occasion, even hiding behind the coat stand. Basically, hiding.

After almost an hour of this, he clearly decides he's had enough. I see the moment when he looks right at me, frowning, the confusion clear to see. Beneath the confusion, a layer of hurt that makes me feel like absolute crap. I am behaving like a child – a selfish, nasty child. I understand my motivations but he doesn't, and it's not fair.

I freeze under his gaze, and I know that what he's most likely to do now is leave. He doesn't feel particularly comfortable here with all these people anyway, and now I'm giving him the cold shoulder too.

I expect him to turn around and exit stage left, pursued by a bear. Or by Laura, who I can see has been watching all of this with a great deal of disapproval. I'm guessing her inspirational pep talk about how we all have to be brave enough to let love into our lives was supposed to have a different effect.

Instead, he pauses for a moment, disengaging from a dance with one of Edie's nieces to 'Ballroom Blitz', and keeps his eyes on me as the next song turns out to be 'Can't Hurry Love'. Hah.

Debbie Johnson

I think he's about to go, and I don't know how I feel about that. Part of me would just be relieved but part of me would be devastated to leave things like this. To let the Cowardly Lion win over. Sadly, the rest of me has now turned into the Tin Man, and I feel so stiff I can barely move my feet.

I watch as Tom walks towards me, glued to the spot, having no idea at all how I'm going to react when he finally crosses through the crowd and reaches me. I am potentially planning to hide under a table, or run out onto the balcony at the back of the building – but that only leads to cliffs, the bay, and a fall to certain death. And I don't want to avoid him that badly. I'm not sure I want to avoid him at all. I'm not sure of anything.

Everyone else has started dancing again, buzzing around him, Madam Zelda yelling and beating time with her cane, Mateo swirling across the room with a delighted Edie in his arms, Frank and Cherie surprisingly nimble on their toes for two such tall people. Sam and Becca are managing to quickstep with a baby held between them, and Laura and Zoe have given up on the men and decided to dance with each other.

Tom makes his way towards me, his eyes never leaving mine, as though he's daring me to run away again. When he reaches me, he doesn't say a word – just grabs hold of both my hands, puts me in the quickstep hold, and chasses me all the way across the room to the door. He dances me out of the café, down the winding path, and even across the car park. All without a single word.

240

I have very little choice but to go along with it, as there is no way he's letting go of me. He looks deadly serious, completely determined, and is a lot stronger than me. Truth be told, it's kind of sexy.

We end up on the beach, which is completely deserted apart from us and the sound of the waves fizzing onto the sand. It's a warm night, but I definitely notice the drop in temperature after the packed confines of the ballroom.

Tom finally lets go of my hands, and we stand there, looking at each other in the moonlight. I notice those flecks in his hair again, and really want to reach up and touch it.

'No,' he says firmly, taking hold of my hand and walking me towards the big boulders that litter the cliff edges. 'You cannot stroke my hair. It's off limits until I get some sense from you. What's going on? Have I done something to upset you? If I have, just tell me – I can't handle game-playing.'

We sit down next to each other on the rocks, not quite touching, faces staring out towards the sea rather than at each other. I feel terrible, I really do. The physical separation only reflects the mood, and I am full of regret at how I've behaved. I'm not the kind of person who plays games, or manipulates, or pretends – I wasn't raised that way, and I've never lived that way, and it's painful to think that that's how he's seeing me right now.

But I have to face it – from his perspective, that's what's

happening. We kissed. We kissed well. And now, I'm freezing him out. What's he supposed to think?

'Tom, I'm sorry,' I say, as it seems as good a place as any to start. 'I'm not playing games, honest I'm not. And to use a good, solid cliché – it's not you, it's me.'

'I need more than that, Willow. If you regret what happened between us, that's okay – I'll live with it. It won't be the first time in my life I've dealt with rejection. I'm a bloody expert at living with it.'

My guilty feet have definitely got no rhythm by this stage, and I kick my boots into the damp sand, angry with myself. Of course it's not the first time he's dealt with rejection – that started when he was just a kid, and nobody in his extended family cared enough to offer him a place in their hearts when his parents died. If my cowardly lion routine has made him feel even the tiniest fraction of that again, I'll never forgive myself.

I reach out, and snake my fingers into his. He's stiff at first, and I can only imagine what must be going through his mind, but eventually he relaxes, wrapping my hand in his.

'Okay,' I say, edging slightly closer towards him with a classy bum-shuffle. 'This is the thing.'

'What's the thing?'

'The thing is, I've acted like a bit of a dick, and I'm sorry. I don't regret what happened between us. In fact, I've not stopped thinking about it. I've not stopped thinking about you. Laura gave me a big talk tonight about needing to be brave, and I thought it was nonsense – but she's right. I'm scared of this. I'm scared of what's happening, and might happen, and might not happen. I'm scared of how it will affect my life if it goes wrong – and I'm even more scared of how it will affect my life if it goes right. I'd written off me and men. I'd willingly given up on it all, because I have too much else going on. You know that. And then, you . . .'

'And then I come along and mess everything up. Is that it?'

'Yes! But that makes it sound too harsh. You haven't messed everything up. You've just messed me up.'

'Messed you up in a bad way? Because honestly, that wasn't the intention. I don't go around kissing women just to mess with them. And they usually seem to like it.'

Oh God, I think. I liked it – I liked it too much. That's the whole problem, I suppose. I liked it so much I could get addicted, and I don't have time for rehab.

'Of course I liked it,' I reply, squeezing his fingers to show him I mean it. 'I was walking on air for days afterwards. I can't get you out of my head, Tom, and my head is already a pretty crowded place. I'm just not sure I have space in it for anything else. Or anyone else.'

He turns to look at me, one half of his face in shadow, the other bathed in moonlight. With his short hair and aquiline nose and the cheekbones, he looks like a Roman warrior, rather than a good-looking geek. He also looks

243

frustrated and I can't say that I blame him. He sighs, shakes his head, and pulls his fingers from mine.

'That,' he says, standing up and towering over me, 'is the story of my life. Don't worry about it.'

He leans down to drop a quick kiss on my head, and strides off down the beach, heading for God knows where but obviously needing to get away. I've said exactly the wrong thing again, and I need to fix it. I jump to my feet, and run after him, grabbing hold of him from behind and turning him around to face me. I reach up, and stroke his cheeks, and wrap my hands around his neck so he can't escape. His body language says angry – but his face says sad.

'Don't go,' I say, quietly. 'Especially don't go down there, because there's nothing apart from the old boat house and some really steep paths and a load of nettles. But don't go anywhere. I'm saying this all wrong, and I'm sorry. Give me a chance to try and explain – it's hard, because I don't even really understand it myself.'

I feel his arms go around my waist, and my body brought in to his, and he nods, once. I let my hands drift up into his hair – it's sawdust – and I wipe the smudge of dirt from his face. I take a deep breath. I remember that talk that Laura gave me. I remind myself that Auburn is at home with my mother – that my mum is safe.

That my mum, of all people, would never want me to avoid an adventure. And adventures come in many different shapes and sizes, don't they? Not all of them involve paragliding over the Andes or walking the Great Wall of China. Some of them are right on your own doorstep.

'I like you, Tom – I like you a lot. I have done right from that first day we met. You make me laugh, and you get me, and you're kind and clever and understanding. You love Rick Grimes, and you love Briarwood, and you're sweet and shy with everyone else, and open with me, which makes me like you even more. Plus, in case you hadn't noticed, you're hot. I'd been trying to ignore that bit – and then we kissed, and I felt like it changed everything.

'Since then, you've constantly been in my thoughts. I think about you when I wake up, and when I'm at work, and when I'm lying in bed at night. I've tried not to, but it isn't working. And that is scary. I'm not going to apologise for being scared – I can't help that. But I will apologise for behaving like an idiot tonight, okay? I just . . . freaked out. I saw you, and I was nervous, and I don't like feeling nervous, and . . . this is all new to me, all right?'

He thinks about this for a moment, and puts his hands on the back of my hair, and nestles me into his chest. He smells of wood and work and man, and it's a glorious place to be nestled. We stand there together, wrapped in each other's arms, the sounds of the bay all around us. If life came with a freeze-frame button, I'd probably use it right now.

'All right,' he says, his breath whispering past my ear. 'I understand. I've been the same. I've been playing the Willow Show in my mind ever since that night. I've been binge-watching the Willow Show, in fact. And this is all new to me as well, you know?

'You've seen how I live. In my own space. That's behaviour I've learned over the years, and it's not easy to step outside that. I'm scared too. But I'm at least willing to try, if you are – because I think it would be a bloody waste not to, don't you? Let's just take this slowly, for both our sakes. Try and enjoy each other, and enjoy the here and now, rather than torturing ourselves with what might be. Neither of us knows that, do we? Unless you really do have Romany blood.'

I shake my head, and burrow even deeper, wiping my face against his T-shirt.

'Are you crying down there?' he asks, tipping my chin up so I'm forced to look at him.

'No,' I reply, knowing that the moonlight is probably reflecting off my tears and making me look a bit like a sad clown. 'I just have allergies.'

He uses his thumbs to gently wipe away the tears, and kisses the marks they've left. He looks at me, smiling. 'What are you allergic to?'

'Emotional intimacy, apparently. Look, I am sorry, honestly. I didn't want to hurt you – I was just protecting myself, and that's stupid. I can't live like that. My life is complicated, but you know that. And . . . I trust you. That's a big deal, so don't screw it up, all right?'

He nods, and promises he won't, and then he kisses me. He kisses me for what feels like an eternity, and by the time he stops, my head is spinning, my knees are weak, and the waves are starting to lap at our ankles as the tide comes in.

'Come on,' he says, holding me steady in his arms. 'I'll give you a piggyback up to the café.'

'Promise you won't drop me?' I ask.

'Never,' he replies, so firmly I dare to believe him.

Chapter 22

My sister is driving us in her Ford Fiesta, and this is making me nervous. She drives like she lives – full on. Her nervous energy and constantly moving limbs translate into an aggressive journey, sharp jolts of the gears accompanied by abrupt turns and last-minute brake-slamming.

Her constant yells at the lunacy of other drivers, as she cuts them up and fails to indicate at roundabouts, is only matched by the loudness of her singing along to Adele.

'We're rolling in the deeee-eeee-eep!' she bellows, as we bounce along A-roads in darkest Cornwall.

'You have the singing voice of an angel,' I say, looking back at Bella, who is curled up in a ball behind us, one paw over her face as though she's trying to block out the noise.

'I know, right? I should audition for *The X Factor* . . .'

I snort at the thought of that – she's just crazy enough to do it, Auburn. She's certainly crazy enough to have planned this outing for us, and I guess her crazy must be infectious, because here I am, sitting right by her side as we head on an odyssey into the past.

Mum is on a day out with Carole and the team at the day centre. It's a special day that's been organised for dementia sufferers, focused on memory work and creative ways to support it. There'll be crafts, classes, and music – basically it seems right up her street. Carole had seemed a little flustered when we dropped her off, stressed about the latest funding crisis, but Mum didn't pick up on that and was looking forward to her outing. To be specific, she was looking forward to 'helping the old people'.

Tom is busy at Briarwood, and it's the day the café is closed, so Auburn and I found ourselves in the very rare position of having time to ourselves. Heaven forbid we spend it lounging around in our pyjamas, eating a tub of Cadburys Heroes and watching a Spongebob marathon – my first choice. Oh no, we had to *do* something. Go on an adventure. Stir up trouble.

'Tell me again why we're doing this?' I say, sipping coffee from my flask and watching the rolling green hills slide by from the window. It's been raining this morning, and the landscape looks like it's just come out of a wash cycle. It's not that different from Dorset out here in the wilds of the West Country, but I still feel like I'm in a foreign land.

'Because I want to? Isn't that enough?' she says, beeping at the car in front, who is daring to drive at the actual speed limit.

'Nope.'

'Okay, we're doing this because . . . because Mum is changing. She's kind of disappearing in some ways. She remembers some of the past really vividly, but we get a distorted view of it. And because her past is part of ours, I just want to reconnect with it.'

'Reconnect? That's a terrible word,' I reply, frowning at her. 'Next you'll be saying you're going on a journey. Have you become American?'

'Well, I did watch an entire series of *The Biggest Loser* last night, so I'm feeling quite at one with the motivational life coach lingo.'

'That sounds like an exciting night,' I answer, cringing as she takes a whole branch off one of the hedgerows.

'We can't all be out razzling and dazzling with our dashing inventor boyfriends.'

'We weren't razzling or dazzling – we were having a pint with Matt after dog training classes. And he's not my boyfriend.'

She turns to give me a sarcastic look, and I gesture for her to look at the road instead. Driving with Auburn is possibly the most terrifying experience of my life.

'Whatever . . . Anyway. Look, I want to do this, okay? We've never been a very conventional family, have we? It's not like we have a lot of background history, or a family tree in an old bible. If I was asked to go on *Who Do You Think You Are?* – the non-celeb edition – I wouldn't have a clue where to start.

'I remember my dad, and I remember life at the

commune, but only just. Pre-digital so hardly any photos. It's hazy, and I'm never sure when Mum's talking about it how much is real, and how much is a construct. I swear to God the other day she started talking about something I thought was a family story, and halfway through I realised she was describing a plot from *Emmerdale* in the nineties. I only noticed when she started talking about the aeroplane crash.'

I have to laugh at that one. She's done the same with me before, telling me what I thought was a sad and revealing story about her childhood, that turned out to be a synopsis of an episode of *Tracy Beaker*.

Auburn has a point – we don't know much about our background. I, in particular, know very little. Mum was a free spirit, and obviously classed little things like marriage and naming dads on birth certificates as boring technical-ities she could live without.

'Besides – doesn't it bother you?' she asks. 'Not knowing who your father is?'

I shrug, and sip some more coffee. I may have had one pint too many last night.

'I don't think about it that much,' I say, honestly. 'I've never believed that I am the sum of my parents' private parts, you know? But I suppose as Mum's Alzheimer's has progressed, I have thought about it all a bit more.

'She's always been evasive, and now she has a condition that completely lets her off the hook – even now, she clams up, and looks a bit embarrassed if it ever comes up. I think everything that's happened with her has made me a bit more . . . aware, maybe? Aware of the fact that we can't take what we know, or what we think we know, for granted. It's one of the reasons I started keeping a notepad as well.'

Auburn's tapping her fingertips on the steering wheel, listening to me and also to the sat nav, and suddenly whirls the wheel to the right to change lanes and take a turning into a quiet one-track country lane. God help any fool who dares to be driving in the opposite direction.

'Well maybe we'll have more material for you after this,' she says, narrowing her eyes as she looks ahead. 'And you can write about things other than Tom, and how dreamy he is. Look – I think that's it . . .'

I ignore her comment about Tom – this is a key survival tactic with Auburn – and follow her gaze as we approach another turning. The mud has been churned up after the rain, and thick tyre tracks have been left where off-road vehicles have driven in and out. There's a sign, hand-painted on what looks like driftwood, that tells us we've arrived at the Twisted Sisters Artists' Retreat, with a picture of an eerie stone circle beneath it.

'The Twisted Sisters – is there a stone circle here?' I ask, as Auburn pulls into the car park.

'From memory, it's less of a circle, and more two lumps of rock on a hill. Maybe there were more, once. God, this is weird . . .'

We get out of the car, and I leave the back doors open in case Bella wants to get out. She doesn't. Auburn is standing still, hands on hips, looking around her. Her hair is loose and shining, and she's wearing her biker-boots-and-skinny-jeans combo, along with some kind of ethnic knit with brightly coloured stripes and geometric designs. She looks completely at home in this place.

I give it a quick once-over, and am actually a bit surprised by what I see. I suppose I have these inherited folk memories of camp fires and feral children and mush-room tea, and expect it all to be a lot more . . . seventies.

In reality, it's all pretty neat and well-kept, with a couple of rows of old brick terraces, a central courtyard dotted with baskets and pots full of flowers and lavender sprigs, and a building that seems to be an office.

'Is this how you remember it?' I ask, raising my eyebrows.

'Kind of . . . but it seems smaller. Or maybe I'm bigger. And it seemed a bit wilder in my mind as well. It definitely seems a lot more business-like than it used to. And did you notice the sign said it was a retreat, not a commune? Maybe these days they do mindfulness workshops and help rich people improve their watercolour techniques.'

'Maybe. Only one way to find out, I suppose . . .'

I head towards the office building, and she follows behind, suddenly more quiet and timid than I'm used to. I suppose this must be, to use a technical term, a bit of a head-fuck.

I push open the office door, and find that it's also a shop. There are framed paintings hanging on the walls, tiny price tags hanging from their corners, as well as all kinds of home-made produce – jam and honey and free-range eggs and mead and elderberry wine and gnarled loaves of bread. It smells of incense, and there's wafting hippy background chanting playing, and I can totally imagine my mother in here.

Auburn browses around the shop, while we wait for someone to emerge from the back room in response to the tinkling of the doorbell.

When that someone does emerge, again it's not quite what I expected. I've been anticipating someone who looks like a Cornish Gandalf, or a woman wearing a tie-dye kaftan – instead, a tall, good-looking guy dressed like a farmer pops his head around the corner. He looks to be in his forties, and is wearing clean, pressed cargo pants and a white shirt with the sleeves rolled up over sinewy arms.

He gives us both a big, beaming smile, and basically exudes a healthy, outdoorsy vibe, his thick brown hair still damp from the morning's rain. He looks a bit like the George Clooney of the artists' commune world.

'Good morning!' he says, walking out into the shop space. 'Welcome to the Twisted Sisters! How can I help you today?'

I can see Auburn gazing at him, mouth slightly open, and just know that she's about to make up some crazy story that involves her watercolour skills and the need to be naked in a teepee. I step right in to head her off at the lying pass, because there simply isn't any need for it.

'Hi there – we were wondering if it would be all right to have a look around? My sister here lived on the commune when she was a child, and fancied a trip down memory lane. Would you mind?'

He stares at Auburn some more, as though trying to place her, taking in her height and her hair and obviously attempting to make some connections that aren't quite falling into place. She would have been, what, five or six when she left? I'm guessing she's changed a bit.

'Of course it would – feel free. But before you do, why don't you come in for a cuppa? I've just put the kettle on. I was probably living here then, so maybe I can help?'

We nod, and follow him through into the back room. I catch Auburn eyeing up his arse as he goes – it is, to be fair, a good arse – and nudge her hard to tell her to behave herself. She grins, and makes a little bump and grind gesture with her hips to let me know exactly what she's thinking. Just in case, you know, I was completely stupid.

The office is not at all what I thought it would be. It's clean and uncluttered and the bare brick walls are painted entirely white, giving it a cool antique minimalist look. There's smooth blonde wood furniture, a MacBook Air, and a tidy pile of papers he's obviously been working on.

He disappears off into yet another room – maybe they get smaller, like in Willy Wonka's Chocolate Factory – and we hear him clunking pottery and pouring water. He comes back carrying the drinks, all in mugs bearing the name of the Twisted Sister Retreat. It's a lot more corporate than I thought, and I find myself looking around in curiosity as we settle into the guest chairs across from his desk.

'Not what you expected?' he asks, noting my inspection and smiling. He sounds amused, not insulted.

'No, it's not.'

'Cleaner? Tidier? No topless women wrapped in Aztec blankets?'

I nod, and smile, uncertain how to react.

'That's okay. I keep them all in the back room, ready for our campfire orgies. My name's Robert, by the way. I run this place – by which, of course, I mean I lead the co-operative. I was born here, and took over from my dad, Malcolm, a few years back. When was it you were here?'

He looks at Auburn, who is fidgeting with the hem of her jumper and staring at him intently. Her face breaks out into a grin, and she says: 'I remember you! You were a lot older than us, but I remember you – Blister Bum Bobby!'

I groan a little inside, but he bursts out laughing, and points at Auburn like she's caught him out in something. He has a good laugh, one of those that you catch.

'Right! That's me . . . I had an unfortunate incident when I was doing a daring backwards slip-and-slide off the rocks into the lake, when I was about ten, and got called that for years afterwards. What can I say? Happy times – but please call me Robert in public, I've got a rep to protect! So, that dates things. What's your name, and who were you here with? You're far too young to have been here on your own.'

'Why, thank you, kind sir,' says Auburn, actually batting her eyelashes at him. 'I'm Auburn Longville, and I lived here with my brothers Angel and Van, and our dad, who died when we were little, and our mum—'

'Lynnie Longville,' he finishes for her, the words coming out as something of a sigh. We look at each other in confusion as we watch his face go from jovial and welcoming to something altogether more wistful. Robert gazes off into the distance, over our heads and through the window at the fields beyond.

He realises he's been quiet for too long, and snaps himself out of it.

'Sorry – lost in space for a minute there. Yes, I remember you now – your hair was a lot shorter, and you looked like an angry boy. Van was older, wasn't he? And Angel was the cherub with the blonde curls. It was so sad when your dad died. Lynnie . . . well, she did her best. She always did. She was an inspirational woman. I missed her when she left. I mean, we all did. She never even said goodbye, and I always wondered what had happened to her . . .'

He drifts off again, and I look at Auburn as she mouths the words 'what the fuck?' to me. I shrug, and make a haven't-got-a-clue gesture.

'Your mum and dad were really good friends with my mum and dad,' he says, explaining. 'When your father passed, we all spent a lot of time together. I was only nineteen or twenty at the time, but, well . . . she was a special lady. I'm sure I don't need to tell you two that. Is she . . . still around?'

He sounds ridiculously hopeful as he says this, and it's obvious that the younger Robert had a massive crush on Lynnie Longville. My mother – the femme fatale. I think it's sweet, but Auburn is starting to look horrified.

She pauses, chews her lip, and stares, before finally, she nods, abruptly. She starts to tap her fingernails on the desk, and then slugs down all her tea in one go, like it's medicine she doesn't like the taste of. She stands up quickly, and looks agitated. I have no idea what's wrong with her, but I get up as well. Looks like our trip down memory lane is coming to an early finish.

'She is,' replies Auburn. 'Alive and well, thanks for asking. And thanks for the tea. And thanks for the talk. And . . . well, thanks. I think we'll go and have that wander, now, if that's still all right? We need to get home in time for our cheese and wine tasting.'

Robert looks confused by the sudden change in mood, and I'm confused by the sudden appearance of a cheese and wine tasting. He nods, and stands up to see us out.

'Of course. It was lovely to see you again, and to meet you – I'm sorry, what's your name?' he asks, holding his hand out to shake mine.

'She's Willow,' says Auburn, quickly, bustling me out of the room, through the shop, and into the courtyard so fast I barely have time to wave goodbye.

'Say hello to her for me, won't you? To Lynnie?' shouts Robert from the doorway, as we leave.

'Will do! Bye now!' Auburn yells back, saluting him, and practically running off into the distance. I scoot after her as fast as my boots will carry me, eventually catching up at the foot of a hill behind the buildings. I look up to the top, and see the two Twisted Sisters, smooth stone glinting in the sunlight.

'Race you up . . .!' she says, and starts to jog before she even finishes the sentence. I chase, and overtake, and am standing at the top of the hill laughing at her by the time she reaches the crest.

She sits down on the grass, ignoring the fact that it's damp.

'I really must give up smoking . . .' she says, as she lights a cigarette and takes a deep, desperate puff. I clamber down next to her, grimacing slightly as I feel my leggings go all moist – and not in a good way.

I give her a minute to smoke, and look down from our perch. It really is a beautiful view – the rolling fields and hills a patchwork of every shade of green nature has to offer; the blue sky crashing down to meet them; the distant Norman castle in the little market town of Launceston clear on the horizon.

I amuse myself making a daisy chain until she finishes the cigarette, waiting for her to stub it out on the damp grass. She looks around, realises that there isn't a handy ashtray up here by ye ancient stone circle, and pops the end into her jeans pocket with a little shrug.

'So,' I say, eventually. 'What was that all about? One minute you're flirting with him, and the next you're galloping out of there like your knickers are on fire!'

She looks at me disbelievingly, and shakes her head as though I've just won the World's Greatest Moron championships. Yay, I'm a winner.

'You really didn't figure it out?' she says, sounding shocked.

'Figure what out? That you're bonkers? Because, yes.'

'No! You didn't notice the way he looked when he talked about Mum?'

'Of course I did – he turned into a lovestruck teenager, which is weird in a man who seemed otherwise sensible, and must be, what, in his mid-forties? He was obviously completely ga-ga about her.'

Auburn nods, and waits. And waits some more. And pulls a face at me.

'Okay. Let me put my hypothesis into plainer terms,' she replies, starting to actually look amused now.

'Go ahead,' I say. 'I'm just a simple country girl, making a simple daisy chain . . .'

'Right. Here goes. Pay attention, country girl. Robert, when he was nineteen or twenty, was clearly in love with our mother. Are you with me so far?'

'Yes, sir,' I reply.

'Good. So then my dad died, and as we've both gathered from her, she struggled afterwards. And then, not too long after, she found out she was pregnant with you and for some reason, she uprooted us all and did a runner two counties over. We never got an explanation for that – she literally just bundled us all up in a moving van one day, it was kind of horrible to be honest.'

'That wasn't my fault . . .'

'I know,' she says, looking at me like I'm mad. 'Nobody thinks it was, as you were a foetus at the time – it was still horrible though. Anyway, that's not the issue. The issue is this – I don't think the Angel of the Lord came down to create you, Willow – I think Bobby Blister Bum did.'

I drop my daisy chain, and stare at her, eyes wide. I want to tell her it's nonsense – but now she's pointed it out, I can't argue with her logic. I mean, the timing fits at least.

'Don't you see?' she asks, prodding me. 'It explains it all. Why she left in such a hurry. Why she cut ties with the place. Why she's always embarrassed and avoids the issue. It's because our mum was a cougar, before the word was even invented – she had a fling with her friends' kid, and then ran away to hide the evidence! And the worst thing is, I was even considering shagging him myself . . .'

Chapter 23

'So, are you going to tell him?' asks Cherie, leaning so far forward I can see down her top. I avert my gaze, and think about the question.

'I don't know,' I reply honestly. 'I mean, we don't even know there's anything to tell, really. It's all just a theory.'

'A good theory,' pipes in Auburn, looking up from the magazine she's reading. *Dorset Life*.

'Yes, but still just a theory. What am I supposed to do – waltz in there and demand a paternity test? Plus, you know, what does it really matter? Our family's always been weird.'

'All the best families are weird,' says Edie, looking up from her iPhone. She's recently become embroiled in an online Boggle community, and is forever on the hunt for new and exciting six-letter words.

'My family, for instance,' she continues, putting the phone down on the table. 'Well, my mother's older sister and her husband died in the Spanish flu epidemic, so her children were raised by aunts, uncles, even friends from the village. There was no official adoption, or anything done through the courts – they just stepped in and took them. By the time I was born, I had two older sisters who were actually my cousins. The others went elsewhere. They lived in different homes, but all in and around the village, so they could stay in touch. As a result they had about five different sets of parents.'

Zoe is sitting quietly next to her, head buried in a book as usual, but she looks up at this.

'Wow,' she says. 'That's really interesting – and complicated.'

'Yes, dear,' replies Edie, patting her hand. 'It's not just your generation who does complicated. The films might have been black and white back then, but our lives weren't.'

We all nod at this – feeling slightly told off – and make space as Laura approaches with a tray of drinks and salted caramel cookies. We're having our usual end-of-day catch-up, and the whole café smells heavenly – Laura's been making Bakewell tarts, and the aroma of almond is so thick you could lick it.

Mum is here with us, but sitting in bookshelf corner with Saul, colouring in. Katie has started a college course, and we're all chipping in to help her out with childcare.

We'd lowered our voices when we were discussing Paternity Gate, so Mum wouldn't overhear, but to be honest I don't think she's tuned in to us at all.

I glance over, and see her colouring book flat on the

table. I note that she is very much not staying within the lines – which is par for the course, it seems.

I'd tried dropping the name Robert into the conversation the night before, asking if she remembered anyone called that. She'd screwed her face up in confusion, and stared off into the distance as though trying to recall, and then finally shrugged and said: 'No, sorry – my poor sick brain must have blanked it out!'

Now, I'm used to seeing the way that Alzheimer's affects my mum. The way it befuddles her, and leaves her searching for words, and lost in a jumble of memories that are only related in her own mind. I've seen the genuine pain and confusion it causes her, and the way she tries to fight it.

I've seen enough of it to know that on this occasion, she isn't suffering from Alzheimer's-related memory loss – she's just plain lying to my face. My mum is one of the most honest people I know. She doesn't care enough about normality or other people's approval to lie for it – so this is quite a surprise. Also, something of a confirmation that Auburn might be on the right track.

'What was he like, then?' asks Laura, once she's passed out the refreshments and settled herself down on the chair next to me. She's had her hair trimmed, but because it's so curly, it now just sticks out from her head like a dense, springy triangle. I want to touch it, and realise I may be developing something of a problem with feeling up other people's hair.

'He was sex on a stick,' says Auburn, sticking her tongue

out at me. 'Kind of like George Clooney crossed with Negan.'

'Who's Negan?' asks Cherie, frowning.

'He's the baddie in *The Walking Dead*,' supplies Edie, the almost ninety-two-year-old. Of course. 'He's a very handsome man, but pure evil.'

'Hopefully Robert's not the same . . .' utters Auburn, flicking through the pages of her glossy. She looks up, and glances around the table at us all. I'm dressed in my favourite black top, which I decorated with stick-on purple sequins myself. Laura's face is covered in flour. Cherie has her Wonder Woman apron on. Zoe is wearing Cal's cowboy hat, and Edie is in her usual beige cardigan with her neon orange Vans backpack still on her shoulders.

'You lot,' she says, wagging her fingers at us. '. . . would not cut it in the pages of *Dorset Life*.'

'What do you mean?' asks Cherie, sounding offended. 'I'm a well-respected local businesswoman! I could be in *Dorset Life* if I wanted!'

'Yeah,' adds Zoe, smirking. 'We could be, easily. In fact, we could have our own reality TV show – the Real Housewives of Budbury Village.'

'None of us are housewives, though,' Laura adds, looking slightly disappointed that we've failed at the first hurdle in our bid for TV fame.

'True – but we're all very real!' responds Zoe. We all like this compromise, and exchange a small round of satisfied high-fives.

'Cal would love it,' she continues. 'Can you imagine him in front of the cameras? He'd be strutting around in his Levis, wearing this hat, laying on the Crocodile Dundee act, accidentally finding reasons to ride a horse topless . . .'

We all pause for a moment to give that image the respect it deserves.

'And Sam,' says Laura, sipping her coffee. 'He'd be down at the beach, surfing and showing off all his tats, and throwing his hair around looking like a L'Oreal advert. Not Matt though. He'd be the stern, solitary one who only gets caught on film by accident.'

'So would Tom,' I reply. 'They probably wouldn't get him out of his camper van. He likes you lot, but he still isn't keen on the social whirl.'

'He's like Matt,' says Laura, grinning at me over her cup. 'I bet he's completely different with you than when he's in public, isn't he?'

Everyone is suddenly taking a keen interest now, as they're all desperate for some titbit of loveliness about our relationship. I look around the table, and see a row of puppy dog eyes.

'He is,' I answer, smiling. 'Completely different.'

They sigh as one, and look eager for more.

'Well, for starters,' I go on, 'he dresses as a woman – including the high heels. Sometimes knee-high boots in patent leather. And he walks around Briarwood in one of those turbans made of fruit, like Carmen Miranda used

266

to wear. And he has a fetish for bathing in mango smoothies. Honestly, the man's a mystery to me . . .'

Cherie reaches out and swats me across the head with the magazine she's grabbed from Auburn, and Edie cackles out loud.

'Carmen Miranda! My goodness!' she says, clapping her hands together. 'That's bananas!'

'Seriously, though,' says Zoe, nudging me. 'How is it going? You seem really happy together. And now Auburn's here, you at least have the space to see where things lead, don't you?'

'For the time being, anyway,' chips in Auburn, looking thoughtful. 'I'm due back at work before too long, so I need to make some decisions. I could come back for weekends, or I could look for work closer to here. I've been keeping an eye on job sites, checking for anywhere in the area that needs a pharmacist.'

I see Laura frown at this, and notice the look she swaps with Cherie. I know what's coming, but there's nothing I can do to stop it. I cringe a little inside, and suddenly find myself fascinated by the cookie crumbs on my plate.

'But we need a pharmacist!' exclaims Laura. 'Right here in Budbury – how do you not know this?'

There's an awkward pause after that, where everyone slowly realises that I've accidentally not mentioned this serendipitous fact to my sister, the pharmacist. That we've had several conversations about her future, and her role in our lives, without me ever casually dropping in the fact

267

that our local chemist's shop is currently uninhabited. In fact, I've distracted her every time we've walked past it, which I'm sure she's now remembering.

'Oh!' says Laura, blushing as she knows she's dropped a clanger. 'Willow must have forgotten . . .'

Auburn folds her arms across her chest, and smiles. She smiles, but I see the hurt flicker across her face even as she covers it up, and I feel terrible. Why haven't I mentioned it? Why am I still such a bloody control freak? Why can't I just accept the fact that she's back in our lives, and wants to stay there? Lots of questions, and no answers that don't involve a hefty dollop of self-loathing.

'It's okay, ladies,' says Auburn, going for cool as a cucumber but still sounding shaky. 'Don't worry about it. It seems I'm still on probation with my sister. I'm a big girl, I can handle it.'

Cherie gives her a hug. Laura kicks me under the table. Even Edie is looking distressed by this stage, which is absolutely unforgivable. I have breached the number one rule of Budbury life: Thou Must Not Upset Edie May. And, yeah, upsetting my sister feels pretty crappy too.

I reach out across the table, knocking the sugar dispenser over as I go, and grab hold of her hand. She doesn't meet my eyes, but she doesn't spit at me either.

'I'm sorry,' I say, simply. 'Honestly, I am. I'm so used to doing all of this on my own, it's taking me ages to accept that I might not even have to. I'm clinging onto it all far too hard, and that isn't your fault, okay? It's mine. I've let my whole life be defined by the fact that I look after my mum – and she's actually *our* mum, not just mine. I want you to stay. I really do. I might want to kill you at least three times a week, but I want you to stay. Forgive me? Please?'

Auburn stays silent for a moment, as does every other single person around the table. All I can hear is Saul and Mum chattering away in the background, and the gentle hiss of the temperamental coffee machine, and the sound of my heart banging away in my chest.

She squeezes my fingers, and blinks her eyes rapidly, and finally says: 'Okay, sis. I can do that.'

There is a group exhale of relief, and I realise that I'm crying a little bit. So is everyone else, even Zoe, who's normally tough as nails.

Just at that moment, Becca walks through the doors, pushing Little Edie in her buggy. She pauses. Stares at us all, with our leaky eyes and trembling lips, and says: 'Oh God. What did I miss? Did someone finally break the news to Laura that Santa Claus isn't real?'

Chapter 24

My name is Willow Longville. I am twenty-six years old. I live in a village called Budbury, with my mum Lynnie. I work as a waitress at the Comfort Food Café, and I run my own cleaning business called Will-o'-the-Wash. I have a dog called Bella Swan, and I love my life. In the last twenty-four hours, the following things have happened . . .

1. I have spray painted an old pair of Doc Marten boots neon pink, to go with my outfit for Edie's party. We are making our own dresses, which could be interesting.
2. I have managed to source a life-size cardboard cut-out of *Strictly Come Dancing*'s Anton du Beke, also for Edie's party.
3. I have learned how to make choux pastry from Laura and I rock at it – am now considering becoming a chef.
4. I cleaned a small apartment building that's just been renovated from top to tail, which was very satisfying.

5. Carole broke the news that the day centre is cutting back to one day a week for dementia patients, which was bad news, but not as bad as it would have been before Auburn came.

6. Auburn has contacted Ivy Wellkettle, and is looking at ways to get a business loan to buy her out of her pharmacy in Budbury. Cherie is considering chipping in and running it as some kind of village co-operative, joking that Frank needs somewhere to get his Viagra. At least I think it was a joke – I didn't want to think about it too much.

7. I watched a TV show called *Descendants* with my mum, which was all about the children of fairytale heroes and villains. I haven't stopped singing the songs since – there are so many ways to be wicked.

8. It has rained and rained and rained, for three days solid, and Cal threatened to start building us a very big ark. Today, we woke up to glorious sunshine and not a cloud in the sky.

9. I have cyber-stalked the man who might be my dad, discovering that he is single, otherwise childless, and has a pet pig called Stanley.

10. I have decided that Auburn is right, and I can possibly now take a risk and have a night away – she has promised me she will look after Mum. She's told me to stay with Tom and explore the Big Bang Theory. I pretended to have no idea what she meant, but am fizzing inside.

Chapter 25

It's been a beautiful day. The land around us has started to dry out after the storms, and looks fresh and wild and green because of them. Superwurzel is still looking very sorry for himself though, his felt hat drooping and his bright red pants askew.

I came home after the lunch shift at the café, and was immediately ordered to go and 'turn into a girl' by my sister. Mum isn't quite sure what's going on, but understands I'm going for a sleepover. She seemed most concerned that I remember my pyjamas, take my toothbrush, and let her know what time I need picking up in the morning.

I've kept a careful eye on her, checking in case this is unsettling her, but she doesn't seem distressed – she might think I'm twelve and going to a friend's house, but she's not distressed. In fact, she packs me a goody bag for my 'midnight feast', which consists of some Babybel cheese, a packet of organic cashew nuts, and an entire head of celery. Whoo. Party time. This explains why I never got invited to many sleepovers as a kid.

Auburn has also packed me a goody bag – but hers consists of a bottle of vodka, a multi-pack of Mars Bars, and a big box of glow in the dark condoms. Subtle.

It takes me quite a long time to actually leave, because I am easily the most stressed person in the cottage. I go over the night-time routine with Auburn again and again, making her repeat things out loud, which she does patiently – for a while, at least.

Eventually, she snaps, and stamps on my toe to shut me up. Sisters, eh?

'Just go, will you?' she says, physically pushing me out of the door and onto the pathway. 'I know what I need to do. I'm not an idiot. I can call you if I need you, but it'll all be fine. Stop being a Worrying Winnie and bugger off.'

I smile at that one. It's a mum classic – don't be a Worrying Winnie, or a Stressed-out Susan, or a Fretful Fanny. Always girls' names, which makes sense – the boys never seemed to worry about much at all.

Tom arrives just then to pick me up, and Rick Grimes leaps out of the back of the Fiat and streaks towards the cottage. Tom tests out one of his obedience commands, and the huge creature actually stops mid-lumber, and drops to the ground, shaking with the effort of restraining himself. We are all delighted, and Rick gets a treat, which he gulps down before dashing off to find Bella.

Rick Grimes is also having a sleepover, at the cottage. That's probably for the best, because if we do decide to explore the Big Bang Theory, I'm not sure I want a slobbery Rottweiler cross to be taking an interest.

I give Auburn a hug, wave at Mum, who is smiling at us through the window, and get into the car.

'You okay?' asks Tom, as he pulls out of the drive. He's wearing an especially fine Goonies T-shirt today, stretched over his body in a far sexier way than its designers probably ever anticipated.

'Yeah,' I say, smiling. 'Just being a bit of a Paranoid Patsy. I've not left her before, you know?'

'Well you don't have to now,' he says, beeping his horn at Frank as we pass him in one of his fields. 'This is a no-pressure situation. I won't take it personally if you want to come back later – in fact, I won't even drink, so I can drive you. How does that sound?'

It sounds like pretty much the sweetest thing a man has ever said to me, and I feel a sudden rush of affection for him that translates into me placing my hand on his thigh and leaving it there.

'That's really kind. But I'll be okay – I just need to get a grip, and let myself decompress. I'm looking forward to a night away, honestly. It'll just take me a little while for my brain to accept that fact.'

He nods, and we spend the rest of the drive in comfortable silence. When we arrive at Briarwood, I immediately see that the transformation is well and truly underway.

There's a new roof, and the brickwork has been repointed. The driveway has been cleared and laid with fresh, pale gravel, and the gardens look less like a jungle. The fountain has been fully drained and all the moss and gunk cleaned out, and there's a new front door. There are building supplies around, and some scaffolding at the side of the house, so everything is still ongoing.

'Wow,' I say, climbing out of the car and gazing at it all. 'It looks so much better already. Where are all the work dudes?'

'I gave them the day off,' he says, winking at me. 'Told them I might get lucky with a hot chick.'

'No you didn't.'

'No, I didn't – obviously I turn into a wimp every time I'm around a man with a tool belt. Male banter is completely beyond me. I did give them the day off, though. Do you want to look inside?'

'Of course I do!' I say, skipping ahead, excited. I know he's pouring his heart and soul into this project – why wouldn't I be excited?

As soon as I step into the hallway, I see the difference. The dark, gloomy wood panelling is now glinting, and the cloakrooms are being opened up to create more space and light. The floor is covered in sheeting to protect it, and the whole place is scattered with discarded tools and buckets and ladders.

'Still a work in progress,' he explains, leading me up the stairs. I nod, and look into one of the rooms. There are new windows, and new sinks, and the horrible old carpets have been pulled up so the floorboards beneath can be sanded down.

'I was going to make them all en-suite,' he says, as we wander. 'But I ended up deciding it was too much hassle. Instead I'm going to add extra bathrooms on each floor, as well as a kitchen and communal living space. It'll cut down the number of places, but that's okay – it's not like when I was here, and they needed to fit as many kids in as they could.'

We walk up to the top floor, and again I see new windows, new sinks, and the beginnings of re-decorating. The damp patches have gone, as has the football wallpaper. Instead, the rooms that have been completed are painted cream, making them feel brighter and airier and bigger. It now feels less like something from a horror film, and more like a posh character hotel.

I ooh and aah at appropriate places, and we make our way back downstairs, where he wants to show me the ballroom – or what used to be the communal dining hall.

The changes here are obvious. The plasterwork on the ceiling has been repaired, and the beautiful bay windows have been fixed, not replaced. The fireplace has been restored to what I have to imagine was its former glory, as have the chandeliers.

The floor has been stripped back to bare wood and polished, and the whole room looks magnificent. The walls are still covered in hideous green wallpaper, but I'm guessing that's next for the chop.

'Wow again,' I say, standing in the centre of the room and spinning around to create a panoramic camera effect through my own eyes. 'This is gorgeous. I swear it still smelled of boiled cabbage last time I was here. What will you use it for?'

'This,' he says, strolling around and stroking the dado rails, 'will be where the magic happens. It'll be an open-plan workshop, where people can focus on their projects, and hang out and chat, and where we can hold meetings and events. Because I'm adding in the kitchens and lounges on the floors above, it will never need to smell of boiled cabbage again.'

'That's a blessing. I can just picture it. All your mini-geniuses, hard at it, music coming from the speakers, cans of Red Bull everywhere – it'll be amazing.'

He seems delighted at my response, and it makes him look about twelve.

I grin at him, and say: 'There's just one problem with all of this . . .'

'Oh? Go on, then, what is it?'

I walk up to him, wrap my arms around his waist, and nuzzle into his chest. Because I'm a big fan of the Goonies.

'The problem is, I did all that bloody cleaning for nothing, didn't I? Why did you let me clean all those windows and sinks and carpets when you knew you were going to replace them?'

He kisses the top of my head – I still can't used to the fact that he's tall enough to do that – and spins me around the room in a loose version of the waltz hold.

'That's not a problem,' he says, as we whirl around.

'That was me being sneaky. I just wanted to keep you around a bit longer.'

'But I got paid for work that didn't really need doing!'

'Money well spent,' he answers, twirling me all the way towards the bay window, where we sit in a slightly crumpled heap on the love seat. 'I got me a hot chick, didn't I?'

I laugh, and look around the room once more. It really is lovely, and now it doesn't feel like a prison mess-hall, I can at least partly picture it the way Edie remembered it back in its hey-day.

'What are you imagining? I can see your eyes doing that dream-sequence thing they do when you're lost in thought.'

I make wavy lines with my hands, which is my physical interpretation of a dream sequence, and reply: 'I was just picturing Edie here, when she was a young gal about town. It must have been quite something, don't you think?'

'Definitely. I found quite a few boxes of stuff in the cellar actually, that she might be interested in. Loads of documents that would have seemed boring at the time, but are fascinating now – details of the servants' pay, what food they produced in the gardens, how many pheasants they shot that season, that kind of thing. Lots of photos, too – I might ask her to help me go through them, see what we come up with. It all needs archiving, really.'

'Then Edie's your woman. She was the village librarian for years. There might even be some of her, who knows?'

'That would be a treat . . . and, now the work here is progressing all right, I did have another idea.'

'You are just one big lightbulb moment, aren't you?' I say, nudging him.

'Yep. Practically my own strip light. I was thinking we could possibly hold Edie's party here. There's almost two weeks to go, and by that time, I could have the decorating done. The rest of the building would still be a disaster zone, but I could at least make it safe. The café is lovely, and I get it if you think this is a dumb suggestion, but it will be crowded with everyone there. And Edie's face . . . well, she had her own lightbulb moment when we talked about this place, didn't she? What do you think?'

I glance around the room – at its grand, high ceiling, the ornate plaster coving, the magnificent fireplace and glittering chandeliers. I imagine it, back in Edie's youth, filled with the light and music and laughter of the pre-war generation. I imagine it now, filled with the light and music and laughter of 2018 – and it feels perfect. Just perfect.

'I think,' I say, kissing him gently on the lips, 'that it's a brilliant idea. I'll speak to Cherie about it, see what she thinks. We'll have to sort some logistics, but Cherie and Laura live for that kind of thing. We could give Edie an actual ball in a ballroom. I think she'd love it.'

'You do? You don't think it might mess with her head? With the whole . . . fiancé thing?'

I ponder that, and shrug.

'I don't know. I don't think so. Edie's head is a mystery

to all of us, to be honest. She didn't seem at all sad when she was talking about it in the pub – she seemed keen to visit. But again, leave it with me. I'll consult the village elders and see what their opinion is. Either way, it's really kind of you. For a socially awkward geek boy who claims to dislike people, you're surprisingly thoughtful.'

He makes an 'aw-shucks' gesture, and stands up. He holds out one hand to me, and I take it. We practise our tango, banging heads with a thud at one point, and then our quickstep. It's much easier not to fall over things or crash into tables in an empty ballroom than in a café, I have to admit.

By the time we've danced, we're both hot and sweaty, and I have the perfect suggestion for how we can cool off.

It's time to live the dream – and finally go skinny-dipping with him, rather than stalking him from the bushes.

Chapter 26

The water in the pond is clear and fresh and absolutely bloody freezing. It might be a warm day, but it's still only spring, and the temperatures are skin-puckeringly low.

I cling onto Tom, shivering and laughing, holding onto his shoulders as we both kick our legs to warm up.

'This,' I say, grinning up at him, 'was a lot more romantic in my head.'

'I know,' he replies, pulling me in closer so our bodies are crushed against each other's. 'And in my defence, I'd like to point out that it's freezing cold. That never has a flattering effect on manhood.'

I kiss him, long and slow and luscious, wrapping my legs around his waist. There's an immediate and pretty flattering response in the manhood department. 'I don't think you have anything to worry about . . .'

His hands are wandering across my back, and I'm getting goosebumps for all kinds of reasons now. We kiss again, and finally pull apart when we're both desperate for air.

I reach up, and stroke his hair. It's shining with droplets of water, and now he looks more like a seal than a mole.

'Did you know I've been stalking you here?' I ask, leaning my head back while he kisses the sensitive skin of my neck.

'I didn't, no. I'm guessing you must have liked what you saw, as you're now naked in here with me . . .'

I am naked. So is he. It's all very racy. I don't have a lot of problems with my body – something in the way my mother raised us taught us to see ourselves as complete, however we looked, which is a lesson I really should thank her for. I'm tall and lean and strong, and even though I don't have much in the boob department and will never be considered curvy and cute, like Laura for example, I don't feel unhappy with what I've got. My body does its job well – it gets me through its busy days, and lets me stay active, and right now, is allowing me some pretty amazing sensations on the pleasure front.

As for his . . . well, I've seen it before. But up close and personal, it's even better. Awesome, in fact – pale but perfectly formed, like a Roman statue in an art gallery.

He's also weirdly okay with all this communal nakidity, to use a made up word – I'd expected him to be more self-conscious, a bit bashful maybe, but in fact he was the first to whip off his clobber and do a running jump into the water. Something I think he regretted two seconds later, but such is life.

Perhaps this was the perfect way to do things – we've

skipped the awkward fumbling and bra-unhooking and trying to find a way for two tall people to undress in a camper van with any shred of dignity. We didn't have to hop around on one leg getting pants off, or worry about a slow reveal – we just went for it. The stuff of dreams.

'I did like what I saw,' I reply, running my fingers along the muscles of his shoulders, feeling a childish urge to shriek: 'Mine, all mine!'

'But the first time I saw you, I thought you might be Edward Cullen, so that didn't really count. The second time, you were in here with Rick Grimes, and I was hiding in the bushes. It was the day I delivered Baby Groot, and I was all a-blush while I watched you.'

He finishes nuzzling my neck, and moves back to my lips for a few minutes, one hand on my back, keeping me close.

'Was that the day the rains came? I was actually thinking about you at exactly that moment. The rain started to lash down, and at first I was going to get out – but then I thought, hmm, what would Willow do? She'd tell me to loosen up. She'd tell me to be brave, and live in the moment – so I just laughed and laughed and laughed.'

'You did. I saw you. And while you thought I'd tell you to be brave, I was lurking in the shrubbery, being a coward.'

'Doesn't matter. You're here now, aren't you? All good things come to those who wait. Now, not that I'm not finding this every inch the erotic adventure, but I'm freezing my arse off.'

I give the arse in question a squeeze, and say: 'It still feels all there to me . . .'

'Whatever you just did, I couldn't feel it. My arse extremities have gone numb. Let's go back to the camper and . . . well, let's go back to the camper, and see what happens.'

'I know what's going to happen,' I say, swimming away from him to the bank and clambering out. I strut away from him towards our clothes, and know he's staring at my extremity as well. I give it a little waggle, just to let him know.

'What?' he says, catching me up. I pause, and look at him, wet and glistening and gorgeous. He's there, and he's real. He's not Edward Cullen – he's even better.

'I'm going to take you back there, and do terrible things to you.'

'How terrible?' he says, pulling on his Levis – he leaves his boxers off, I notice, which will definitely save time later.

'Terribly terrible. They might even make Baby Groot blush.'

He grabs hold of me before I have a chance to put my top back on, and wraps me up in his arms, crushing my breasts up against his chest.

'That,' he says, smoothing damp hair away from my face, 'sounds terribly wonderful.'

Chapter 27

Later, after terrible and wonderful things have happened, we are lying together in the bed of the camper van. We're both deliciously tired, and have topped up our energy levels with the Mars Bars. For some reason the celery didn't seem as attractive an option.

I'm in his arms, the duvet cover is tangled around our legs, and I'm feeling such a warm glow I could light up a cigarette. You know, if I smoked.

'What are you thinking?' I ask, poking him in the ribs. He's staring up at the roof, eyes distant, with a look of intense concentration on his face. Other men, I'd guess, would be asleep and snoring by now – but as ever, his brain is whirring away.

'Well, I was thinking . . .' he says, grinning at me. 'About those glow in the dark condoms.'

'Okay. They were useful. But how much thought can you really give a glow in the dark condom?'

'I was thinking,' he says, laughing at himself, 'that they would be extremely handy in the case of our much-discussed zombie apocalypse. You know, if the electricity was cut, and we hadn't been able to raid a supermarket for batteries?'

'You're right,' I reply, laughing with him. 'All we'd need to do is keep you in a permanent state of arousal, and you could lead our rag tag gang of maverick survivors to safety.'

'Ah, well, that's what I was thinking about – me being in a permanent state of arousal isn't practical, is it? Much as I adore you and have no doubts that you could make that happen, it would be tricky. It'd also give the zombies a really obvious target, and I don't fancy that at all. I was thinking that we could put the glow in the dark condoms on sticks, and use them like lanterns. What do you think?'

I run my hands over the firm planes of his stomach, and kiss his chest. The combination of this body and that totally unique brain is completely irresistible.

'I think you're a genius. We'd definitely all survive if you were in charge.'

'Good,' he says, kissing my hair. 'I feel like a proper alpha male now.'

We lie quietly, both happily lost in our thoughts and our fatigue. It's dark outside, now, and the only light comes from a small lamp in the shape of Yoda's head. It lets off an eerie green glow, just enough to show me that Baby Groot is in the windowsill, watching us. I half expect him to wave his little pipe cleaner arms and do a funky dance.

The rest of the camper . . . well, it looks like it's been hit by Hurricane Willow. My bag is dumped on the floor, various items of my clothing are strewn around, and my two goody bags have been emptied onto the table. It all looks a lot less tidy than it usually does, and I have a brief moment of anxiety when I wonder if I'm his Auburn, and all this chaos will drive him nuts.

'Is this okay?' I ask, suddenly concerned. 'Me being here, and messing up your space like this?'

He turns my head up to face him, and kisses my nose.

'What do you mean? It's more than okay. I needed a bit of mess in my life – you know that.'

'Yeah, but . . . it's annoying when someone comes along and does things differently, isn't it? Changes everything up? Even if you're happy to have them, it can be annoying.'

'I don't think you're talking about me any more,' he says, accurately. 'And honestly, no – I like it. I like the fact that your knickers are hanging off the taps, and your bag is set up like a booby trap by the door, and your celery is weirdly staring at me from the counter, like it's planning my death. I like it all. I've lived alone for so long.'

He sounds so wistful when he says this, and I wrap my legs around him so he's completely engulfed in me. Even before his parents died, I get the impression that his was a solitary life. He might never have had brothers and sisters who drove him nuts, and he might always have had his own room, but he also missed out on all the good stuff – the chaos and the camaraderie and the shared lunacy of family life.

The stuff that the rest of us take for granted. Even my

siblings tormenting me was better than being alone, at least they knew I existed. I was always at the heart of a big, loud, bonkers world – one that wasn't perfect, but was always vibrant and alive.

'This must be a big change for you,' I say, quietly. 'I understand why you haven't exactly been at the heart of the social whirl. You've basically been alone your whole life.'

He cuddles me tighter, and I hear him sigh in the darkness.

'It is a big change. But it's a change for the better. I know you've been scared . . . worried about how we'd manage this, given everything else you've got going on. But, at the risk of blowing my newly found alpha male image, I've been scared too. I've never had this before. I've never felt this kind of connection before. I've been happy enough, in my own weird way – but meeting you? Being here, in this place? It's like I've suddenly woken up in a whole new world.'

I fight the inappropriate urge to sing the Aladdin song, and reply: 'Well. We're both taking a risk, aren't we? On life. On each other. On glow in the dark condoms.'

'On killer celery.'

'On catching pneumonia in ponds.'

'On Baby Groot filming us and putting a sex tape on the internet.'

'On everything . . .'

'Yep,' he says, tugging the duvet up so it's actually covering us. 'On everything. I'm a regular daredevil these days, thanks to you. I've . . . well, I've had a wonderful day. An even better night. So – thank you, Willow.'

At that point my phone beeps, telling me a text has landed. I climb on top of him, so I can reach it on the floor, and stay there, straddling him, while I read it.

'Everything okay?' he asks, his hands on my hips.

'Yeah,' I answer, putting the phone back down. I stay on top of him though – because why not? 'Just Auburn, telling me they're both still alive, and sending me an assortment of 2,000 emojis. She's like a teenager.'

I lean down, and kiss him, my hair swishing around both our faces. I hear an owl hooting outside, and I know what it's telling me – it's telling me to go for it. That life's too short for playing games. That this man is worth going all out for. Or maybe it's just seen an especially juicy field mouse for its tea, who knows? I'm not one to ignore the wisdom of owls though – they're famous for it.

'Tom Mulligan,' I say, sitting upright and placing my hands on his chest. 'Inventor of the flange bracket. Owner of Briarwood, and the world's best collection of movie-related T-shirts . . . I love you.'

I see his eyes widen, and have a momentary jolt in my tummy, like I've driven over an especially bouncy dip in the road. I'm going to shoot that owl if this goes bad.

He reaches up, and holds my hair back, and pulls me down for a deep, sensual kiss. When he's finished, he says: 'Willow Longville, owner of bright pink hair and the most generous heart I've ever encountered – I love you too.'

I collapse down onto him, and he rolls me to his side, and wraps me up in his arms, head resting on his chest. The owl hoots, telling me well done, and I close my eyes, smiling against his skin.

I feel suddenly exhausted, in the nicest way possible. My breath slows, and my limbs turn to liquid, and I know I'm going to have the best night's sleep I've ever had. Because I have never, in all of my life, felt quite so safe – or quite so happy.

Chapter 28

I'm in such a deep sleep when the phone wakes me up that I haven't even been dreaming. I've been utterly comatose, snuggled up with Tom under the duvet, lost in our mutual calm.

I have my phone set to sound like one of those old phones – the ones with dials instead of buttons – and for a moment it feels like I'm in a scene from a black and white movie; that I'm Sherlock Holmes about to be called in to consult on a case at Scotland Yard.

Tom murmurs and moves beside me, and slowly my conscious rises to the surface. Damn that fiendish Moriarty and his dastardly ways.

I clamber over Tom, and grab my phone from the table. I'm still groggy, and wiping sleep from my eyes, and see that it is just after 5 a.m. – just after 5 a.m., and Auburn is calling me.

I suddenly sober up, the traces of sex and sleep fleeing my body to be replaced by an unpleasant surge of adrenaline – the kind you get when you trip up, even if you manage to stay upright.

'It's me! I'm here!' I say, as soon as my fumbling fingers manage to answer the call. 'What's wrong?'

I don't think I'm being presumptuous asking this – there's no way Auburn would call me this early just to ask where the granola is. At least I don't think she would.

'She's not here!' Auburn says, the panic in her voice immediately communicating itself to my brain. I take a deep breath, and try to stay calm – both of us freaking out isn't going to help anybody. I'm sitting on the edge of the bed, naked, and now shivering. I hear Tom moving around behind me, and nod at him gratefully as he covers my shoulders with the duvet.

'Okay. Do you mean she's not in the house?'

'What else would I bloody mean? I got up for a wee, and checked in on her, and she's not there. Her bed is empty!'

'Calm down, Auburn,' I say, even if I don't feel it myself. Tom has realised something is afoot, and is quietly getting dressed, pulling on his jeans and flicking the Yoda lamp on.

'Is the bed still warm?' I ask.

'What? How would I know? What does that matter?'

I feel like reaching down the phone line and throttling her, but luckily technology isn't that advanced yet. I remind myself that she's a novice at all this, and that's not her fault.

'Go and check. Just touch the sheets. If they're still warm, it means she's not been gone long, and won't have made it far.'

I hear her make a 'humph' sound as the logic hits her, and the sound of her walking through the house. A few moments later, she says: 'No. Stone cold. Oh God. What does that mean? What should I do?'

'First of all, stop going nuts. That won't help Mum, or you. This has happened before, and there are a few places she usually aims for. The café, the Community Centre in the village, and possibly this place – Briarwood. I'm here already, so I'll start at this end. I'll call Cal and Zoe, they're in the village and can look there. You set off for the café – she takes the footpaths over the field and then the coastal track. If we don't find her straightaway, I'll get the others on the hunt. Don't worry. We'll find her. It'll be okay.'

I hear her sucking in air, trying to calm herself down, and the sound of her pulling on her boots. I also hear the sound of rain, hammering away on the roof of the camper van – looks like April is living up to its reputation, and bringing us more showers, just when we least need them. A million thoughts flit across my mind: is she wearing shoes; did she take a coat; is she lying in a ditch; will we find her by the side of a stream all grey and sickly like E.T. . . .

I take control of all those thoughts, and instead I say: 'Keep your phone with you, and on. I'll call you soon. Be careful.'

Tom has not only listened in and put two and two together, he's already on the phone to Cal, telling him what's happened and asking for their help. I hear Cal's sleepy but reassuring Aussie drawl over the line, as he tells

Tom they'll get right on it. I wonder whether to call Cherie and Frank now, but decide to give it a bit longer. We might find her straightaway, and I don't want to cause a huge drama for no reason.

I can feel the guilt starting to seep through my mind as I get dressed, hopping around trying to get my leggings on, fumbling with the laces of my boots. I sit down on the edge of the bed, frustrated at my sudden bout of clumsiness. Tom kneels down in front of me, and ties the laces for me.

'It's okay,' he says quietly, holding onto my knees and looking up at me. 'We'll find her.'

I nod, abruptly, unable to speak. Unable to speak because right now, I'm almost paralysed by it – the guilt. What if I hadn't had a sleepover? What if I'd stayed where I belong, with my mum?

She hadn't seemed upset, but maybe I just chose not to see it, because I was so desperate for my night with Tom. And now my mother is lost, out there in the rain, just so I could have a shag. I cringe a little even as I think it – it's an unfairly crude way to describe what happened between me and Tom last night – but the fact remains. I left, and she went walkabout.

I stand up, and grab my phone. Tom gives me a waterproof to wear, and we share one small, sad smile, as though marking the end of the happy times, at least for now. I escaped reality for one night – now it's caught up with me, and is punching me in the face.

I'm feeling awful, and he knows I'm feeling awful, and he knows why – which must also make him feel awful. This has gone from blissful to bollocks in the space of one phone call, and I want to reach out to him – but I can't. I need to concentrate now, to be practical and calm and clever. I need to find my mum, and sort out all the other crap later.

He opens the door to the camper, and it looks spooky outside. It's that weird false dawn, a little while before true sunrise, when the light seems to filter through in a strange pale silver that stripes the sky. The rain is torrential, flattening the broad-leaved branches of the trees, splattering off the table in huge fat droplets, pooling in the dips and valleys of the grass.

I step down, and the ground squelches beneath my feet. It's cold, but not by any means freezing, which is something of a blessing. If she is out there, stranded, she'll be chilled but hopefully not hypothermic. I turn around, and say to Tom: 'Can you bring a bag with you? A blanket, some water? Just in case.'

He nods, and turns around to get them. I shelter under the canopy, and text the same to Auburn and Cal. She may well be absolutely fine – sitting in a bus stop thinking she's about to get the express to Lyme Regis, or waiting outside the Community Centre ready to start her yoga class, or sitting on the bench that overlooks the bay, waiting for dawn so she can do her sun salutations. I have to believe that, or I'll go mad.

Tom emerges, the hood of his jacket pulled over his head, carrying a torch. He takes my phone from my hand, and silently wraps it in a small plastic bag, the kind you keep sandwiches in. Ever the inventor. I give him a quick smile, and we set off, plunging through the darkness and the rain.

It's heavy going, the pathways slick with mud, gnarled tree roots slippy and covered in moss, leaping up to snaggle our feet. I feel like I'm in some weird episode of Bear Grylls, hacking my way through the Amazonian rainforest. Eventually, we emerge out into the clearing at the front of the house.

Briarwood looks menacing in the half-light, shrouded in shadow, rain drops bouncing off the plastic sheeting at the side of the building. The fountain is filling with water, and the newly laid gravel is sodden beneath our boots.

We split up and do a quick circuit of the house – it was left unlocked, and part of me wonders if she's made it in there. There's no response to our calls, so we leave again, back out into the wilderness.

'If she was coming here, where is she likely to be? What route would she take?' Tom asks, as we regroup by the front door, hiding beneath the porch.

'Last time she tried to make it here, she was on the main road up the hill, thank God. There are all kinds of short-cuts and pathways, but she stuck to the main road. Let's try there next. I'll just check in with the others.'

Tom ushers me back into the hallway of Briarwood, to

the smell of sawdust and paint, while I check my phone. There's already a text from Zoe, telling me she's not at the Community Centre, but they're carrying on looking around the village. I tap out a quick reply, asking them to look in the Pet Cemetery, in case for some reason she's gone to visit Pickle, our late, great Border Terrier. I add in a thank you and several kisses, remembering at the last minute to be grateful, before I call Auburn.

'Anything?' I ask, when she answers after a couple of rings. I can hear her panting and wheezing, and guess that she's run the whole way from the cottage to the café. Her poor ciggie-addled lungs are not happy.

'No! I'm here now, in the garden, and she's nowhere. I even checked in the dog field, and in the sheds where they keep the barbecue, and around the back of the bookshop. Nothing. Where else should I go? I'm so scared for her, Willow – it's bloody awful out here, anything could have happened!'

'Thinking like that won't help,' I reply, as it's exactly what I've been telling myself. 'Check down by the bay – she likes sitting on those big rocks and watching the sea. It can come in quite high, so be careful. If she's not there, walk up the pathway along the side of the cliffs – there's a little bench there where you can look down at the beach. She likes that too.'

'I know the one,' she replies, and I can hear her moving off again. 'We went there the other day and she told me the names of all the birds. I think she was making them up though – I'm not sure the Snozz-Wozzle Puffin-Pie is real . . .'

I have to smile at that – our mother, channelling her inner Roald Dahl. I say goodbye to Auburn, and Tom and I set off again.

He leads me towards his car, and I try to shrug him off.

'No,' I say, shaking my head, seeing raindrops fly from it with the gesture. 'It's better to walk, so we can check out the footpaths as well.'

'It's not,' he replies firmly, opening the car door, and bundling me inside. 'You said she took the main road last time. There's no reason to assume she hasn't this time, and this will be quicker and drier. We can do a quick circuit in the car, and if we don't see her, we can double back and do it again on foot. Trust me, I'm a mad scientist.'

I can't argue with his logic, and am grateful that at least one of us still possesses some. I'm trying to sound level-headed to my sister, but inside, I'm coming apart. Tom flicks the heating on full, and I'm even more grateful when warm gusts of air start to cloud out onto the skin of my wet, trembling hands.

'Does she have a phone?' he asks, putting on the lights, carving out two tunnels of yellow in the gloomy air around us. The rain stripes down through them, neon blobs against the darkness.

'No,' I say, regretfully. 'We tried – I thought it would be sensible. But she just couldn't get the hang of it at all, and it made her feel bad about herself, so we gave up.

Maybe we shouldn't have, maybe I should have tried harder . . .'

'Stop doing that,' he says, frowning as he negotiates the car through the gate posts and heads for the main road.

'What?'

'Stop beating yourself up. We can set aside some time for that later, if it makes you feel better. But for now, concentrate on looking through the windows – I have to concentrate on not crashing.'

I nod, because he's right. I can't let my self-pity party get in the way of the mission.

He drives at a snail's pace, because he can – it's not like there's any other traffic out here at this time of day.

I wind the windows down, because I can't see out of them properly when they're steamed up, and the rain lashes in, slapping my face and his. He doesn't say a word, just blinks it away, because he obviously knows why I'm doing it. Killer brain, three steps ahead.

I look out of my window, and out of his, and out of the windscreen, the wipers flashing away on the highest setting. I shine the torch out into the hedgerows, startling a fox, who stops what he's doing and stares up at me, the light reflecting from his eyes before he scampers away, fur flattened and wet.

Tom stops at each of the footpaths, and I examine the gates and stiles, looking for any evidence she's passed this way. Auburn calls from bench, to say there's no sign of her – I tell her to head to Frank and Cherie's farmhouse.

Mum's never gone there before, but at the very least, I know they'll look after Auburn – who is now sounding so desperate and anxious that I'm almost as worried about her as Mum. She's been tense ever since she got here – I've noticed all the twitches and tics and nail biting and the constant movement. This might be enough to push her over the edge, and nothing will be more effective in preventing that from happening than getting some TLC from Cherie.

I see texts have landed from Laura, and from Scrumpy Joe, and realise that Zoe and Cal must have raised the alarm to spread the search more widely. Becca and Sam are left alone as they have Little Edie to care for, and Big Edie is automatically immune due to being almost a thousand years old.

I feel my eyes fill up a little with truly pathetic tears – this is a terrible situation, but I am so grateful to have such friends around me. Out here, in the middle of nowhere, the police force would consist of two bobbies in a patrol car if we were lucky – hopefully it won't come to that, and this lot are likely to be even more effective. Their help means the area around the Rockery and the outer edges of the village are now also being checked.

'No news?' asks Tom, eyes still glued to the road. The light is starting to filter through the rain clouds now, as the sun at least tries to rise. The world looks grey and miserable, but those first fingers of brightness chase the shadows from the trees and begin to dispel at least some of the apocalyptic gloom.

'No, not yet,' I say, resuming my eagle-eyed surveillance out of the side of the car. I feel his hand reach out and squeeze my thigh, but don't have it in me to respond beyond a small smile.

'It'll be all right,' he says firmly, following the curve of the road down the hill.

'You don't know that,' I reply, feeling unfairly annoyed – it's exactly what I've been saying to Auburn, but for some reason, I don't want to hear it myself. 'You don't know it's going to be all right. Look at this weather. It's dark, it's dangerous – anything could have happened to her. I never should have left her . . .'

He ignores that, but keeps his hand on my leg. I leave it there, because none of this is his fault, and I already feel bad for snapping at him.

My mind is working overtime, conjuring up every hideous scenario it can – the flip side of having a vivid imagination is the way it can mess with you. I see Mum lying in a heap on the beach, pale and still as the waves wash over her lifeless form; I see Mum collapsed and in pain on one of the treacherous cliff-side paths; I see Mum kidnapped by human traffickers and on her way to Marrakesh . . . and finally, miraculously, I see Mum.

Not in my imagination – I actually see her. We're crawling down the hill, me shining the torch through the open windows, and I catch a glimpse of something that doesn't quite belong. It stands out from the soggy green shades of the bushes and hedgerows and the black tar of the road. It stands out because zebras do not roam wild and free in the Dorset countryside.

'Stop!' I yell, trying to pull open the car door before he's even had time to brake properly. 'I think I see something!'

I almost fall over as I clamber out of the car, and he is by my side in seconds. We abandon the Fiat, doors open, headlights cutting a path through the grim dawn morning. I run over to the side of the road, and see one leg stretched out – a leg dressed in a zebra-print onesie.

My relief only lasts for a few seconds, because as I reach her, scrambling through the bushes, overhanging branches tearing at my face, I see that she is in a bad way.

She's curled into a foetal ball, her arms wrapped around herself to try and stay warm. Her onesie is soaked through, clinging to her body, her hair a slick tangle around her face. Her cheeks are pale and glistening with rain, and her ankle is swollen and twisted, skin shining white around the bruises. She's wearing her fluffy moccasin slippers; one is still on, coated in mud and clinging leaves, the other cast off from her injured foot.

I throw myself down next to her, aware that Tom is right behind me, and cradle her head. I drop the torch, and it lands next to us, casting a bright light over the bushes and sending a flurry of scared wildlife away in a sinister scuttle.

I stroke her hair away from her face, hold her cold hands, and call her name, praying that she responds.

'I'll get an ambulance,' says Tom, reaching for his sandwich-bagged phone. The rain isn't letting up.

'Wait a minute,' I say, rubbing her hands, and hoping for her eyes to open. 'It'll take forever for one to get here – if she's conscious, we're better just getting her in the car, warming her up, and going straight to the hospital.'

He nods, and takes off his coat, covering her with it to shelter her from at least some of the rain. His Goonies T-shirt is immediately soaked through as the storm continues, but he doesn't seem to even notice.

'Mum . . . Mum, wake up! It's me, it's Willow!' I say, desperately.

Her eyelids flicker, and her fingers weakly grasp mine, and eventually, she opens her eyes and looks up at me. She stares, and smiles, and finally speaks.

'Willow. I was looking for her,' she says, her voice tiny and low. 'I was looking for Willow. The one with the pink hair. My baby girl. She went for a sleepover, and I had to go and collect her.'

I realise that my hair is plastered to my scalp, dark with rain, and to her, probably doesn't look even the smallest bit pink.

'It's me, Mum,' I say, sounding ragged, 'I'm Willow, the one with the pink hair. I'm here. I've got you. It's all going to be okay now . . .'

Chapter 29

'Where are we?' asks Mum, clinging on to my hand. 'Why are we here?'

She's lying in a hospital bed, and I'm sitting next to her on one of those hard plastic chairs that's already made my bum go numb.

'We're at the hospital, Mum,' I say, calmly. 'You had an accident, and you needed some X-rays, so we brought you here. Everything's all right.'

She nods, and settles, letting her damp head fall back onto the pillows. This is approximately the fifteenth time that she's asked me this, and each time, I have to explain again.

She was rushed through triage and on to an assessment ward, where she was warmed up and given pain relief before being taken through for the X-ray. They're holding off on giving her anything to eat or drink until we know if she needs surgery, but the staff here seem to think she'll be okay. She was cold but not hypothermic, and other than the ankle, doesn't seem to be hurt.

I've not left her side since we got here, apart from a quick trip to the loos to get changed. Laura turned up with spare clothes, which I'm now wearing – the red tartan jumper is way too big on the chest, and way too short on the arms, and the green leggings end just below the knee, but at least they're dry. I'm finally starting to warm up, and have been force-fed hot coffee and choco-late croissants.

Cherie has opened the café early, and Laura's headed back there now – sounds like it's turned into a refugee camp for survivors of the Great Lynnie Longville Escape Plot, with Matt and Laura and Cal and Zoe and the teen-agers and the Scrumpy J Jones Collective all retreating there to eat and drink and reassure each other.

Laura looked relieved to see we were all alive, but couldn't get out of the place quick enough – I know from Cherie that she hates hospitals, a throwback to the time her husband David was on a life-support machine and she had to decide to switch it off. I appreciate the fact that she's faced her fears, and done a charity run anyway, bless her.

Tom has also changed – Laura brought some of Matt's things with her as well – and is modelling the same clownish look as me, in jeans that end above the ankle. Serves us right for being stupidly tall. Just like I've not left Mum's side, he's not left mine.

Auburn arrived half an hour after us, wet and bedrag-gled, her long hair snaked over the shoulders of her

Berghaus coat, her face pale and stressed, and her huge eyes panicked.

'How is she?' she'd asked, running over towards us, her wet boots sliding on the floor.

'She's going to be all right,' I replied, smiling. She looked terrible, and Laura hadn't brought spare clothes for her because she didn't know she was there. She was dripping all over the lino, looking far from fine, and once she was reassured that Mum was okay, I persuaded her to go off with Tom and find the canteen.

He didn't want to go, but I insisted.

'Please,' I said, holding his hand. 'She needs to calm down, and warm up, and you'd be doing me a favour. She needs a break and she won't go alone.'

He'd nodded, and led Auburn away in the direction of the lifts. I watched them go, and felt a sense of relief that I wasn't proud of. Truthfully, I needed a break too. I needed a break from worrying about Auburn, and a break from worrying about Tom, and a break from simply being around people. Obviously, I was still around people – even in the morning the hospital is busy – but they're not people I need to do anything for.

I've towel-dried my hair, and taken off my boots, and can finally feel my toes again, snug in Laura's fluffy red bed-socks. I lean back in the chair, and look at Mum.

She seems so small and vulnerable, tucked up in her bed. Her hair is bunched up around her like a halo, and her eyes are closed. I can tell she's not asleep, but at least she's resting and not in pain. I cling onto her hand, as much for my reassurance as hers.

Now that I'm finally alone, I let myself breathe. I let myself acknowledge how close I came to losing her, and how terrifying that was. I know that I'll never, ever forget that sight – the sight of her, curled up in a ball in the mud in a zebra-print onesie, looking for all the world like she'd gone forever.

I feel the trauma seep through me, as chilling as the rain, and screw up my eyes in fatigue. Hospitals are always so bright, aren't they? My eyeballs are sore from exhaustion and strip lighting.

Mum stirs slightly, and looks up at me. I know what's coming before the words even leave her lips.

'Where are we?' she asks, her gaze darting anxiously around at the other cubicles and the passing nurses and the squeaky-wheeled trolley of tea being pushed by an auxiliary. 'Why are we here?'

'You had an accident, Mum,' I reply, again. 'You hurt your ankle, and we needed to bring you to the hospital for an X-ray. It's all fine, honest. I'm here.'

She nods, and accepts what I've said.

'Can I have a cup of tea?' she asks, like a child begging for pudding.

'Not just yet,' I say, looking around for someone to bother. I see a harassed-looking doctor walking towards me, and stand up to get his attention.

He nods, and walks over, and I see the effort it takes

for him to smile. He's probably been on shift all night, and even in Dorset, has most likely been dealing with more than his fair share of drunks, drug addicts, and car crashes. We were probably just the cherry on the cake.

'Good news, Mrs Longville,' he says, patting my mum on the shoulder. She smiles at him, but I can tell she's feeling uncomfortable – she doesn't know who he is or what he's talking about. Her short-term memory seems to be completely shot to pieces by the events of the night. All she knows right now is that she wants a cup of tea.

'The ankle is broken, but it doesn't need surgery,' he tells us both. 'It's just a minor fracture, and should heal well. We're going to keep you here for a day or so, Mrs Longville, with a splint on, until the swelling goes down. After that, if all goes to plan, we'll fit you with a very stylish support boot – we have them in different colours, you'll be the envy of all your friends!'

Mum looks at him like he's mad, and I hold back a laugh. He's trying to be nice, obviously, but it isn't working.

'I can't imagine that I will,' she replies, frowning. 'If I'm wearing odd boots, that's not going to get me on the Britain's Best Dressed list, is it? Plus, it's "Ms", not "Mrs". Can I have a cup of tea now?'

The doctor looks slightly taken aback, but agrees to the tea, which is when she loses interest in him completely. She lets out a mammoth whistle to attract the attention of the auxiliary with the trolley, and all seems to be well with her world, at least for the time being.

I let her get on with it while the doctor takes me to one side and explains more – she'll take at least six weeks to heal completely, he says, but once the swelling is gone and the boot is on, she'll be able to walk on crutches. She might need to use those for a couple of weeks, or possibly be able to bear weight sooner, depending on how it all goes.

'She's actually in very good physical condition,' he adds, glancing at her sadly. I feel his pity, and decide I don't like it. I like it even less when he carries on.

'If you need more help, I can arrange for a visit from social services. You shouldn't have to deal with this alone,' he says, sympathetically.

'I'm not alone, and we already have a social worker, and I'm fine. Thank you.'

My tone is maybe a little sharper than it should be – the man is only trying to help – and he raises one eyebrow at me.

'Well, it's not just about you, is it?' he replies, not unkindly. 'It's about her. She was lucky tonight. These things happen, and it's nobody's fault – I'm just saying that if you need help, then get it. For both your sakes.'

I nod, and shake his hand, and keep my mouth shut – because of course he's right. We were lucky. This could have all ended so much more badly than with a stylish boot, and I know I'm only being waspish because I'm feeling so guilty about everything. That's my load to carry, not his.

I sit down next to Mum, who is gratefully sucking up

milky tea from a plastic beaker and a straw. She finishes it off, and passes it to me with a satisfied sigh.

'That was disgusting,' she says, 'full of sugar. My teeth might fall out immediately.'

I glance at the beaker – she's drained every last drop – and decide it can't have been quite that disgusting.

She seems exhausted after the effort of drinking the tea, and I press the button on the bed controller so she can lie flatter. Obviously I get it wrong first time and we spend an amusing few moments with her going up and down. It makes her laugh at least, and eventually she gets settled, sore foot propped up, head comfy, one hand still in mine.

She looks up at me, and around at the ward, and I can almost pinpoint the moment she loses her grip on the here and now.

'Where are we?' she says, tiredly. 'Why are we here?'

I puff out a long, slow breath, and give her the usual reply, and encourage her to close her eyes and rest. I know she can't help it, but I'm really very tired myself now, and it would be a relief to us both if she could get some sleep.

She nods, and closes her eyes, and seems to drift off. I tuck her hand back beneath the blankets, and stand up to stretch. Laura's jumper rides up with the movement, and I flash the auxiliary with my belly button. Lucky devil.

I see Tom and Auburn heading back from the lifts, and smile as they walk over. I make a 'shhh' gesture with my fingers, and point to Mum, who at least appears to be sleeping.

Auburn has taken off the Berghaus, and also her jeans, which were soaking. She's wearing a long shirt-dress over the top, which protects her modesty, if not her knee caps. Tom, I can see, has donated Matt's socks to her cause, his bare ankle bones peeking out between his jeans and his still-wet Converse. I hope he doesn't get trench foot.

Auburn is holding a plastic coffee cup, and her hands are so jittery, she's splashing the liquid over the sides and onto her fingers. Tom notices, and takes it from her without a word. He puts it down on Mum's table, and wraps me up in his arms for a hug.

He kisses me briefly on top of my head, then lets me go. I feel strangely distant from him – from everyone in fact – and slightly as though I'm having an out-of-body experience. Hospitals will do that to a girl. I think it's the incessant beeping; it makes you feel like you're in a science fiction film.

'She okay?' he asks, quietly.

'Yeah, she'll be fine,' I reply, gazing at Auburn with some concern. She looks as though her head might explode sometime soon, like that scene in *Scanners*. Crikey. I really am losing it.

'It's just a minor fracture,' I explain. 'She'll be all right, really. Thanks for all your help tonight, Tom.'

'Don't be silly,' he says, also looking at Auburn now. She's moving from one leg to the other like she needs the toilet, and is chewing her lip so hard I can actually see it bleeding. She's staring at Mum intently, tearing at the skin inside her mouth.

'It's all my fault,' she whispers. 'She could have died, and it's all my fault. I'm bloody useless, and you'd both be better off without me.'

Tom glances over at me, and we both share a 'WTF?' moment. I reach out, and take her hands in mine. They're shaking and cold and feel fragile, like brittle twigs. Her nails are bitten and the skin around them is raw and tattered and red.

'Like Tom just said to me, don't be silly, Auburn,' I say, trying to steady her. 'This isn't your fault. If anything, it's mine for being away from home. I should have known it was a mistake.'

I cast a quick eye towards Tom, realising as I say this that it sounds harsh, but he shakes his head to let me know he understands what I mean.

'No, it's my fault,' she insists, eyes filling with tears that spill out and paint silvery lines down her grimy cheeks. I think I'm a bit grimy too, and definitely have a few scratches on my face from dashing through those bushes. We all look like we've been fighting a guerrilla war.

'Why do you think that?' I ask. 'These things happen – she's made a break for freedom before, you know. Even with all the security precautions we take, she sometimes manages it.'

'That's the thing,' Auburn mutters, staring at the floor. 'I didn't. I locked up and everything, just like you told me.

I got her settled off for the night – she seemed absolutely fine, she really did. I was a bit hyper, so I stayed up, arsed around on the internet for a while. Watched a bit of *Grey's Anatomy*. Then . . . well, then I went out for a smoke, didn't I? In the garden. It was before it was raining, and I sat out on the bench, and talked to Wurzel, and had a fag. I even felt quite pleased with myself for managing everything without you around. That's when I texted you. And when I came back in . . .'

'You forgot to lock the back door?' I finish for her, trying to keep any judgement out of my voice.

She nods, pathetically, looking at me with her tear-stained face and tangled hair and aura of utter desolation.

I know I need to reassure her. Tell her it's okay. That nothing disastrous happened, after all. Tell her we all make mistakes; that she won't make this one again; that we're all learning how to cope with a difficult situation. That she's only human, and none of us are perfect.

I know I need to do this, but it takes a few moments for me to be able to actually translate that into words and actions. Because – in all honesty – I don't want to. I'm wiped out, and exhausted, and angry, and kind of want to kill her. My one night away from home – my first night with Tom – was ruined, and Mum was put in a horrendously dangerous situation, all because of Auburn's need for a nicotine rush.

I can only imagine what this morning would have been like if she hadn't. Maybe I'd have woken up in Tom's arms, and we'd have had naughty morning sex, and eaten the rest of the Mars Bars, and everything would have been different.

Now, though, I can't even imagine being alone with him again – because this has been too much of a scare. I know I might change my mind, but at that precise moment, I can't imagine feeling confident enough to leave Mum on her own at all.

I'm angry, and sad, and tired, and wired, and all over the place. I force myself to calm down, and squeeze Auburn's hands.

'It's okay,' I say, trying to sound genuine, trying to remember the lines that will make me the kind of human being I want to be, instead of the resentful cow I actually feel like. 'We all make mistakes. You're only human, and none of us are perfect.'

She examines my face, my forced smile, and I know she sees through it.

'I know you don't mean that. I know you're upset,' she says, pushing me just a tiny bit further than I am willing to be pushed.

'I will mean it, later,' I reply, sadly. 'I know I will. For now, this is the best I've got, so please? Let's just leave it. We're all tired, and stressed, and there's no point making it worse, is there?'

She opens her mouth to argue – because she's Auburn, and she always argues. Because my big sister has never been able to let things lie. Because she always needs to take everything to its absolute limit.

This, more than the cigarette thing, annoys me – that she can't just let it drop. Can't just allow us all a moment to regroup. Can't leave me alone even when I feel like I'm at breaking point, because it doesn't suit her and her need for redemption.

I close my eyes, and pray for patience, and shove my hands under my own elbows.

As Auburn starts to say her piece, to carry on the self-flagellation that I just don't have the energy to cope with, Mum wakes up. We all see her come to, suddenly, eyes snapping wide open. She looks around, at the cubicles and the nurses and the other patients, and she says: 'Where are we?'

'We're in the bloody hospital!' I shout, before she gets to the second part of the same sentence I've heard over and over again all day, on a constant repeating loop.

She stares at me, looking shocked. Auburn stares at me, looking horrified. The auxiliary stares at me, looking strangely sympathetic. Tom stares at me, looking incredibly sad. He reaches out to hold me, and I push him away. I can't take his kindness, not right now. I don't want it, and I don't need it, and I certainly don't deserve it. I wasted the very last shred of my patience on Auburn, when I should have saved it for my mother.

I ignore them all, and dash to Mum's side. I take hold of her hand, and kiss her forehead, and whisper to her: 'I'm sorry I shouted. I was upset and tired. We're in the hospital, Mum. You had an accident, and we needed to get some X-rays done on your ankle. It's broken, but you're going to be fine. You'll get a stylish boot, and it'll all be okay. I'm sorry I shouted.'

She reaches up, and strokes my hair away from my face, tucking it behind my ears just like she used to do when I was a little girl.

'It's all right,' she says, smiling at me. 'You look like you need a sleep. You go off now, and have a rest. I'll be fine here. My daughter Willow will be back soon. She's just been for a sleepover at a friend's house.'

Chapter 30

I smile, and nod, and move away as quickly as I can. I don't want her to see me cry, and I don't have the energy to explain who I am again just now.

Tom holds out his hand, but I can't take it. I can't take anything at all. There are no vacancies in Hotel Willow's Brain.

'I'm going for a break,' I say, not meeting his eyes. 'Can you and Auburn stay with Mum for a minute?'

'Auburn can. I'll come with you,' he replies, firmly.

I place one hand on his chest, and look up at him. He's so perfect, in every way – but I can't be around him. Or Mum. Or Auburn. Or the kindly auxiliary. I need to be alone, just for a moment.

'Please, Tom. I just really need a few minutes on my own.'

I see him process this; see the conflict of emotions run across his face, his need to protect me battling with his need to respect me.

'All right. What will you do?'

'I don't know, go for a run or something.'

'In red bed socks?' asks Auburn, pointing at my feet.

'I'll jog on the spot. Look, I'll be fine – obviously I need to decompress. I'll be back in ten, and I have my phone with me if anything changes.'

I don't give them time to argue. I don't actually care what they think anyway. I know myself well enough to realise when I'm reaching bang-bang levels, and I'm teetering right on the edge. I stride off towards the lifts, and make my way to the foyer. I check my phone as I go, and see a text from Cherie, and one from Laura, which I ignore – I'll read them later, when I'm less insane.

Outside, it's the middle of the morning, which for some reason surprises me. You lose all sense of time and space in hospitals – they seem to exist in their own little reality bubbles; bright lights and loud noises and no windows and constant activity.

People are standing having cigarettes beneath the 'no smoking' signs, visitors are getting out of cabs, staff are scurrying around with lanyards around their necks, carrying Costa coffees in their hands. Just a normal work day for them.

The rain has faded to a drizzle, and the sun is dazzling. It's one of those days where the sky is going to end up constantly bejewelled with rainbows.

I breathe in the air – not exactly fresh, with all the traffic out here, but at least cool and clear – and do indeed jog on the spot. I realise within seconds that I'm too close to the automatic doors, which start to frantically open and close in response, and move further out, onto the pavement.

I do a few simple yoga poses, and it feels good to stretch out my limbs, feel my muscles strain, my spine expand, and my breathing flow through my body. I get a pitying look from a man in a wheelchair, a wolf whistle from a passing workman, and a thumbs up from a paramedic. Go me.

I stretch, and I clear my mind of everything: of Tom, of Auburn, even of my mum – all of it needs to go, if only for a nanosecond. I need to be Willow again, not a girl-friend or a sister or a daughter.

I let my thoughts drift to other times, other places. I think about the bay and the café and the bluebells in the woods. I think about Bella, and remind myself that someone really needs to go and let her and Rick Grimes out for a toilet break.

I think about the commune in Cornwall, and the view from the Twisted Sisters, and the time I went on a rib boat to see a seal colony off the coast of St Ives. I always felt like they were watching us, not the other way around, preening their whiskers and laughing at the exhibits in the floating human zoo.

I think about my friends in the village, and wonder how I'm going to wrap up a life-sized cardboard version of Anton du Beke for Edie, and how I really feel like watching all of the *Twilight* films in a row while drinking hot choc-olate with marshmallows and flakes.

I'm thinking about so many things, I barely notice when a jeep pulls up right outside the hospital entrance. It looks a bit like one of Frank's from the farm, and I wonder if it's Cherie, bringing me hugs and cake.

The jeep pauses for a second, engine running, and the door opens. I hear a brief exchange between the driver and the passenger, before he gets out.

He bangs the jeep door with his fist, and the driver beeps his horn in acknowledgement before pulling away and joining the queue of traffic waiting at the lights by the exit. I see the vague outline of a hand waving at me as he drives off.

The man stands still for a second, looking around him, as though slightly confused by the amount of people and cars. Like he's been dropped there from outer space. He hoists a backpack over his shoulder, and as he walks towards the doors, I see that he looks familiar. Different, but familiar. Bulkier than I remember, chestnut hair cut brutally short, skin brown and weathered from years living in a much hotter climate than rainbow-strewn Dorset.

He pauses, stares at me, and grins, looking me up and down and taking in my outfit.

'Hey sis,' he says, once we've eyeballed each other for a few seconds. 'You look like an elf who got shrunk in a hot wash. Where's your jingly-jangly hat?'

'Van,' I say, sighing tiredly. 'Just fuck off, will you?'

Chapter 31

I really don't need an extra layer of complication right now, but here it is, standing right before me, wearing cargo pants and an amused expression. Part of me wants to run into his arms and let him look after me, to feel as safe as I used to in days of yore – but I'm not a little girl any more, and anyway, by the time Van left, he was a snarky pig who constantly made fun of me. Small stuff, and nothing I still hold against him – but enough to make me wary.

'How is she?' he asks, dropping his backpack at our feet and giving me a hug. I hug him back – because I'm not completely immune to my big brother's charms. Just aware that there's a flip side.

'She's all right,' I reply, standing back and examining him. His eyes have big crinkles at the side of them, from smiling and laughing in the sun, and his hands are rough and calloused from outdoor work. He smells of coffee and spices, which tells me he's been to the café.

'Good,' he says, giving me a similar once-over. 'I turned

up at the cottage, and there was nobody home. The door wasn't locked, and when I went in Bella ignored me, as usual, but this other giant dog jumped all over me. Honestly, I thought I was a goner but he just wanted to lick my face. I let them both out into the garden to do their business, then headed over the fields to Frank's farm. Nobody there either, so I went to that café – Auburn told me you were working there.'

'And let me guess,' I say, smiling at the image. 'You found half of Budbury there on a sugar rush. Some of them also wanted to lick your face, and then they sat you down and gave you cake while they interrogated you?'

'That's about right, yeah. They told me what had happened, but that everything was under control, and that I should stay and eat cherry scones for five minutes – which, as I've spent the last three days in transit, I was happy enough to do.'

He pauses, and scratches his head, looking vaguely puzzled.

'It was weird actually – seeing Frank again, after all this time. He's in good nick, isn't he? And that Cherie one he's married – I just about remember her. And Joe, the cider guy, was there, with his kid, who I really don't remember. And Edie, the woman who ran the library, I can't believe she's still going. Then that Aussie bloke – Cal – gave me a lift here. I suspect the minute I left, the whole place exploded, and they all texted you at the same time.'

Ah, I think, caressing the phone I'm still clutching. He's

right, of course – and that explains the texts from Laura and Cherie. Cherie's will be straightforward, Laura's will feature an inappropriate amount of kisses and exclamation marks.

'I doubt it,' I lie, blatantly. 'You're not that interesting. What are you doing here anyway?'

'Auburn managed to get a message to me. I was overdue a trip back to the UK, so I thought I'd come and see you all. Maybe . . . well, maybe stay for a bit, see if I can help. I've been living in Tanzania, building a school. Unless you need a well digging in the garden, I might not be much use – but, anyhow, I'm here. Do with me what you will.'

I raise my eyebrows at that one – part of me would quite like him to turn around and get on the next plane back to Africa, but I know that will pass. Just like it did with Auburn. I'll start off guarded and cynical, and he'll win me over, and before I know it, I'll be completely dependent on them both.

Given the events of the last twenty-four hours, that doesn't exactly fill me with joy. I know Auburn made a simple mistake, but it's going to take me a while to forget about it. To feel safe leaving her with Mum again. To let my defences down and relinquish some of the control for Mum's care – because the first time I really did it, it all went spectacularly tits up.

'You look delighted to see me,' he says, nudging me so hard I almost trip over his backpack. 'Not.'

'I'm sorry,' I say, shoving him back – I learned long ago

not to let any of these swines push me around – 'I'm just tired. It's been a bad day. A bad year . . . look, I don't know how she'll react, okay? She might welcome you home like the prodigal son. She might tell you off for leaving your PE kit at school. She might not have a clue who you are. She might accuse you of stealing her chamomile tea bags. She's not at her best right now, and if she's asleep, it's probably best we leave her that way, all right?'

He shrugs, and accepts what I say without arguing. That's a good thing, given the state of my mood.

'Whatever you say, Will. You're the expert. Can we go in now? This might feel like spring to you, but I'm bloody freezing.'

Chapter 32

The next few days pass in a blur of discomfort, weird dreams, and hospital coffee. Mum takes a slight turn for the worse due to a bladder infection, but is finally allowed home after three days – wearing her very stylish boot.

She's accepted Van's presence without too much disruption, and in some ways, her Alzheimer's makes the change easier to accept – she simply behaves as though he never left. I don't know whether she's doing that deliberately, or if in her mind, this is all a continuation of some far-off weekend in 2001.

I have to admit it's handy having a big bloke around, getting her in and out of the car and helping her into the cottage. And I'm sure if we need a well building, he'll be brilliant.

Auburn is thrilled to see him, and the two of them lapse straight back into their usual banter. A tiny part of me shrivels at that – the not-very-mature Willow that lives inside me immediately feels left out again.

I'd just about started getting used to having Auburn here, and to enjoying her company, but now I'm slightly surplus to requirements as they laugh at each other's jokes and reminisce about their travels and swap stories about airport toilets in faraway lands.

Still, I have my hands full anyway – Mum is on the mend, but she's a long way from better. As I'd have expected, she discards the crutches as soon as she's home, and insists she can get around absolutely fine without them. She even does a mock moonwalk around the kitchen, announcing in a booming astronaut voice that she's taking one small step for womankind, clomping across the stone floor in her mighty boot.

I stayed in the hospital with her while she was recuperating, and have spent three nights almost-sleeping on a chair. The staff did at least manage to find me one with a cushion, but it wasn't the world's most restful.

I'm relieved to be home, and even more relieved to be in my own bedroom, surrounded by my own things, snuggled up with my own dog. Bella Swan has obviously missed me – I can tell by the fact that she lies on my chest instead of next to me. I stroke her furry little head, and let her lick my nose, and feel so much better now we're together again. Auburn and Van can bugger off to Timbuktu to save endangered peregrine falcons for all I care – I have my little Bella again.

I've left my siblings and my mother to it for an hour, while I chill out. No use trying to do more than I'm capable of, and as I'm still in the cottage, they'll hopefully be able to avoid disaster for a little while.

Having Van back is good, but it's going to be tough for him. He'll have to go through the same learning process that Auburn did, figuring out how to cope with our brand new mum – and all the sadness and frustration that brings with it. But as the pair of them are getting on so famously, maybe they'll be able to help each other.

Laura has been round while we were bringing Mum home, and the whole place is filled with fresh wildflowers in vases, as well as enough food to last us a week: home-baked bread, vats of soup in the fridge, a springy raspberry sponge on the kitchen table, almond and chocolate chip cookies in a tin, steak and ale pies with crusty pastry to go in the oven, creamy mashed potato that just needs warming up, a big jug of gravy. She's showing her love the best way she knows how.

Everyone else has been in touch, with offers of lifts to the hospital and pints in the pub and promises to do our shopping and weed our garden and walk the dog and basically do absolutely anything a human being could possibly need. Katie's popped in with Saul, who now wants a big boot just like Mum's, and Carole from the day centre sent us a lovely card signed by all the staff and clients.

There's been such an outpouring of affection and support that I feel a bit overwhelmed by it all – lucky, but overwhelmed. Like between all of that, and Van and Auburn, I might just disappear entirely.

I burrow down beneath the duvet, listening to the sounds of music flow in from the kitchen, accompanied by the wonderful tinkling of my mum's laughter, and close my eyes. Bella is snoring gently, letting out little puffs of air with each snort.

Disappearing, I think, might be a very pleasant thing – at least for a little while. Or sleeping, anyway, without getting jolted awake by somebody's heart monitor going off, or nurses brushing past me to check blood pressure, or the sad, solitary sound of someone crying alone in the night.

I'm just about starting to drift off into a blissed-out state of trance when Bella suddenly sits up, and dashes to the edge of the bed, dragging part of the duvet with her. Her tail points up in the air and wags frantically, and her nose sniffs and twitches.

Approximately thirty seconds later, my less sophisticated senses kick in as well – and I hear the car pull up on the gravel of the driveway. That's followed by a car door thudding shut, and an almighty great woof that booms all the way through my open window.

Bella, once she's confirmed who our visitor is, immediately curls back up in a ball and pretends like nothing has happened. No fuss, no excitement, no wagging tail or twitching nose – she's acting all cool as though she doesn't care about Rick Grimes coming for a play date.

I blow a huge raspberry just for my own amusement, and wonder if the same might work for me. Or if I could maybe get away with hiding in the wardrobe, or putting on a felt hat and standing in the garden, like a scarecrow.

I've not been alone with Tom since the night Mum went missing. He's been attentive and supportive and wonderful in every possible way – but we've always been chaperoned. By Mum, by my siblings, by nurses and doctors and other patients, by passing ladies selling hospital pens to raise funds for a new scanner.

Of course, we could have found ways around that. We could have built in time to sneak off to the canteen, or had a cuddle in the hallways, or even ridden up and down in the lifts together doing that thing where you jump before you reach the bottom to give your tummy a jolt. We could have escaped to the local pub for half an hour, or walked around the building, or even just sat in the car and watched the seagulls fight over discarded crisp bags.

We could have done many things – but we didn't. To be more specific, I didn't. I clung to all of my various chaperones with an air of desperation that now fills me with embarrassment and regret.

I avoided being alone with him deliberately, because I simply don't know how I feel about everything any more.

The joy of my night with Tom was so quickly overshadowed by the guilt at what happened with Mum that the two now seem to have become inseparable in my mind. I know that this makes no sense and has no logic – but emotions are notoriously bad at following rules. At least mine are, it seems.

I hide my head under the duvet for a moment, as I hear Auburn opening the front door, and welcoming him in. I hear Mum say something about a flange bracket, and Bella finally gives in and jumps off the bed.

There's the gentle hum of small talk, and I hear the door to my room creak slightly open. I know that if I stay under the duvet, and possibly snore or drool, he'll assume I'm asleep and leave me alone. He knows how tired I've been, and he won't disturb me.

I'm half-tempted, but I couldn't live with myself. Days ago, I was sitting on top of this man telling him I love him. Tom has had enough bad treatment to last him a lifetime, and he doesn't deserve me hiding from him and hoping he goes away.

'It's okay!' I shout, shuffling myself upright. 'I'm awake! Come in!'

I run my hand over my hair, and remember that I haven't brushed my teeth that morning. I might be confused by how I feel about him at the moment, but I still seem to be a girl.

He walks into the room, smiling hesitantly. He's sporting a black T-shirt with the *Jurassic Park* logo on the front, and his trademark Levis and Converse combo. I feel the usual urge to stroke his head, and realise that now I've seen him naked, I actually find him even more attractive. Thrown into the mix of the way my brain is eating itself, it's quite a maelstrom.

He perches on the side of the bed, and gazes around.

He's never been in here before, and I see him taking it all in: the knick knacks and paperbacks and dream catchers and photos and the papier-mâché Stonehenge I made in art class and the scattered assortment of Doc Martens. It's the complete opposite of his living space, but I can tell he likes it.

'The inner sanctum . . .' he says, grinning.

'Yep. It's a mess, isn't it?'

'It is a mess, but I bet you know where everything is.'

He's right – I do. It's chaos, but it's my chaos.

'How are you?' he asks, reaching out to stroke the side of my cheek. I let my face rest on his palm for a second, enjoying the touch of his skin on mine.

'Not too bad. Just very tired.'

He nods, and replies: 'I can imagine. I can go if you like – I just wanted to see you, check how you and Lynnie were getting on. In fact, I've just given her a present. I made it myself.'

'Is it a flange bracket?'

'No,' he says. 'It's a necklace.'

I raise my eyebrows at this, as it is an unexpected gift.

'Oh – that's nice. She does love a bit of bling, as long as it's from the hippy dimension . . .'

'It is,' he says, letting out a quiet laugh. 'I made it from rose quartz crystal, which is—'

'Associated with love, peace and healing, amongst other things. Obviously I couldn't grow up in this house without knowing my crystals, Tom.'

'Fair point. I see some amethyst chips on your dream catcher over there. Anyway – it is pretty, and she will like it, but that's not the point. It's actually also a gift for you. I put a tracker in it.'

I stare at him for a moment, wondering if I heard him wrong. Something about that whole sentence didn't make much sense.

'I put a tiny chip in it,' he explains, when I obviously don't understand. 'A bit like the technology they use in phones these days. And I can send you some details for an account it's connected to, where you can log on and see where she is. Or, at least, see where the pendant is. I just thought . . . it might help. Give you a bit of peace of mind.'

'Wow,' I say, shaking my head. 'You've put a tracker on my mother, using a crystal? That's like a human rights abuse – but . . . it's also brilliant. Thank you. So much. It's so kind, and clever, and awesome.'

He shrugs, and replies: 'Well. That's my job, ma'am – being kind and clever and awesome. Anyway, it might not work. She might just hang it on Wurzel the minute I leave, but who knows? If it can avoid anything like the other night happening again, it'll be worth it.'

I nod, and stare at the string of amethyst chips on the dream catcher in the window. Protection, cleansing of the spirit, and maintaining a sober mind. Maybe I should swallow it.

'I can't let anything like that happen again,' I say,

eventually. I'm struggling to meet his eyes, because that will feel too big. Too serious.

He reaches out and holds my hand, stroking the skin of my palm with his fingers.

'I know,' he says, quietly. 'I understand that. But it wasn't your fault, you know that, don't you? You being with me . . . that wasn't a mistake.'

I hold onto his hand, and force myself to look at him. Smiling, though – that's beyond me.

'Being with you was wonderful,' I say quickly. Whatever happens next between us, I don't want him to doubt that; to doubt that it was as real for me as it was for him.

'It was heavenly, in fact. It was the best night of my life, Tom – right up to the point where it turned into the worst. And now, whenever I think about lying there in the camper van, wrapped up in you, warm in that bed, I can't help seeing her. Seeing her lying in the mud with a broken ankle while I . . . well, while I was distracted. I know it doesn't make sense. I know it's stupid – but it's the way I feel, at least for now.'

He nods, and now he's the one avoiding my eyes. I feel terrible, because I know that being so honest is hurting him – but being dishonest would be even worse.

'I know. I might be socially inept, but I picked up on that in the hospital, when you were avoiding being alone with me. I think it was the time you offered to help the nurses collect the bed pans when I'd asked you to come for a walk that drove it home.'

I bury my face in my hands, and cringe. I'm such a knob sometimes.

'Oh God, Tom, I'm so sorry!' I say, my voice muffled through my fingers and hair. 'I really am. The last thing in the entire world I want to do is upset you, but I can't pretend like none of this happened. I've always been so focused, I've always looked after her, and we've always managed. Then Auburn came along, and I fell for you, and just for a moment there, I let my focus slip – I let myself think my life could be different.'

'Your life could be different,' he says, pulling my hands away and forcing me to look at him. 'Auburn is still here. Van is here. I'm here. I don't expect you to leave your mum any time soon. I'm not planning to kidnap you and keep you in the camper as my sex slave. I love you, and I'm here to help you, not pressurise you. I want to make your life better, not worse. The way you feel now . . . you're exhausted, and traumatised, and full of misplaced guilt. It's not the time to make decisions. It's just the time to rest, and recover, and sleep.'

I nod, my lips quivering with the effort of keeping my wrecked emotions under control, and let him gently lay me down on the bed, head on the pillow. He pulls the duvet up to my neck, and leans down to kiss me. I want to reach up, to wrap my arms around his shoulders and pull him in there with me. I want to pretend, at least for a few blissful hours, that everything can be okay, just like he says it can.

I want to do that – but I don't. Because it wouldn't be right, and I'd be doing it for such selfish reasons.

He tucks me in, and closes the curtains. The sunlight is still seeping around the edges, making the room hazy, misty with half-light and dancing dust motes.

'I'll speak to you later, Willow,' he says, from the doorway as he leaves. 'I love you, and I refuse to regret that, whatever happens. Now get some rest.'

Chapter 33

My name is Willow Longville. I am twenty-six years old. I live in a village called Budbury, with my mum Lynnie. I work as a waitress at the Comfort Food Café, and I run my own cleaning business called Will-o'-the-Wash. I have a dog called Bella Swan, and I love my life. In the last twenty-four hours, the following things have happened . . .

1. I have argued with my brother about the TV remote control approximately 3,457 times.
2. I have cleared out my wardrobe, and thrown away precisely nothing – it was just to keep me busy.
3. I have read a book about mindfulness, and learned precisely nothing – it was also just to keep me busy.
4. I have realised that doing things to keep me busy is silly, as I actually am busy.
5. I have cried. A lot.
6. I have stopped myself from driving over to Briarwood to see Tom about as many times as I've argued with Van about the TV remote.

7. I have cried even more.
8. I have felt sad and lonely, even in a house full of noisy people.
9. I have come to the conclusion that the 'I love my life' part of my diary entry might not be completely true any more.

Chapter 34

It's the very last dancing session before Edie's party. The party itself has now been relocated to Briarwood, after much discussion with the planners and the birthday girl herself.

By 'much discussion', I mean the twenty seconds it took for Edie to clasp her hands together in delight, pronounce she was fit to swoon at the very thought, and demand smelling salts to revive her. Once she'd made her feelings clear, the rest of us would move mountains to make it happen – there aren't many Edie Mays in the world, and if you're lucky enough to have one, you need to keep them happy.

Cherie and Laura have gone into organisational over-drive, and although I'd normally be involved, they've obviously had some top-level carrot cake meeting and decided that they'll do it all without me, as I have enough on my plate.

I'm grateful, because they're really not wrong. Mum's mental state has been erratic since she got home, and we're all hoping it's still because of the accident and the infection. She's had entire days where even my pink hair doesn't work, and where she suffers from spells of paranoia so vivid that she becomes terrified even in her own home.

On the days she has been more like herself, she's struggled to find words for the simplest of things, and has been confounded by such activities as making tea, brushing her teeth, and putting her shoes on. It's horrible to watch as she suffers, so obviously embarrassed and confused, lost in a private torture that we can only imagine.

She reads and re-reads her old notebooks incessantly, as though trying to find her way out of a maze, looking for clues as to who she is and who we are and how we should all be relating to each other.

The only bright spot has been her becoming obsessed with a TV show about American football called *Friday Night Lights*. She's sucked us all into her evil web with this, and I even caught Van shedding a tear after poor Tim Riggins got his heart broken. Mum declared after that episode that she was in love with Tim Riggins, and if ever he was in the neighbourhood, she'd kidnap him and lock him in the shed. Luckily, he's fictional, and lives in Texas.

Auburn is moving things along with the pharmacy and seems excited about it. She hasn't quite recovered from the night Mum had her accident, and I think is possibly even more affected by it than me. It seems to have knocked her confidence completely – I'd already made a vow to myself that I wouldn't be leaving Mum alone with her anytime soon, and she is totally on board with that. She doesn't want to be left alone with her – it's like she doesn't trust herself any more.

I suppose it will all take time to settle down, and maybe we'll find our balance again in the future – but with Alzheimer's, it's hard to anticipate a time when there will be any balance at all.

Van is making himself useful in any number of ways – he's taken over the garden and veggie patch completely, installed a rain butt and several bird feeders, and has been doing jobs around the cottage that I hadn't even noticed needing doing, like fixing leaky taps and oiling gate posts and putting new coat hooks up so Mum can see all her jackets without having to root through them all to find the one that takes her fancy.

I think it's his way of contributing to a situation that still makes him deeply uneasy. Of all of us, he seems the most disturbed when Mum has a bad episode. Again, it will take time – although I'm not sure how much of that we have.

I heard him today, out in the garden, on his phone. The kitchen window was open and he didn't know he was being listened to. He was talking to the airline about his ticket to Tanzania, so I have the feeling he might be leaving us sooner rather than later. I walked away as soon as I heard him – that's his business, and I've tried hard not to get used to having him around anyway. I need to accept his help while he's here, but not become dependent on it.

He's at the café tonight, along with Mum and Auburn, and everyone else who is about to graduate from Zelda and Mateo's *Strictly* masterclass. The three of them are set up at a table in the corner, along with Katie and Saul. Saul has clambered up onto Van's lap, and seems determined to stay there. Van, who I don't ever remember being especially patient with kids younger than him – by which I mean me – has obviously changed. His years living abroad, and working in a school, have left him softer, more responsive.

I've been helping Laura and Cherie set up the refreshments, and in all honesty can't wait to get the night over with. Mainly because of Tom.

I haven't seen him alone since the day he visited me at the cottage. Life has been both stupidly busy and stupidly tedious at the same time. I've done a couple of shifts at the café, with Mum there, and a few small cleaning jobs that she's come along to as well. She's not wanted to go back to the day centre yet, and I'm not going to push her – hopefully she will at some point.

He's called into the café a few times, or met Matt there for dog training sessions. There was a breakthrough with Rick Grimes when they finally exposed him to Midgebo, and even a bouncy black lab didn't push him into throat-tearing mode. We all watched over the fence by the field as Matt took the younger dog in, on a lead and well-controlled, and introduced him to Rick.

Rick clearly wasn't overjoyed with the whole experience – but he remained in sit position, Tom's hand on his head to reassure him, and managed to at least ignore Midgebo. No reaction at all is obviously much better than a reaction that involves bloodshed, and Tom was delighted. He even hugged Matt, which both of them regretted about one second in.

Other than these communal encounters, I've simply not seen him. He's called around at the cottage a couple of times, but I've always been with Mum or Van or Auburn, and we've not had the opportunity to talk properly at all. The way my mood has been, that's probably for the best.

I just feel like so much of the joy has been knocked out of me right now, and I can't find a way to get it back. The easy banter we used to share feels more strained; the casual touches that used to thrill me now make me feel awkward; the intimacy and closeness that once brought me to life now terrify me.

As seems to be my mantra these days, it's going to take time – but for now, I can't deal with anything more than my home life and my work. I hope that one day, I'll be able to look back on my time with Tom, and smile. Be able to feel my heart soar like it did that night. To remember it in all its glory, and revel in it.

But for now, none of that is happening – because every time I do let my mind drift in that dangerous direction, it automatically fast forwards through time, to finding my mum.

I don't know when – or even if – I'll feel differently, and I certainly don't expect Tom to hang around like a devoted puppy, waiting for that mythical time to come. I don't know what I expect from him, and that might be why I feel so tense and nervous the minute I see him slip through the café doors.

The room is packed, and Zelda has set up salsa music. I see my mum get up and do a few moves by her table – which is impressive given the size of her mighty boot.

Tom, as usual, sneaks in as though he's hoping nobody notices him – which is silly when you consider the fact that he's easily the tallest person in the room. I see him slink off to the side, and pretend he's interested in cupcakes, when actually he's just trying to be inconspicuous.

I see him cast his eyes around the room, and know he's looking for me, and my heart breaks a little for him. I wave, and head in his direction – I might be confused about our relationship, but I'm not made of stone.

'Yo,' I say, grinning at him. 'Salsa tonight. Got those snake hips ready?'

'My snake hips were born ready,' he replies. 'Ready to dance extremely badly. I see your mum's giving it a good shake, despite a fractured ankle.'

I glance over at her, and have to smile. She's doing the steps with one foot, the other planted steady, swivelling her body in time to the music. Van is jigging Saul up and down on his lap, and I can see them both giggling.

'Yeah, well,' I say, turning back to him. 'She always did have moves like Jagger. How have you been? I'm sorry I've been so . . . busy.'

He shakes his head, dismissing it, but I know he's pretending. I know he must be confused, and hurt, trying to understand it all. Everything changed so quickly, both our heads are still spinning.

'That's okay. I've been busy too. Moving on with the work at Briarwood, getting the place ready for Edie's party, planning world domination. The usual stuff. Are you all ready for the event of the decade?'

We're making small talk, and it sucks. This man means so much more to me than small talk – but it feels like all I can give him at the moment.

'Oh yes. The dresses are made. Anton has a big ribbon tied around his neck. Mum loved her necklace, by the way – she's barely taken it off. It goes perfectly with the frock, so if she does a runner during the party, she won't get far.'

He nods, then looks over at her again, and smiles.

'That's good. I want her to be safe. And I want you to be happy. You know that, don't you? I want you to be happy with me, but . . . well, if not, I'm a big boy. Don't beat yourself up about all of this. You're carrying enough of a load at the moment without adding me to the list. Just tell me what you need, and I'll try to make it happen.'

Just like that, he leaps out of small talk and into big talk. Big talk that isn't going to make either of us feel like getting our salsa on.

I reach out, stroke his arm, and wait until he looks back at me.

'Thank you,' I say, leaning up to give him a quick kiss

on the cheek. 'For everything. And in all honesty I don't know what I need. For someone to find a cure for Alzheimer's. For world peace. For someone to stop Mateo doing a bump and grind with Edie. I don't know. Tom, I don't regret anything that happened between us, I don't want you to think that – but for now, I think I just need a friend. Do you think you can manage that, or is too much to ask?'

I bite my lip as I wait for him to respond. I would totally get it if he decides it is, and walks right out the door.

Instead, he gives me a quick hug, and replies: 'A friend . . . well, I've not got much experience of that kind of thing, but I've seen examples on TV. I'll give it my best shot – as long as you let me be Joey.'

'I think,' I say, laughing, 'that you're all three of them – geeky like Ross, funny like Chandler, and sexy like Joey.'

He swaggers away, gives me a thumbs up, and drawls, 'How *you* doin'?' as he disappears into a mass of unco-ordinated Latin kings and queens.

I know he doesn't mean it. He couldn't quite hide that brief glimmer of heart-wrenching pain when I dropped the 'F' word on him. But he's trying – he's faking it, just for me, and I love him even more for it.

Chapter 35

On the day of Edie's party, the weather breaks again. The sunshine decides it's time for a rest, and tag teams rain in instead.

It's been falling in a steady drizzle all day, and ups its game to official Met Office 'bucketing it down' status by 8 p.m., when the party is due to begin.

It's added some logistical problems to the whole event, with more people driving, but Cherie has got around this by hiring a coach and driver to ferry people back and forth. I've driven us, in Auburn's car, after much faffing around and unusually high levels of girl-dom in the cottage.

The dresses have turned out well, if I do say so myself. All three of us are wearing the same design, as we have similar builds – simple satin sheath dresses with thin straps. Mum is in a beautiful dove grey that makes her eyes shine and is perfectly complemented by her secret spy tracker pendant.

Auburn looks amazing in deep green, her hair shining and loose, flowing over her back, wearing killer heels that make her as tall as Van. If not for the chewed nails she could pass for a retired supermodel.

Mine is black, because it clashes brilliantly with the neon pink hair and the matching boots. I have some black fishnets on, and have a full face of make-up, and I look okay. Which is good, because I'm feeling pretty shitty.

I've not seen Tom since that night in the café, and I miss him. I've tried analysing all of this, and making lists, and writing about it in my notepad, but it's that simple – I miss him. He brought something to my life that it's poorer without, and I don't just mean spectacular sex. I miss the chats peppered with geek references; I miss having someone to be myself with; I miss the sense of comfort and security I got when I was around him – the sense that no matter how bad things got, I'd always be able to slip my hand into his, and feel better.

And – let's be honest – I also miss the spectacular sex. It's all very sad, and blue, and miserable, and other words that I don't want to be associated with a party.

I pretended I was okay while we all got ready, and Van – handsome in a tux he borrowed from Frank, one with a distinct Seventies air with its wide lapels – set up the camera on a timer to take a group shot of us before we left.

'What a handsome bunch,' Mum said, as we all froze, like those families you see in sepia prints from a hundred years ago. 'Beautiful inside and out.'

I'd topped up Bella's water bowl, and left the TV on for

her. She doesn't mind being left for a few hours, but I always feel bad, and assume the voices will give her some company. This is undoubtedly silly, as Bella Swan is very self-sufficient – but to make myself feel better, tonight she cán watch *Animal Planet*.

We arrive at Briarwood a little early, so we can deposit Anton du Beke in the hallway, where he will be greeting the birthday girl in person. He spent the journey lying over Van and Auburn's laps in the back seat, and seemed perfectly happy with that.

By the time we pull up outside the house, the coach, along with several cars and jeeps, is already there – Cal and Matt have been on Big Man Furniture Moving Duty, and Laura and Cherie have been setting up all the catering.

Lizzie and Martha and Josh and Nate have been employed as waiting staff, and are all looking splendidly smart in black and white uniforms. Both the girls are wearing tuxedo-style outfits as well, with their hair slicked back in the style of a Fred Astaire film – perfect for the occasion.

Their job is to keep everyone's glasses topped up, and make sure nobody chokes on a chicken wing. Lizzie seems relaxed and happy, prowling around the outside of the house, taking photos on her phone – I'm assuming she's smoothed over her worries about Josh and Martha leaving, or at least managed to ignore them.

Briarwood itself looks spectacular. Tom has rigged up some projectors in the gardens, which are casting ever-moving spotlights over the front of the building, like the opening credits of a 20th Century Fox movie. The fountain has been dressed up with fairy lights in rainbow colours, and matching lights have been draped over the surrounding bushes and shrubs. The fact that it's wet just seems to make it look even more magical, the bright glimmers cutting through the darkness and the rain.

Inside, I see, as we all traipse through, is even better. The pots of paint and discarded tools and dust-sheets are gone, and although the side of the building with the old cloakrooms is closed off, the rest of it looks awesome.

Mr and Mrs F's old living quarters have been given a quick lick of paint, and completely emptied out. Now, the rooms are filled with trestle tables covered in damask cloths, heaving with every imaginable kind of party food – mini pies, vol-au-vents, platters of smoked salmon slivers, a whole roasted ham spiked with cloves, home-made Scotch eggs with piccalilli dip, skewers of tender seasoned pork, tiny glasses filled with rich chocolate mousse, dainty little marzipan tarts, a huge chocolate fountain surrounded by chopped strawberries and marshmallows and brazil nuts.

Another table is laden with drinks, and even ice buckets filled with bottles of bubbly and white wine. There's a whole selection of cider from Joe's cave, spirits and mixers, every kind of juice, and a small pile of Guinness cans that must be for Matt. One table has been set up as a cocktail bar, which Becca has promised to man with help from

Lizzie. The teenagers are here, filling up flutes with champagne, arranging them on silver trays so they can circulate among the guests with a welcome drink.

Edie's birthday cake – made by Laura of course – is lush. It spells out her name in giant sponge letters, coated in chocolate ganache, with tiny icing birthday wishes all over it. She's been bagging each of us in the café, getting us to pipe our own message on there, all week. I snap a quick picture of it on my phone – it's a work of art, and a tribute to Edie's much-loved presence in the village. It seems a shame to even eat it.

I realise as I gape at it that I've not eaten since breakfast – being girly takes way too much time – and barely restrain myself from diving right in.

The others drag me away, and into the ballroom. We all pause in the doorway, and look around, eyes wide. The only word I have for it is 'wow'. The chandeliers are lit, sparkling over the whole room, and the walls have been stripped and painted in one of those quiet, tasteful tones you see in National Trust properties. Tom has somehow managed to set up glitter balls, just like on Strictly, dangling from the ceiling, spinning and shimmering in the low light, casting dancing shapes on the polished floorboards.

A few tables and chairs have been scattered around the edges of the room, so people can rest between dances, and the love seat in the bay window has been set up as Edie's own personal space. It's filled with cushions and a sparkly sequinned blanket and even a footstool. The banner overhead pronounces: 'Happy Birthday Edie – you get a 10 from us!' in colourful letters.

I smile as I imagine Edie sitting there – the Queen of the Dance – and decide that this is the perfect place for Anton. I call Van over, and he sets him up, looking lovely in his top hat and tails, waiting for his 92-year-old date.

All of the café crowd are already here, dressed to the nines in fancy frocks and suits, dashing around making sure everything is as perfect as it can be in advance of the Queen's arrival. Laura is wearing a blue dress that shows so much cleavage she keeps staring down at it and hoisting the top half back up, her hair pinned and curls cascading around her neck like a curvy Jane Austen heroine. Cherie is magnificent in a vintage '70s frock covered in sunflowers, and Zoe has gone with the teenagers, and opted for a dinner suit instead.

The menfolk are looking approximately two billion times smarter than they usually do, and Frank is especially dashing, his silver hair Bryll-creamed into place. He's such a vibrant man that it's easy to forget how old he is – and he fits these clothes, and this scene, in a way that seems to come naturally to him.

Edie's nieces and nephews and extended family are here, as is pretty much the whole of the rest of the village, as well as some of her former colleagues from the library and her friends from the Community Centre. The table next to her throne is already heaving with gift bags and brightly wrapped presents. How absolutely brilliant to be as old as

Edie, and have this many friends. It's enough to make a girl feel emotional.

I pat Anton on the cheek, pull myself together, and ask if there's anything I can do to help. Cherie pauses, thinks, and passes me her phone.

'You can be on look-out duty,' she says, pointing outside. 'Becca's bringing Edie. Little Edie's staying at home, Katie's babysitting – she chickened out, despite being the best dancer in Budbury. Says she'd rather stay in with Saul and the baby. Anyway, they should be here soon. She's going to text us when they're five minutes away so we can get ready.'

I nod, and take the phone, suddenly nervous in case I miss the code word. Not that there is a code word. No, hang on, this is Becca we're talking about. There will be a code word.

I wander around the room, admiring the decorations, keeping an eye on Mum, and pretending not to do what I'm actually doing – which is looking for Tom.

I finally catch a glimpse of him on the far side of the room, and let out an audible sigh when I do. Like the rest of the men, he's dressed up, in a suit and bow tie. But unlike the rest of the men, the sight of him makes my heart rate bump and my breath catch in my throat. He's gorgeous, and I want to run across the room, knocking people out of the way as I go, and throw myself into his arms.

As though he senses my gaze, he looks up at that exact

moment, and we live out a perfect cliché – our eyes meet across a crowded room. I see him stare at me, look me up and down, and know that he feels exactly the same as I do. This whole 'just friends' thing is truly rubbish.

Just as I see him start to make his way towards me, the phone in my hand beeps. It takes me a few seconds to react, I'm so lost in Tom, but I soon snap myself out of it and read the text from Becca.

'The beagle is landing,' it says. 'Battle stations.'

I dash across to Cherie, who is standing at the centre of all the activity surveying her kingdom, and shout: 'Five minute warning!'

Cherie claps her hands, and bellows at Frank and Cal: 'Roll out the red carpet! Get the music on! Get your umbrellas!'

Everyone jumps to attention, and I see the two men head into the hallway, carrying a big bundle. They stand on the steps, and together let it flow out into the garden – a proper, full-length, actually-like-Hollywood red carpet.

Tom disappears off to the corner of the room, where he has various gadgets that I presume are to do with sound and vision set up, and the rest of the guests all make a mad dash towards Cherie, who has pulled a big cardboard box out from beneath Edie's gift table. She is handing out umbrellas, all of them in bright primary colours, like a sergeant major issuing ammo.

I have no idea why, but I learned a long time ago not

to question Cherie's actions – she usually has a plan. I join Mum and Van and Auburn in the umbrella queue, and once we've all been supplied, Cherie leads us outside.

She directs us perfectly, taking into account different height levels and the need not to get poked in the eye by random spokes, and within a couple of scurrying minutes, we're all in place. We stand along the edge of the red carpet, umbrellas aloft, a perfect canopy of red, green, blue and yellow forming a sheltered archway over the carpet.

For a second, we all stand there, rain hammering down on our brollies, the random spotlights playing across our faces in the darkness – then everyone bursts out laughing when we realise how brilliantly silly we look. But hey, we're keeping Edie's red carpet dry, and that's what counts.

Just as we hear Becca's car pulling into the driveway, Tom hits the music, and the theme tune from *Strictly Come Dancing* belts out from the speakers just inside the hallway.

It's impossible to resist the temptation to start doing a silly dance, and none of us are good at resisting anything – so pretty soon after the opening notes, the whole umbrella-wielding entourage starts to bop and wriggle, brollies twirling and shaking as Becca parks the car.

Sam gets out of the passenger side, dressed in a dapper suit jacket that seems to be made of velvet, and dashes round to open the doors for the ladies. Becca steps out first, giving us all a thumbs up as she looks at the umbrellas shimmying in the rain, and is followed by Edie.

Sam already has a big striped golfing umbrella up and

open above her head, protecting the perm she obviously had touched up today.

Edie pauses, and looks at the crowds, and the red carpet, and the sight of us all dancing to the theme tune of her favourite TV show beneath our undulating archway of umbrellas. She gazes at the beautiful lit-up facade of Briarwood, and the roaming searchlights, and just for a moment it seems like it's all too much for her.

She stands still, perfectly turned out in a baby blue dress and matching sequinned cardigan, and clasps her cheeks in both her wrinkled hands. She stares at us all, and I see her take off her specs and wipe tears from beneath her eyes as she takes it all in.

She says something – I can't tell what, because the music is too loud – and within seconds Becca and Sam are on either side of her, offering her their arms. She smiles, radiant with happiness, and links her arms with theirs, looking like a child between them.

Then, God bless her, she struts down that red carpet like the star she is.

Chapter 36

We all cheer and shout, and bounce our umbrellas up and down, showering raindrops, until Edie is safely inside. Everyone follows her through, and you can see how overwhelmed she is when she is escorted to her throne in the ballroom. Her face lights up as she casts her gaze around the place, and I can only imagine how many decades' worth of memories are playing across the show reel of her mind.

I'm thrilled when she walks up to Anton and places a kiss on his smiling face, and know as she disappears among a crowd of friends and family that she's going to have the night of her life.

I stay on the periphery, letting Edie enjoy her moment, smiling as the reflection from the glitter balls dazzle their way around the room.

I can see my mum, sitting at one of the tables with Auburn and Van, sipping a glass of champagne that's just been delivered by Martha in her waiter's uniform. I note that Auburn isn't actually drinking, which is unusual in a social situation, and that Van is perched on the table, looking at his phone, distracted.

The music starts – a nice easy waltz to begin with – but nobody seems quite ready to dance just yet. Without Zelda and Mateo bossing us around, it's entirely possible that we'll all just decide to rebel, and break-dance or do the Macarena instead.

I glance over at the corner of the room where the music lives, and see Matt in there, staring at buttons and looking slightly confused. I decide to make his life easier by fetching him a can of Guinness, which I open, and pour into a champagne flute. He's a man of simple tastes.

'Ah,' he says, accepting it gratefully. 'At last, a proper drink!'

'Plenty more where that came from,' I say, passing him the rest of the can.

We stand together for a few moments, silent, watching the party unfold before us. Edie is unwrapping her presents with glee, and Cherie is stuffing the used paper into a bin bag next to her. Anton is looking very pleased with himself next to them.

'Are you looking for Tom?' asks Matt, suddenly. He's a quiet bloke, Matt, but not unperceptive.

'No. Yes. Maybe,' I reply, laughing at myself by the end of it.

'Well, it's good to have a plan,' he responds, smiling at me. 'He left once he'd put the music on, and we all trooped outside to make Edie's rainbow arch. Looked like he had a lot on his mind. So do you.'

'No, honestly – my mind is completely empty,' I reply. 'A blank canvas. Nothing in there but tweetie birds and unicorns.'

He raises his eyebrows at me, and obviously doesn't believe me. I'm shocked – I think I look exactly like the kind of person who has tweetie birds fluttering around in her head.

'You should go and find him,' he says simply. 'Take him a drink. Not the Guinness though – that's all for me.'

I grin, and walk away. He's probably right. I should go and find Tom – even if it's only to say thank you for helping us all organise this night for Edie. Without him and his lightbulb moments, we'd all be crammed into the café right now, sweating our fishnets off.

The problem with that plan soon becomes clear – I can't actually find Tom anywhere. He's not in the ballroom, and he's not in the food and drink room, and he's not outside in the garden – which is lucky, as he'd need a flotation device. I check a couple of the side rooms, and even sneak past the tape that cordons off the cloakroom area. I lurk outside the toilets for a while, because I'm classy like that, and am rewarded only by the sight of Laura doing that weird jumping around dance us ladies do when our tights are falling down in the gusset region.

I check the ballroom and the other rooms again, and even in the big storage cupboard under the stairs, in case he's done a Harry Potter.

After all of this comes up empty, I have a lightbulb

moment of my own, and suddenly have an idea as to where he might be. Where a man like Tom might go off to if, as Matt said, he had a lot on his mind.

I stand at the foot of the stairs for a moment, fondling the wooden pineapple-shaped bottom-stopper and admiring the polish of the banister, and come to a decision.

I run up the stairs, quickly before I can change my mind, and make my way up to the second floor. To that same corridor where all of this began – the corridor where my once-evil and now-just-annoying older siblings goaded me into opening the door of a room they'd persuaded me was haunted.

I still feel nervous now but for different reasons. I walk past the other doors, the smell of fresh paint still strong up here, and down to the end of the hallway. I pause outside, and wonder whether I should knock. Eventually I decide I don't need to – I certainly didn't last time, and anyway, he's probably not even here.

I take a deep breath, and turn the handle, and push the door open. It still bloody creaks, like something out of a horror film.

Sure enough, there he is – sitting alone in the window-sill, shrouded in moonlight. He glances up as the door opens, and I see I've caught him deep in thought. At least this time neither of us screams or runs away in terror.

'Hey,' I say, edging into the room and closing the door behind me. I can hear the sound of Queen's 'We Will Rock You' coming up the stairs, the one we practised the paso doble to, and wonder if Cal is doing his bullfighter thing again, making little horn shapes with his fingers.

'Hey back,' he says, quietly. It's dark in here, apart from the moonlight, but for some reason I don't flick the magical switch next to me. Something tells me we might both be better off in the shadows.

He's tugged his bow tie loose, and it's hanging around his neck unevenly. His jacket is still on but unbuttoned, and the laces on his proper grown-up man shoes are undone.

'You look like James Bond after a heavy night at the casino,' I say, walking towards him slowly.

'And you look better than all the Bond girls put together in a blender and mixed up,' he replies.

'I should hope so,' I answer, pondering the image. 'Even Pussy Galore wouldn't look good if she'd been run through a blender. Are you all right? Why are you hiding away up here?'

'I'm not hiding away. I'm . . . Okay, I'm hiding away. There are a lot of people down there, and I've done my bit. Nobody needs me hanging around making very bad small talk.'

'What about me?' I say, reaching out to stroke his hair. Soft and velvety as usual. 'I might need someone to make very bad small talk with.'

He takes my hand in his, and holds it steady. He looks into my eyes, and he's not smiling. He's not smiling, or laughing, or looking like he's in the mood for banter. I feel my breath catch in my throat, and suddenly feel even more petrified than the time I burst in here as an 8-year-old.

'You don't need me, Willow,' he says, sadly. 'And that's okay. I understand why you're making the choices you are – but I'm not sure how easy it's going to be to live with. I thought it would be all right. I thought I could be Joey, and you could be Phoebe, and it'd all be fine in the end. But when I saw you tonight, looking like you do . . . well, I realised it's not going to be easy. In fact, it's nothing to do with how you look tonight – you could have walked into that room wearing a bin bag and reindeer ears, and I'd have felt the same.

'It's you – being around you, but not being with you. I think I can get there, in the end. But I'm not there yet, and I—'

'Need some time?' I finish for him, knowing exactly where that sentence was going. Time. It's what I keep telling myself will cure everything – but right now, there seems to be so little of it.

I lean forward, and kiss him gently on the forehead. I understand – I have to. This man, like all of us, still carries traces of the time when he was a child – when he was a boy, growing up in this very room, feeling unwanted and unloved. And now, I can tell, he feels that way again, and it's all my fault. I didn't set out to hurt him, but I have.

'Yes,' he says simply, wrapping his arms around my waist and pulling me in close. He buries his head in my chest, and I hold him there for a moment. I am the one causing the pain, and the one attempting to console him. There is something truly screwed up about that.

'Yes,' he repeats, pulling away from me as though he realises the same. 'Some time. I'm going to go back to London for a bit. Not forever, I promise – I'll be back here at some point. And I'm only a few hours away, if you need me, for anything. I won't disappear on you – I just need a break. I just . . . need a bit of time to get my head sorted. Then when I get back, I'll be the best friend you ever had.'

I nod, to show that I heard him, but I can't risk speaking out loud. If I speak, I'll say the wrong thing. If I allow myself to open my mouth, I'll tell him I don't want him to be my friend. I'll tell him I love him. I'll beg him to stay, and be so much more than my friend. I'll let my desperation persuade me to make promises I can't keep, and make demands that I can't justify.

I can't speak, because I know that doing that wouldn't be fair. I know it wouldn't, no matter how much I want to. I can't expect him to hang around waiting for my life to get simpler. Waiting for me to have less responsibility. Waiting for me to feel able to commit to anyone other than my mother – because that probably isn't going to happen.

So I stay silent. I nod again, and I kiss him one more time, and I leave him – alone there, perched on the window-sill, in that room he grew up in. Shrouded in moonlight.

Chapter 37

By the time I stagger back down the stairs, after a brief sobbing pit-stop on the first floor, the music has changed again. 'Always A Woman' by Billy Joel. I stand in the doorway to the ballroom, and see that Zelda and Mateo have arrived – which means that everyone is now dancing, for fear of getting hit by a big stick.

Auburn is actually in Mateo's arms, high heels kicked off, swirling around in her stockinged feet. She gives me a wink over his shoulder, and I wonder if she'll be giving him marks out of ten by the end of the evening. I laugh, and give her a thumbs up – why the hell not?

Van is dancing with Mum, in the corner of the room, obviously persuading her to stay far from the madding crowd because of her very stylish boot, and everyone else seems to be coupled up and getting jiggy with it – in a very old-fashioned way.

Everyone except Edie, that is, who sees me in the doorway, and beckons me over to her throne. She's perched on all her cushions, and has her feet on her stool, and is surrounded by gifts of all shapes and sizes.

'Have you seen my swag?' she asks, eyes sparkling, pointing at the table full of goodies. 'I don't know how I'll fit it in the house! I might have to get one of those rental units, like you see on that *Storage Wars* show in the afternoon.'

I smile, nod, and make admiring noises about her pot pourri selection and cuddly rabbit hot water bottle and fluffy slippers. I don't feel in much of a party mood any more, but this is Edie, so I do my best to look happy. Obviously, being Edie, she sees right through me. I don't suppose you get to spend over nine decades on the planet without learning a few things.

Peering at me over her glasses, she holds out one tiny hand, and says: 'Would you do me the honour of this dance? I need to show these whippersnappers how it's done!'

'But of course, birthday girl,' I reply, helping her up and walking to the dance floor.

'I'll lead,' she whispers as we start to move. 'You don't look like you're capable of counting to three right now.'

I nod – she is correct – and try not to tread on her feet as we waltz. She usually wears quite sensible and sturdy shoes, but tonight has on little blue ballet pumps decorated with pom-poms. My Docs would squash them flat, along with her toes, which wouldn't be very celebratory.

'Nice posture,' she says, as we pass Frank and Cherie. 'You can tell he learned as a child, can't you? Now . . . come on, tell me all about it. I can see you've been crying, and you look miserable as sin. I might be being a nosy old biddie, but it's my party, and I'll pry if I want to!'

She seems delighted with her pun, and I have to admit it's a good one. I sniffle a bit, and am glad that the room is lit by chandelier and glitter ball rather than anything more revealing.

'Is it about your nice young man?' she asks.

I nod, and sniffle some more, and finally say: 'It is, yes. It's all very complicated, Edie.'

'I see,' she replies, dancing me back towards the window seat, obviously fearing for the safety of her metatarsals. We both sit down, and she passes me a glass of champagne – she has about six lined up in front of her, the old lush.

'Complicated, is it?' she repeats, taking a sip. 'But not impossible, eh?'

'It feels impossible right now,' I answer. 'And anyway, it's your birthday party – I don't want to spoil it.'

She reaches out, pats my hand, and smiles kindly at me.

'Oh no, dear – you brought me my very own Anton du Beke. Nothing could possibly spoil that! I suppose, perhaps, that you think you can't find time for him, young Tom? Because of your mum, and work, and being so very busy all the time? And perhaps you blame yourself for your mum's accident, because, I heard tell – scandalous gossip I'm sure! – that you were with him here when it happened?'

I can't help it – I actually blush. The only thing worse than a ninety-two-year-old talking about my sex life would be a ninety-two-year-old talking about her own sex life. This delights her, and she cackles into her hands at the look on my face.

'Goodness – you youngsters! You didn't invent sex. None of you would be here if the older generation hadn't discovered it first, would you? Now, look at your mum, Willow. Does she look unhappy?'

I glance over, and see her and Van, still dancing. She doesn't look unhappy. She looks thrilled to be out, to be dancing, to be here. Even with everything that's happened to her, she's never quite lost her joy at being alive and out in the world. Sometimes she misplaces it – but it always seems to come back, like a river that's been dammed and diverted but eventually bubbles back to the surface, irrepressible and full of energy.

'No, she doesn't,' I agree. 'But it's not that simple, is it? And we have no idea what will happen next with her.'

'None of us do, my love. And believe me, I've seen people with Alzheimer's over the years – my sister, God bless her, suffered terribly. So did my own mother, though back in those days, it didn't really have a fancy name. I do understand what it's like, and how hard it can be. You don't know what pain feels like until your own mother forgets who you are, even though you spend every living moment looking after them.

'But I also know this – your mother would be the last

person on earth who would want to feel like she was stopping you from living your life. It would absolutely break her heart.'

I remember now, from things that Frank has said, that Edie cared for her own parents until their deaths. I give myself a brief telling off for forgetting how much experience she has, and for falling into the trap of assuming I am totally unique in my suffering.

'I know, Edie – you're right. So I try not to think like that, or to see my life as not being lived. I'm just . . . adjusting it, that's all. The day centre might close – it's already down to one day a week. Auburn is staying, but she'll probably be busy working in the pharmacy soon. And Van, well, he hasn't said anything, but I don't think he'll be staying too much longer. There are only so many hours in the day, and it's not fair to Tom to expect him to hang around, waiting for more than I can give.'

She wags her finger at me, just to warn me that I'm about to get a telling off.

'Well, maybe you ought to talk to your brother and sister about all of that before you think you know what's going on. And as for Tom, he didn't strike me as an idiot. He seemed very bright.'

'Yes, he is. Very bright. What do you mean?'

'I mean, Willow, that he's old enough to make his own decisions about what is and isn't right for him – it's not up to you to make them for him. He's a grown man with a fine mind, he's capable of weighing up the pros and cons.

And as for Van and Auburn, it doesn't even sound like you know what they're up to – which leads me to conclude, in Miss Marple style, that you're basing your whole future and Tom's on the basis of absolutely bloody nothing. Excuse my French.

'Now, while you give that some thought, be a dear, and fetch me a slice of cake, will you? Not the birthday cake – that's for later, hurrah! – but some of that lemon meringue that Laura does so well? Maybe a smidgeon of cream? No, actually – make that a lot of cream! You know what they say – you're only ninety-two once!'

I stare at her, shell-shocked by that whole speech. Miss Marple indeed. I can't argue with her logic, and know that it's only stubbornness and self-pity that's even making me want to. I wasn't happy with the course I was taking, but I was set on it – now Edie's come along and blown me way out to sea again.

It's a lot to process, this different perspective, and it effectively smacks me out of my assumptions of what is right and what is wrong. I need time to think – but as ever, I don't have that. Maybe I should stop thinking so much, and start feeling. Maybe thinking is over-rated. And the way I'm feeling is desolate. I can't fix some parts of my life – but perhaps I can work on others.

I reach over the pile of bath sets and paperbacks and photo frames, and give Edie a quick hug, before getting to my feet and saying goodbye.

I climb past Anton, and collar Lizzie, who's passing with

a tray of canapés, and tell her to go and fetch Edie the biggest slice of lemon meringue she can cut, along with a whole boat-load of cream.

'Okay . . .' she says, frowning, crinkling up her eyeliner as she does. 'But what kind of boat? A kayak full of cream? A catamaran? An ocean liner?'

'Think *Titanic*,' I reply, grinning at her. 'Without the icebergs and Jack and Rose.'

I pat her arm, and dash off to the corner, where Mum and Van are finishing their dance as the song draws to a close. Auburn heads back in our direction, looking flushed and wafting her face with her hands to cool down. She slips her high heels back on, and flashes us a smile.

'Wow. That Mateo has some moves – he even makes a waltz feel like foreplay,' she says, sounding impressed. 'I might need to sign up for some private lessons!'

I ignore her blatant invitation to talk smut, and instead look at her and Van, my face set and serious.

'What are you two planning?' I ask, simply. They both look at me blankly, then look at each other, and I realise I need to be more specific.

'Auburn – you're staying, aren't you? How will it work, with the pharmacy? Will you be doing long hours?'

She lifts her hair up from the back of her neck to let the air in, and gives me a crooked smile.

'That's not the plan, no,' she replies. 'I mean, what would be the point? I didn't come back here just to work, and leave you to look after Mum. I'm planning to work part-time, and I've been talking to Katie about her taking on some hours. She's a nurse by training, and she's been doing a top-up course at the college. Saul's starting pre-school soon, so she's looking for flexible work.

'I'll have to have set hours that people know in advance, when there's an actual pharmacist available – you know, so I can tell them what creams to put on their warts and such like. But the rest of the time, it'll open as a shop and for over the counter stuff. I'll be here, sis. I'll be able to help – if you want me to.'

Her voice fades a little as she says this, and I know she's still suffering from the guilt even more than I am. I clasp hold of her hand, and reply: 'Of course I do. Thank you.'

I turn to Van, who is downing a lager and still fiddling with his phone. I raise my eyebrows at him. 'What about you? No bullshit, Van. If you need to go back to Tanzania, I understand. I appreciate you coming back, and I won't hold it against you at all if you leave – I know you have a life there, and I don't expect you to give it up. But I do need to know, so spill.'

He gives me a mock salute, and replies: 'Aye aye, captain! Well, I'm in. I'm staying. I've had to cancel flights, and make a lot of arrangements, and that's why I've been a bit cagey. I needed to sort it all out first. But if you want me, I'm here – I'll pick up some farming work or some labouring. It's a busy time of year. I'll try and work it so it fits in with your schedule. I mean, why would I want to leave? Isn't it every man's dream to be sleeping back in his childhood bed, in the same room as his little sister? I really think, if I'm staying, that you and Auburn should—'

'No way!' I say, interrupting him. 'I'm not giving up my room for any of you. I've earned that room. But . . . that's great. And yes, of course I want you to stay. Thank you. Right, I have to skedaddle.'

As I leave, I hear Mum – who has politely watched our conversation like it was a tennis match, turning her head from this way to that – finally speak.

'Tanzania?' she says, sounding impressed. 'When did you go to Tanzania, Van? What an adventure!'

Chapter 38

I sprint out of the ballroom, and gallop up the stairs, taking them two at a time. I run along the hallway, and fling open the door to his room.

It's dramatic and silly, and also completely useless – because the room is now empty. Some time between my leaving and my potentially life-changing chat with the wisest woman in Budbury, he's disappeared.

I stare out of the window, seeing the fountain outlined in the moonlight, the rain still slicing through the night sky in jagged sheets. I remember the first time I saw him out there, with Rick Grimes, and think of all the ways my life has changed since that day.

I feel the desperation seep through me, and run all the way back down the stairs. I bump past Scrumpy Joe at the bottom, briefly apologise as I dash towards the front door, and leave him with one of those 'huh – women!' looks on his face that men get when we confuse them.

Outside, the rain is thundering down, and the red carpet, no longer sheltered by dancing umbrellas, is soggy beneath my feet. I pause by the fountain, and decide to head towards the camper van. Maybe I'll find him there, watching a *TED* Talk on YouTube or something, and I can turn up on his doorstep like a damp Cinderella and make everything right.

I use the torch from my phone to light my way, and squelch along the footpath past the pond; around the ghosts of skinny-dipping past and the echoes of old laughter. It's incredibly dark beneath the canopy of trees, and I keep getting whacked in the face by over-hanging branches, raindrops shimmering all over my hair. I drive myself on, swearing beneath my breath with every near-miss with a gnarled tree root, until I finally arrive at the clearing.

I slip and slide towards the camper, and see that it too is dark. The tables and chairs from outside have been packed away. There are no lights on inside, and no sound that implies any kind of human or canine habitation. I shine my phone up towards the window, and see that Baby Groot has gone, little pot and all.

This isn't a good sign. If Baby Groot is gone, then he's gone. If he was in there, sleeping, or thinking, or binging on fig rolls, Baby Groot would still be there, arms waving on the window ledge.

I reach up and push the door, just in case. It's locked, and I am swamped with misery. He's gone, and I've no idea when I'll see him again.

I realisse that the answer to such questions might lie in

the simple use of the telephonic device in my freezing hands – but that's a no-go. Tom, being the inventor of the flange bracket and all-round wunderkind, was clever enough to wrap our phones in sandwich bags last time we were running around in the forest at night in the rain, like extras in *Predator*. I, being the inventor of precisely nothing apart from a stylish range of customised Doc Marten boots, didn't even think of such a thing.

The phone is as soaking wet as I am, and doesn't work. Even the torch is starting to flicker now. I let out a howl of frustration, the kind that will cause anybody who hears it to stock up on silver bullets.

I stay there for a few more moments, rain slicking down my hair and pouring over my bare skin, feeling defeated. I allow myself that – just for those few moments.

Then I hitch up the skirt of my dress, tuck the soggy strands of hair behind my ears, and start running. I know this place like the back of my hand – or better than that, as I've not actually spent a lot of time getting acquainted with the back of my hand, and think that's a very stupid saying.

I know this place, in the way you always know the things you grew up with. Like the adverts that were on TV when you were ten, or the lyrics to *The Fresh Prince of Bel-Air*.

I spent days and weeks exploring these woods, and I know all the shortcuts, and all the footpaths, and all the secret ways. I know there are routes down to the bottom of the hill that might get me there soon enough – the routes I wanted to check out the night my mum went missing, but Tom was sensible enough to talk me out of.

I am going to work on the assumption that he can't have got far. I was only gone for minutes, and he definitely hadn't left that room by the time I got to the bottom of the stairs. While I was talking to Edie, he must have come back here, grabbed Baby Groot and Rick Grimes, and locked up. Then he'd have had to make his way back to the side of the house, where he keeps the Noddy car in a garage, and find a way out through all the parked jeeps and the coach and everyone else's car. I might even have been on my way here by the time he managed that.

I run, as fast as I can, through the dripping branches and the night-coated trees and the mud that seems to try and suck my boots in with every step. I slap cold leaves out of my way, and leap over roots and stones like a Ninja. My dress tears as I clamber over the last stile before the main road, and my hair is so splattered over my face I can barely see. I'm probably freezing cold now – but my adrenaline doesn't know that. My adrenaline keeps me going, as I charge through the deepest, darkest heartland of the woods.

I am a woman on a mission, and by the time I emerge back into civilisation and onto the main road, I am pumped up so much I could probably fly if I tried. I dash into the middle of the road, my eyes adjusting to being out of the dense woodland again, and stare in the direction of Briarwood.

If he's already gone, I tell myself, then it's not the end of the world. He might be lost but I can find him again. I know that's sensible, and I know it's right, but I just can't feel it – I feel like this is my last chance. That if I let him go, I might never see him again, no matter what he promised. And if that happens, I know I'll have made the biggest mistake of my entire life.

I stand, hands on hips, panting with exertion now I've finally stopped. My dress is torn, I'm soaked and bedraggled, and I know I have enough dirt and grime on my face to qualify as camo on an SAS training camp.

I stare up that road, waiting for something that might never come. I stare up that road, praying for him not to have left. I stare up that road, knowing that if he doesn't appear, I have a long, sad walk back up to Briarwood.

I stare, and I stare, and I stare. And I see nothing, apart from the spooky shapes of the hedgerows, and the white lines in the middle of the road, and the man in the moon, laughing at me from his lofty heights.

I see nothing, and hear nothing, and eventually, without even making a conscious decision to, I start to walk – deflated, empty, cold, and miserable.

I walk slowly, each stop a torturous plod in waterlogged boots now heavy with mud – and as I walk, squelching and defeated, I finally see it.

I see light – seeping through the darkness ahead of me.

I stop, and squint, wondering if I've imagined it, or if

it's a spaceship about to land, full of curious alien beings keen to whisk me away on their flying saucer.

It's not. It's a car, coming around the bend in the road, long-range headlights on, heading right for me. I stand still, frozen, until I realise that I probably look terrifying and might well cause any car driving towards me to crash.

I jump up and down and wave my arms, jiggling the flickering light of my phone up and down in a bid to attract attention. The headlights come closer. I hear the sound of the engine, and for one brief moment think that all of this might end with me, splat, squashed on the wet tarmac like a cartoon villain beneath an ACME steamroller.

The car slows, and I'm blinded by the headlights, caught in their beam, hands over my eyes to try and shield them from the glare. The car stops, and the headlights are switched to low, and I hear the car door open.

I still can't see properly, between the dazzle and the rain and the blackness of the sky around me – but I know it's him. I know it's him because I hear Rick Grimes let out a booming woof, and the skittering of his claws as he leaps out of the back seat, and in my direction.

The dog reaches me first, licking and snuffling and shoving his snout up my torn skirt, in the way that dogs will.

Tom reaches me next, and does none of those things. He just stands there, looking at me, obviously confused. He's changed back into jeans and his Goonies T-shirt, and he looks a million times better to me than when he was

dollied up in a dinner suit. Because now he looks like Tom
– my Tom.

'What are you doing out here?' he asks, which isn't an
unreasonable question.

'Oh, you know, I was just passing,' I say, swiping a sodden
rope of hair out of my eyes.

'Just passing?' he says, as Rick disappears off to inves-
tigate the bushes. 'Just passing, on the road, in the rain?'

'No. Not really. I was looking for you. I thought . . . I
thought you'd gone. I thought I'd missed you.'

'You almost did,' he says, reaching out to wipe the rain
from my cheeks. 'Edie was waiting outside Briarwood with
that golfing umbrella, just as I was pulling out. She wanted
to tell me in intimate detail about every single one of her
birthday presents, including the hand-knitted toilet roll
holder doll her great-niece made her. She did go on a bit
– but I had to stay and chat; you can't walk out on Edie,
especially when it's her birthday. You're freezing. Come and
sit in the car.'

I laugh, and he must be fearing for my sanity as well
as my core body temperature. God bless Edie May, I think,
picturing her out there, on the soggy red carpet, three steps
ahead of the world.

'Not yet,' I say, grabbing hold of both his hands. My
fingers are trembling, but I only know that when I see
them – I've lost all feeling in every limb by this stage. 'Not
until I tell you what I need to tell you.'

'Okay,' he replies, rubbing my fingers. 'But do it quickly,

or you'll turn blue, like the people in *Avatar*. Far less sexy in real life.'

I gaze up at him, and see that the thick fuzz of his hair is covered in rain – the sparkling droplets stay on the surface, like on a seal's coat, or like Midgebo when he's been in the sea. He's so beautiful, and I know that I'm making the right decision, even if it's not an easy one.

'I love you, Tom,' I say, simply. 'I love you, and I don't want you to go back to London. I know it might not be fair asking you to stay, but please – don't go. I don't know how all of this will work out. I know it's all messed up. I know it will be hard. But please stay here, with me – and not as my friend. As more than that. As my . . . Tom. My flange bracket. My everything. I know what my life was like before you came – and now I don't think I can live without you.'

He ponders this, and I see the mighty cogs of his super-powered brain at work.

'Technically, you could live without me,' he says, thought-fully. 'You know, if you had food, water, shelter from the elements . . . you could live without me, Willow. And I could live without you.'

'Okay. Yes. That's true. But I don't want to live without you. I want you to stay here. I want us to try. I want to give Baby Groot a proper family, and spend time with you in the camper van, and wake up in your arms on more than one morning. I want us to have stupid conversations that only we understand, and I want to bonk you silly, and

I want to help you zombie-proof Briarwood. I want all of that – and I'm sorry I was ever stupid enough to think I didn't.'

He takes his time responding, and for one heart-stopping second I think he will say no. That my crazy dash through the undergrowth will be wasted. That I've risked pneumonia and ruined a perfectly good dress all for nothing. That he'll get back in the Noddy car, and whisk himself and Rick Grimes and Baby Groot away, back to a simpler life in London, away from insane women with pink hair and complicated families and snooty Border Terriers.

I cling onto his hands, and feel the tears finally flow, and wonder if this is it – the moment I say goodbye to the legendary ghost boy of Briarwood, who will haunt me for the rest of my days.

He reaches out, and wraps me into his arms. He holds my head against his chest, and kisses my hair, and swamps me with his warmth. I feel safe, and loved, and want more than anything for this to last. For this to be a beginning, not an end.

'Of course I'll stay,' he says, his breath warm against my skin. 'Because I was lying – I don't care what the science says. I can't live without you, either.'

Chapter 39

My name is Willow Longville. I am twenty-six years old. I live in a village called Budbury, with my mum Lynnie. I work as a waitress at the Comfort Food Café, and I run my own cleaning business called Will-o'-the-Wash. I have a dog called Bella Swan, and I love my life. In the last few weeks, the following things have happened . . .

1. I have given Superwurzel a brand new look for the summer – a Hawaiian shirt I found in a charity shop, cool shades, and a pair of Van's old football shorts.
2. I have volunteered as a cleaner at the day centre, to help them keep costs down – although their future is looking a bit more shiny after they received an anonymous donation from someone who chose only to be known as 'flange bracket'.
3. I have progressed from choux pastry to filo, but it all burned so I don't think I'll become a chef after all.
4. I have taken my mother for her latest check-up, which was hellish as usual.

5. I have decided to go back to the Twisted Sisters to chat to Blister Bum Bobby, who may or may not be my father.

6. I have had Lizzie over for movie and pizza night, as she did brilliantly in her GCSEs.

7. I have spoken to my brother Angel. He explained that on the day he visited us, his girlfriend Charlotte had also told him she was pregnant, and everything felt too big for him to cope with – he is sad about what happened, and plans to come and visit again. I pretend to be understanding, but am a flawed human being, and secretly hope he rediscovers his backbone in time for his trip.

8. I have left Mum alone with Van and Auburn on three separate occasions, none of which resulted in anything more dramatic than me getting to spend blissful nights with my geek-boy lover in a camper van in the woods.

9. I have watched the whole of *Friday Night Lights*, and have to agree that I, too, am in love with Tim Riggins.

10. I helped Tom stock the Briarwood cellar with essentials like water, beef jerky, glow sticks and antiseptic cream. Bring it on, zombies – you won't stand a chance at the House on the Hill.

Epilogue

It's a gorgeous day in late summer. Frank has had his eighty-second birthday – the theme was Explorers, and we all wore pith helmets and drank gin and tonic in a big tent Cherie had set up in the garden. The teenagers came as lions and tigers, with species-appropriate onesies and matching face paint.

The summer has been busy, with most of the population of the Western hemisphere coming to the Comfort Food Café to enjoy Laura's cakes and paninis and chocolate-flavoured milkshakes. Now it's the end of the season, and there's a real 'school's out' feeling for all of us as the pace of life quietens down.

Things with Mum have been up and down, but that's always been the way. Some of her symptoms are getting worse, and some exciting new ones are springing up as well – but she can still have days where everything feels normal; or as normal as it can with Lynnie.

I've been in regular contact with Robert, after breaking the news to him that his one-night stand with the mysterious

Ms Longville might have resulted in the creation of yours truly. Maybe, at some point, we'll do a paternity test – not live on the Jeremy Kyle show or anything – to find out for sure. At the moment, we're both feeling our way through a tricky situation, and getting to know each other.

Auburn is up and running at the village pharmacy, ably assisted by her glamorous assistant, Katie. Van is working for Frank, and will be at least until harvest is done. He seems happy enough, but I do sometimes catch him sitting in the garden, staring into space, as though his head is somewhere else entirely.

Today, we are all here together, at Briarwood. All of the work is done, and in mid-September, the first of Tom's Baby Boffins will be arriving to immerse themselves in its splendid isolation while they hone their skills. We're all really excited about it – especially Tom.

I am sitting on the edge of the fountain, looking on as he chats to Van about his plans. He's wearing the same Godzilla T-shirt he was wearing on the day we were reunited, all those months ago. He's waving his arms around, his brown eyes shining with enthusiasm. I am completely and utterly mad about him. I know he feels the same about me, because he tells me so all the time. This is a small miracle, and something I celebrate every single day.

Auburn is sitting next to me, tapping her fingers on her knees, jittering around as usual. She's had a few private lessons with Mateo, but it's clearly nothing more than a fling. She's rediscovered her mojo with Mum, though, and finally feels confident enough to be alone with her. We work out our hours together, the three of us, so we are always available for Lynnie adventures.

The sun is warm today, and the air is still and quiet – no breeze, and no sound apart from Tom and Van's chatter, and the mellow hum of the birds and the bees and the tinkling of water in the now-restored fountain behind us.

Off on the edge of the garden is my mum. She has a big tartan blanket spread out on the grass, and she is stretched out contentedly in the sunlight. She's very happy right now, because Angel is here. He's here with his baby, a pudgy little girl called Heather, and they're both on the blanket with her. Heather has her tiny fingers curled around one of Mum's, and Angel is watching them fondly.

He looks up, and sees me, and smiles. I smile back, wave, and sigh out loud. Auburn looks at me, and raises her eyebrows.

'What's up?' she says.

'Nothing. Just happy,' I reply, gazing around at everyone. This is the first time we've all been together in so long, and it's perfect.

Mum disengages her finger from Heather, and sits up, cross-legged. Her grey hair is wild, and she is watching us all, her eyes flitting from one to the other, pausing on each. She smiles, and reaches for her notepad and pen.

Does she even know who we are? Are we friendly strangers or cherished children in her mind? Is she calm because she understands where she is and who she is with, or is she just enjoying the warm day and the company of a cute baby?

I honestly have no idea – but for now, I simply choose not to care. I am here, in the sunshine, surrounded by my family, and a man who makes me insanely happy.

She might not know who I am – but is that really the point? I know who she is. And I love her.

Today is a good day. I feel strong. I feel lucky. I feel whole. My name is Willow Longville, and I love my life.

Acknowledgements

The biggest thank you of all must really go to my readers – the Comfort Food Café fans who love it as much as I do. I've lost count of the number of times I've received e-mails or comments about how much they wish it was a real place – well, so do I. Wouldn't it be great if we could all meet up there, for coffee and cake and a chinwag with Cherie and the gang?? Without your continued support and enthusiasm there wouldn't still be a Café, and I wouldn't still be telling these stories – so thank you, so much.

As ever, a mahoosive great big THANK YOU to my family – you all totally rock. Dom, thank you for at least trying to stop your eyes from glazing over when I tell you my 'fascinating' plot plans and tales of publishing. It's not been an easy year, my love, but we shall overcome. Kids – thank you for being simply the best (and no, I don't know what's for dinner). Much appreciation also to the friends who help keep me practically sane, through their humour, kindness, patience and willingness to sit in pubs with me. I might not have a real-life Comfort Food Café, but I do have the friends, which makes me a very lucky woman indeed.

Extra dollops of thanks to my author friends, who are the closest thing I have to colleagues, and who have been incredibly tolerant of my ups and downs this year: Jane Costello/Catherine Isaac, Jane Linfoot, Milly Johnson and Carmel Harrington.

Giant whoop-whoops and other enthusiastic noises also for Kim Young and the team at HarperCollins, especially Charlotte Ledger – she's the Publisher of the Year, don't you know? Thank you, Charlotte, for being boss-lady, editor, drinking partner, inspiration and cheerleader all rolled into one.

Last but not least, thank you to my superb agenting team – Rowan Lawton and Eugenie Furniss and their lovely squad at Furniss Lawton.

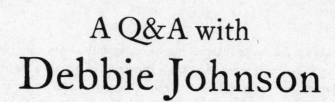

A Q&A with
Debbie Johnson

What is your favourite thing about the Comfort Food Café series?

There are so many things I love about it - the food, the location, the doggie crèche, the book shop, the gorgeous men! Mainly, though, I think it's the feeling that everyone can feel comfortable there - it doesn't matter how you look, or what clothes you're wearing, or what job you have, or how successful you are. People at the café are eccentric in the nicest sense - they all have their hang ups, their weird quirks, their issues, their pasts. Not everyone is confident, or articulate, or perfect, or young, or beautiful - they make mistakes. They have bad hair days. They mess up. They can be anxious, or selfish, or scared - just like we all can. It's the way the crowd at the Comfort Food Café accept their own and other people's imperfections that makes it such a very special place. People can arrive at the café feeling lost, or lonely, or even broken - and leave feeling so much better. It's an idealised version of what we all long for in life: a group of fab, funny friends who accept us for who we are, and force feed us cake! I always used to love that TV show *Cheers* when I was growing up, and think maybe the idea of having a place 'where everybody knows your name and they're always glad you came' stuck with me!

There is a strong sense of community in all the Comfort Food Café books- is this something that you experience in some aspect of your life? Or something that you think is important?

I think it's incredibly important, and something that we seem to have lost to some extent, sadly. I am blessed with a wonderful group of friends, and we meet most weeks for a pub quiz, where we spend the night drinking, laughing, and chatting to the extended community

there. We may or may not also consume vast quantities of alcohol while we're at it. That makes me so lucky - I know a lot of people don't have that. I think loneliness is an epidemic in our society; it makes me feel very emotional, especially when it comes to older people. It's strange how even though we live in a world that technically is more connected then ever, it's so easy to feel isolated and distant. Watching other people's lives on social media sometimes seems to feel as important as getting out there and living our own. We all feel lonely sometimes, don't we - no matter how many people we know and how busy our lives are? A community like the one in Budbury is ideal - supportive and pro-active and so, so non-judgemental.

Do you have a favourite place to write?

I don't really have a lot of choice - my house is full of kids and dogs and chaos. I don't have my own room, or even a desk. My glamorous writing space is on the sofa, usually with two old, flatulent dogs snuggled up next to me! In all honesty, I wouldn't have it any other way.

What do you hope that readers get from your novels?

I hope they come away from reading one of my books feeling better about the world than they did when they started. Whether that's because the story has given them some hope or inspiration, or simply allowed them a precious few hours escapism away from the trials and strains of the real world, I don't mind - I just want to send some positive vibes out there into my readers' lives! There's nothing better than a good, cathartic cry - having a sob at a fictional character's heartbreak gives us the chance to let it all out, and pop any tension bubbles we might be feeling ourselves. I did this recently when watching *Grey's Anatomy*, and one of the leads was diagnosed with a brain tumour - I mean, I don't know her, she doesn't exist, but boy did I cry! I was crying for her, and crying because I needed a good old cry myself as well. I like to think my books have a lot of humour and quirkiness to offset the sad crying, and that it all balances out - hopefully bringing a bit of joy by the end.

What is your favourite thing to do when not writing?

I love spending time with my kids and family and dogs. I love reading - especially the kinds of books I don't write, like crime and fantasy. I enjoy a good binge-watch when I find something good on TV. I like getting out and about in nature - I'm not especially fit and you'd never find me doing anything extreme, but I do like a good romp around the hills or the beach with the gang. It makes you feel so much better about the world. Another of my pleasures - slightly guilty - is planning holidays I'll probably never go on. I have piles and piles of brochures for luxury holiday companies, and cruises, and exotic locations - none of which I can afford to go on, but I do enjoy thinking about it!

How important is location in your books? And why did you choose Dorset?

I love writing about locations, and recreating them on the page and in my readers' minds - for me, the location is somehow like an extra character. I've set books in Liverpool, where I live, which was brilliant to do, and also in places like Cornwall and Turkey and Scotland and New York. Dorset is a place we go on holiday - we stay at a lovely spot called Lancombe Country Cottages which is between the coast and the country, really dog and child friendly. In fact those first few holidays in Dorset were what inspired me to create the café - the scenery, the pace of life, the food, just a generally gorgeous atmosphere. It's a very special place, and I always feel relaxed there - every time we go, I find something new and wonderful about it.

If you didn't write, what would be your ideal alternative career?

Gosh, I don't know - all I've ever really done is write, either as a journalist or an author, apart from all those jobs you have when you're young, like waitressing and catering and call centres and factory work and...actually, I've had a lot of jobs, now I come to think about it! One of the best was working as an usherette in a cinema - selling ice creams

from one of those trays around my neck, collecting tickets, etc. I really loved that, and there was a good sense of community in that job. I'm pretty useless to be honest - I'm like the opposite of Liam Neeson in *Taken*, and have very few skills! But maybe I'd have been okay at something like advocacy or law? I have a good memory for detail and like a good debate!

Do you have themes that you know you want to explore, before you start writing a book?

Yes, kind of. Although sometimes they emerge more strongly as the story progresses and the characters become more clearly defined. Like with Laura, in the first Comfort Food Café book - at first, her losing her husband was something of a plot device for her moving to Dorset and working at the café. But as soon as I wrote that first chapter, I started to really feel it - her sense of loss, of devastation, her need to move on with life. That became an integral part of the whole book - hope, optimism, and her battle to find the courage she needed to make the changes she did. I had some lovely emails from people afterwards, who had lost their own loved ones, saying how real her story felt to them, and how much hope it gave them as well. That was a real honour, to touch people like that. And with Zoe in *Coming Home to the Comfort Food Café*, I was interested in exploring how a non-parent can be as much of a mum to someone as their 'real' mother - the ways that our relationships, and the way we love people, aren't necessarily defined by titles or roles.

Are there any characters in the Comfort Food Café series that you have based on yourself?

None of them are based on me, no - that would be a very boring story! I suppose they all have little bits of me in them. Probably the character I most identified with, weirdly, was Zoe - we have the same sense of humour and love of books. I would love to be Cherie when I grow up - and to last as long and as healthily as the wondrous Edie May!

Sunshine at the Comfort Food Café, and Willow's story, features Alzheimer's as one of the main elements - why did you write about that particular subject, and did you always see Willow as someone who would get their own book?

I always intended to give Willow her own story, from the very beginning. In the previous three books she played a small but significant part, mainly bringing some character and humour. I love Willow - her wackiness and her slightly off-the-wall way of thinking and her odd wardrobe. She's deeply kind, but also very eccentric. In terms of the Alzheimer's, I really wanted to explore this because I have reached the age (I'm in my forties) where a lot of people I know are supporting their parents - that thing has happened where the children become the grown-ups, for various reasons. Both my mum and dad are no longer with us, and with my mum in particular there were a lot of years where she wasn't in good health. I've seen friends and family go through the very difficult experience of looking after older loved ones suffering from dementia, and it's a unique challenge. Not without it's humour, of course - one of my pal's dads lived in a nursing home, but was convinced he was much younger, and was sure he was 'in with a chance' with all the nurses - he was quite happy! It's a very, very hard situation though - and much as Willow struggles to cope sometimes, she has the support of friends and family, a day centre, and access to reliable carers for her mum. In the real world, of course, a lot of carers have none of that, and face these battles alone.

Stay in touch with
Debbie
JOHNSON

Chat with Debbie and get to know the other fans
of the Comfort Food Café series:

f /Debbie Johnson Author

🐦 /@debbiemjohnson

You can also pop over to Debbie's website and sign up to
her newsletter for all the latest gossip from the café,
book news and exclusive competitions.

www.debbiejohnsonauthor.com